Exploring Education and Chil

Education has become dominated by testing, standards, interventions, strategies and political policy. Yet while elements such as these are important, *Exploring Education and Childhood* contends it is childhood – including its sociology and psychology – that is the vital holistic context for teaching and learning.

Written by a team of specialists who combine rigorous research and scholarship, with experience of teacher training and classroom teaching, each chapter examines a topic that is of vital importance to education. The book includes thought-provoking examples of educational practice that illuminate contemporary problems in order to understand future possibilities for education. The authors reflect on educational theory to better understand education policy in the international context. With an emphasis on reflection and deep thinking – something that all the best teachers are able to do – key issues in the book include:

- the voice of the child
- metacognitive strategies
- agency, pedagogy and curriculum
- performativity, standards and school readiness
- educational settings and new technology
- teacher expertise and agency
- diversity and child agency
- families, society and school choice.

Exploring Education and Childhood challenges education professionals, policy-makers and all people with an interest in education to envision a new future. It is ideal for the professional studies reading of student teachers and teachers, and particularly appropriate for Masters-level research and the study of education more broadly.

Dominic Wyse is Professor of Early Childhood and Primary Education at University College London, Institute of Education (IOE), UK.

Rosemary Davis is Visiting Professorial Fellow at University College London, Institute of Education (IOE), UK.

Phil Jones is Professor of Early Years and Primary Education at University College London, Institute of Education (IOE), UK.

Sue Rogers is Professor of Early Years Education at University College London, Institute of Education (IOE), UK.

Exploring Education and Childhood

From current certainties to new visions

Edited by Dominic Wyse, Rosemary Davis, Phil Jones and Sue Rogers

Routledge
Taylor & Francis Group

LONDON AND NEW YORK

First published 2015
by Routledge
2 Park Square, Milton Park, Abingdon, Oxon OX14 4RN

and by Routledge
711 Third Avenue, New York, NY 10017

Routledge is an imprint of the Taylor & Francis Group, an informa business

British Library Cataloguing in Publication Data
A catalogue record for this book is available from the British Library

Library of Congress Cataloging-in-Publication Data
Exploring education and childhood : from current certainties to new visions / edited by Dominic Wyse, Rosemary Davis, Phil Jones and Sue Rogers.
pages cm.
ISBN 978-0-415-84110-8 (hardback) – ISBN 978-0-415-84111-5 (paperback) – ISBN 978-1-315-71582-7 (e-book) 1. Early childhood education. 2. Child development. 3. Early childhood educators–Training of. I. Wyse, Dominic, 1964- editor of compilation.
LB1139.23.E95 2015
372.21–dc23
2014046578

ISBN: 978-0-415-84110-8 (hbk)
ISBN: 978-0-415-84111-5 (pbk)
ISBN: 978-1-315-71582-7 (ebk)

Typeset in Bembo
by Cenveo Publisher Services

MIX
Paper from
responsible sources
FSC
www.fsc.org   FSC® C013056

Printed and bound in Great Britain by
TJ International Ltd, Padstow, Cornwall

Contents

Figures and tables

Figures

Tables

Notes on contributors

Paula Ambrossi MA ICTs in Education, PGCE Secondary Modern Foreign Languages, BSc Honours Psychology/Computing. Born in Santiago de Chile, Paula has lived in the UK since 1988. She worked as a Spanish/French teacher in a secondary school, where she developed her interest in the intercultural and affective aspects of language teaching and learning, and in innovative ways of teaching grammar. Paula has worked as a primary lecturer at the UCL Institute of Education, since 2006. She has explored cross-curricular elements to language learning, for both children and teachers, in particular using video production as media. Her other interests include graphic design and behaviour management.

Lynn Ang PhD researches in the areas of the curriculum and diversity issues in early childhood, international early years policy and early childhood care and education across cultures, particularly in Southeast Asia and the Asia-Pacific region. She is interested in the social, cultural and macro-political contexts of children's early experiences, participatory and ethnographic methodologies and the impact of socially relevant research on policy and advocacy for children and families. Her recent work includes a UNICEF project on early childhood and peacebuilding to inform a research agenda for the Asia-Pacific region. She lectures on the MA Early Years Education programme and supervises professional doctorates (EdD) and doctorate (MPhil/PhD) students at the UCL Institute of Education.

Sue Bodman EdD works at the International Literacy Centre at the UCL Institute of Education, and is a national leader for Reading Recovery. Her research focuses on effective professional learning and professional development for teachers and teacher educators, particularly in the field of literacy learning and teaching. Her most recent publication (*Which Book and Why: Using Book Bands and book levels for guided reading in Key Stage 1*, Bodman and Franklin, 2014) demonstrates her commitment to ensuring that teachers have access to up-to-date theory to inform their practical teaching decisions.

Rosemary Davis PhD is a Visiting Professorial Fellow at the UCL Institute of Education, in Early Years and Primary Education. Formerly a primary teacher, and headteacher of three schools, Rosemary was founding course tutor to the Primary PGCE at UCL Institute of Education. Subsequently, she worked as a consultant or in universities for fifteen years on development education in Botswana, Mauritius, Namibia, Malawi and ten countries in Southeast Asia, mainly with children, teachers and headteachers. Rosemary's five years in Namibia were mainly as part of a team from Florida State University and consultancy work with UNICEF. She has published books and papers on primary education, as well as internationally funded research reports, including for UNDP/UNICEF and WHO.

Tony Eaude PhD was the headteacher of a primary school for nine years. He now works independently and has links with the UCL Institute of Education, and the University of Oxford. He is especially interested in the development of the whole child and how teachers of young children can encourage this. His publications include *Children's Spiritual Moral, Social and Cultural Development: Primary and Early Years, Thinking Through Pedagogy for Primary and Early Years* and *How Do Expert Primary Classteachers Really Work?* His book; *New Perspectives on Young Children's Moral Education: Developing Character through a Virtues Ethics Approach*, is due to be published in late 2015. More details of his work can be seen on www.edperspectives.org.uk

Rosie Flewitt PhD lectures and researches in the complementary areas of young children's communication and literacy development, inclusion and participatory research methods at the UCL Institute of Education, and in the London Knowledge Lab, where she specializes in researching early literacy in a digital age (http://mode.ioe.ac.uk/). The methodological focus of her work lies in ethnographic and multimodal approaches to the study of early learning, particularly how children use combinations of modes (e.g. spoken and written language, gesture, images, sounds and layout) as they engage with written, printed, oral, visual, embodied and digital texts. Recent publications include *Understanding Research with Children and Young People* (with A. Clark, M. Hammersley and M. Robb, 2014).

Phil Jones is Professor of Children's Rights and Wellbeing at the UCL Institute of Education and has published and lectured widely on childhood, children's rights, play, wellbeing and therapy. He is series editor for Bloomsbury's *New Childhoods* and authored books include *Rethinking Childhood* (Continuum 2009) and *Rethinking Children's Rights* (Continuum 2010, 2015), with edited books including *Children's Rights in Practice* (with Walker, Policy Press 2011) and *Childhood: Services and Provision for Children* (with Moss, Tomlinson and Welch, Pearson 2007).

Georgina Merchant started her career in Edinburgh, where she was particularly interested in teaching English. A move to Australia saw her exploring this interest further through study at university in Sydney and specializing in teaching children who are learning English as an additional language. Returning to the UK, Georgina worked in ITE at the UCL Institute of Education. Currently she is teaching both PGCE students and Teach First participants and beginning some research regarding the synthesis between audience, feedback and motivation in improving the writing of Key Stage 2 boys.

Joseph Mintz PhD is Senior Lecturer in Education at the UCL Institute of Education. His research interests include special educational needs; educational technology, including the use of mobile technology with autism; as well as the professional practice of teachers working with children with special needs, including psychoanalytical perspectives on professional practice. He was Principal Investigator on the Best Practice in Special Educational Needs and Disability Education for Teachers project, funded by the English Department of Education. He is particularly interested in the relationship between theoretical and experiential knowledge in the work of teachers with children with special educational needs.

Helen Morris MA has extensive experience of primary teaching and school leadership, both in Australia and in the UK. For eight years, she also worked in school improvement in England, specializing in literacy and literacy difficulties and developing action research with class teachers. Helen is currently a National Trainer at the International Literacy Centre at the UCL Institute of Education, and module leader for Literacy Development in the MA in Literacy and Literacy Difficulties. During the development of Every Child a Reader, Helen worked in a local authority as a link manager for the Reading Recovery Teacher Leader, supporting the rollout and evaluation of the programme. Helen's early research explored multimodal texts as a scaffold for writing, with a particular focus on potential impact on boys' attainment. Her current research interest is in the learning of teacher educators and the ways in which professional learning is shaped, investigating the ways in which close observation and socially constructed learning contribute to the development of critical reflection.

Lynn Roberts MA is a Lecturer in Primary Education at the UCL Institute of Education. Her research focuses on the role of new media in learning, with a particular interest in how technology can support the links between home, school and community. Lynn teaches a New Media Specialism and leads the Professional Practice Module and Computing component of the Primary PGCE programme. Prior to joining the UCL Institute of Education, Lynn taught in primary schools in London, Sweden and Spain.

Guy Roberts-Holmes PhD is Senior Lecturer at the UCL Institute of Education, where he leads the internationally acclaimed MA Early Years Education programme. The main focus of his research is the relationship between early years policies, curriculum, assessment and pedagogy. Guy's recent publications in major journals include critical examinations of recent early years policy changes, and their impact upon the 'datafication' of early years teachers professional roles, and pedagogy. Guy has also written a bestselling early years research methods book.

Anne Robertson PhD has been a primary teacher since the early 1970s, first in Scotland and then in London. She moved into advisory work and from there worked with King's College, London, on Cognitive Acceleration programmes in primary schools. She now works with primary PGCE students in the UCL Institute of Education. Her main areas of interest are the teaching of science and mathematics, as well as continuing to consider how best to develop children's thinking.

Sue Rogers PhD is Professor of Early Years and Primary Education at the UCL Institute of Education. Her main body of research is concerned with pedagogy and the role of play in educational contexts. More recently her research has examined the nature of research use and expertise in early years settings. She has published widely in the field (including three books to date), and has led a range of funded projects in early years settings and primary schools.

Susan Taylor PhD is Academic Tutor in Professional Learning at the UCL Institute of Education. She works predominantly in the Doctoral School. Prior to joining the UCL Institute of Education, she had a diverse range of teaching experience spanning all age phases including nursery, primary, secondary and post-compulsory sectors. Susan's research focuses on initial and continuing professional development, curriculum design for developing generative learning and early literacy acquisition and literacy interventions. Her publications and conference work to date have focused on designing professional development to develop generative learning not only in the education sector, but also in relation to flight safety.

Dominic Wyse PhD is Professor of Early Childhood and Primary Education at the UCL Institute of Education. The main focus of his research is curriculum and pedagogy. Dominic's publications include major international research volumes and bestselling books for teachers and educators. His book *Creating the Curriculum* (written with colleagues) was the first to compare the national curriculum in the four nations of the UK. Dominic is currently an editor of the *Curriculum Journal*, one of the journals of the British Educational Research Association (BERA); he is also an elected member of the BERA Council.

Introduction

*Dominic Wyse, Rosemary Davis,
Phil Jones and Sue Rogers*

It's Wednesday morning; there is no assembly today. The teacher reminds the class of ten-year-olds that the menu of activities that was started at the beginning of the week has to be completed by Friday at midday. One activity on the menu is the collaborative research project, that began at the beginning of term, for which pairs of children decided their research questions. The presentations for the research will be held during the course of the final week of term, and then will be published on the school's digital portal for parents. The children collect the resources they need to carry out the first of the activities that they have chosen to begin the day with. Some children are working with peers, others choose to work alone.

The teacher answers a few queries from children, such as from one or two who want help to decide which activity to start with. Then, having waited while the class settle into their activities, the teacher sits down to discuss the work that one of the children is doing to solve the problem: 'Which is the most likely number to be scored if you throw two six-sided dice?' After that, the teacher moves to the art area of the classroom to discuss the way another child is planning to use some of the colours and shapes of the Matisse *Jazz* images as inspiration for a collage.

The teaching and learning continues in this way until the end of the school day, broken only by lunch and break times.

How did you react to this example of classroom teaching – with curiosity, excitement, disapproval, disbelief, incredulity? The example is a fictional one, but one that did take place in some classrooms in the UK (and some other countries such as the USA) in the 1970s and 1980s. We chose the example because, although it is only very short, it illuminates some of the histories, cultural practices and issues in early years and primary/elementary[1] education. Perhaps the biggest question raised by the example is, could this happen in a primary classroom anywhere in the world today, or more importantly, *should* this happen in primary classrooms today?

The approach that the example exemplifies was called *the integrated day*, a form of classroom organisation that was built on the concept of *child-centred education*. First and foremost was the idea of children as capable autonomous learners, who, it was argued, were able to make significant choices over their learning. This not only motivated them to learn, but also allowed them to set their learning at a pace that was most appropriate for the individual learner. By exercising control over how long they spent on each activity in the menu of activities for the week (or in some cases two weeks) children were also able to prioritise subjects of interest to them so that they could develop specialisms in subject areas.

The role of the teacher was to support children's learning, in the first place by planning activities appropriate to children's development. These activities would also be planned by taking account of the children's views. For example, by asking them about their areas of interest in relation to the 'topic', a theme such as food, ourselves, transport, etc., this was used to bring greater coherence to the learning across different subject areas. Although the theme was designed to cover as many subjects as possible, other areas of the curriculum were still covered discretely, such as number work in mathematics.

At the beginning of a week of activities a greater amount of whole class input was required so that the children were clear about the learning intentions for the different activities. As the week progressed the teacher would use whole class teaching as required, but the bulk of the teaching would be done by working with individuals, with pairs and sometimes with small groups of pupils, responding to learning needs that emerged as a result of the children working on the activities. The teacher's interaction skills were crucial; similarly, so was the ability to perceptively assess the children's learning and development, and take that learning forward appropriately.

As you can see, the example raises profound issues about early years and primary education: children's rights to make choices; teaching styles; pedagogy and teaching approaches; classroom organisation; curriculum design and planning; forms of assessment; time and sequencing of activities and tasks; and many more that we are sure will have occurred to you. However, we are not, at this point in the book, advocating any particular approach to early years and primary education. The use of an example, at the very beginning of a chapter, to stimulate questions is a device used throughout the book. The one at the beginning of this chapter is a seed for the book as a whole, a book that will take you through many issues, some regarded as controversial, towards its concluding chapter where we put forward our new visions and manifesto for education.

The title of the book, *Exploring Education and Childhood: From current certainties to new visions*, itself signals particular ways of thinking. Naturally, in view of our expertise, the book is about education. But education in some people's minds has become dominated by ideas such as testing, standards, interventions, strategies, political policy: encapsulated in Prime Minister Tony Blair's words, 'education, education, education', when elected in 1997 in the UK. But while elements such as assessment are important, it is childhood (including its sociology and psychology), in our view, that is the vital holistic context for teaching and learning. Too often children appear in public discourse to be dissociated, and hence disenfranchised, from the very education that is claimed to be in their best interests. Education is also centrally about people and relationships, relationships that are sustained through interaction between professionals and children.

The *current certainties* in our title are derived not only from the practice of teaching, but also from recent and current educational policy, including at international level. When you work in schools, as a trainee teacher, and as a qualified teacher, you become aware of the customs and practices of a school. If you are curious, you might think: why does the school do things in this way? For example, why are literacy and maths nearly always taught in the morning? Why are there more men in the junior part of primary schools, and more women in early years and infants? Why is the primary curriculum organised in subjects rather than different kinds of areas of learning? Why does the school do spelling tests every week? These customs and practices can be seen as one kind of *certainty*. At a different level there are certainties implicit in what politicians from most main parties say. For example, the idea that national statutory testing and the publication of league tables of schools are good for children's learning, or that because Ontario in Canada, for example, does well in international comparative tests of maths and reading of fifteen-year-old pupils, then countries in the UK should replicate what they do. Or, at the level of the curriculum, the current certainty in England that formal grammar teaching will improve children's writing, apparent in the pages and pages of requirements to teach grammar as part of England's national curriculum for the subject English.

Finally, in relation to the title of the book, *new visions*. This was our greatest challenge. The world of education is, of course, full of new visions. For example, in the world of educational policy every new government brings new visions to education as part of its manifesto, because education is rightly regarded as one of the most important aspects of society. But the new visions brought by governments frequently don't achieve their aims. Too often they seem simply to be a 'repackaging' of ideas that have been promoted again and again without sufficient success. So the challenge for the authors and editors of this book was to establish new visions built on our particular ways of thinking about education through theory, research and practice, supported by the particular processes and frameworks we used in the writing of the book. To this end, each chapter of the book begins by examining some certainties, as a means to arrive at new visions, however modest these may be. And in the final chapter of the book the editors crystallise what appear to them to be the new visions most urgently in need of consideration and direct action, in practice and in policy. More practically, each chapter explores a topic that is a vital feature of being a teacher, and of teaching. The book encourages reflection and deep thinking, something that all the best teachers are able to do.

Each chapter in the book critically explores a controversy or issue that has wide-scale relevance to teachers. The starting point for each chapter is typically a thought-provoking depiction, a vignette, to provoke questions. In order to critically examine issues arising from the depictions that the chapters begin with, rigorous scholarship (theory and research) is also examined in each chapter. Through the explicit comparison of practice and scholarly work the chapters suggest new visions for education.

For any book of this kind, the experience and knowledge of the authors is of paramount importance. There are many significant books about education. The experience of the authors of such books tends to be one of two kinds: a) mainly as a practitioner, or b) mainly as an academic. Edited books, in particular, tend to have authors who are academics. This book brings together authors who were themselves teachers (and who have many years of experience of educating each new generation of teachers) with authors and editors who have international reputations for their research and scholarship. This combination of practical experience of classroom teaching, of teacher education and training, and of rigorous research and scholarship in our view allows a unique perspective on education. In the book we make reference to work in sociology, psychology, philosophy, etc., all disciplines which have important ideas to contribute to understanding education, but it is the experience of understanding the lived realities of education combined with educationists' rigorous research and theory that we hope makes an original contribution to advancing teaching and learning.

All the authors and editors work in the department of Early Years and Primary Education at the University College London, Institute of Education, one of the world's leading centres for the study and practice of education. Unlike any book proposal that we are aware of, this one began its life with an open invitation to any member of the department to become involved as author and/or editor. The sense that true new visions might emerge from such a democratic process of involvement was uppermost in early thinking about the book. All the authors were supported by editors who were more experienced in writing of this kind. The close collaboration between authors and editors resulted in more than 60 chapter drafts across the book as a whole, the number of drafts per chapter varying according to the issues that arose as a result of working on chapters and responding to them.

Developing the proposal for the book began with the team working together to identify what they considered to be some of the most important issues in relation to teaching and learning. Work on the book included regular meetings to share ideas, and presentations of work in progress – for example, in peer-reviewed symposia given at the annual conferences of the European Educational Research Association and the British Educational Research Association. This way of working as a team had many advantages, but particularly in bringing greater coherence to the book as a whole.

To ensure the coherence of the book six themes were established as a result of the ongoing collaboration. The six themes are sometimes addressed explicitly in chapters, and sometimes are more part of underlying thinking that informed the book as a whole.

Identity and agency

The ways in which children's identity is reflected, and included, in their education or not. The perspectives and needs of different societal groups, such as minority ethnic groups, balanced against the richness and complexities of people's individual life histories, and the perspectives about the world that their lives give them. Consideration of the extent to which teachers and pupils have agency over their education, and arguments for and against the desirability of agency.

Surveillance

Consideration of the ways that education is 'measured', evaluated, tested, standardised and used to monitor the work of teachers and children. Recognition that professionals are accountable to society but that the particular ways that they are held accountable makes a difference to the quality of education, teaching and learning.

Performativity

The means by which national, and international, policies influence schools, through testing, target setting and international comparison. Closely tied to the ways that politicians and political parties understand education and what needs to be done to improve education. The links with economic competitiveness and the impact this way of thinking has on teachers as professionals.

Development

The importance of individual child development. But also ideas such as the 'developmental approach' to teaching and learning where it is recognised that, contrary to whole cohort benchmarking, children progress in individual ways. Emphasis on continuous human development, from birth to age eleven, more than the structural historical divides of early years, infant, junior, or primary.

Rhetoric vs reality

With each new government comes the rhetoric of solving the problems of those most in need of high-quality education. Too often the answers to problems seem to be derived from limited personal experience, and familiar political ideology. Yet a more nuanced appreciation based on rigorous understanding of educational history and research could provide a more realistic appraisal of what might work. Reality is appreciated most keenly by those who teach, and those who research teaching and learning from particular perspectives.

Alternatives

Our search for new visions. We build on rigorous understanding of the history of early years and primary education, and we reject the misplaced nostalgia for so-called 'golden' periods of education. Our alternatives are built on recognition of a very long and honourable tradition of innovation (including the so-called 'radical'), from class-rooms and local authorities in the UK and elsewhere.

Each chapter includes a powerful example of practice that raises issues of broad relevance. These examples are used as the basis for exploration in a number of ways. Theory and research are explicitly linked with classroom practice to deepen the analysis. Policy orientations are explored in relation to the examples in order to critique current practice and, finally, to recommend alternative ways of thinking and working with children. The book is organised into four parts which are summarised below.

Part I: The foundations of childhood

Childhood is not only an idea that we have all experienced, but is also a concept amenable to academic study. One modern variant of the study of childhood came from the sociology of childhood. However, in recent years pressures such as globalisation have resulted in the need for reconceptualisation. Jones' chapter is founded on the sociology of childhood but takes this into a new interdisciplinary space in his analysis of contemporary educational documents using a variety of theoretical perspectives. His critique of documents written by the Chief Inspector of Schools in England reveals the troubling ideas that are taken for granted in the education system.

A particularly important way to understand childhood and children's needs is to listen to children, something that is summed up in the book by the concept of 'voice'. Davis shows us the merits of appropriate recognition of 'voice' and reminds us that many children's lives around the world are fraught with danger and abuse. Davis' exploration includes the very important reminder that children have rights enshrined in international law, yet traditionally education systems have been slow to uphold these rights, particularly at the level of classrooms.

A less politically charged idea about childhood and educational practice is child development, although the idea of 'developmentally appropriate practice' that refers to particular traditions of early years teaching has caused debate. Robertson's chapter takes a more cognitive perspective in its examination of children's thinking, and in particular the idea of cognitive acceleration. Her newly published findings reveal important things about children's thinking, revealed by the children themselves.

Part II: Curriculum, pedagogy and assessment

The curriculum is the vehicle through which children experience education. It can even be argued that it is a singularly important element of the discipline of education. Curriculum is inseparably linked to pedagogy and to assessment as the chapters in this part reveal. Rogers and Wyse show how particular moments of interaction between teachers and children reflect different kinds of pedagogy. They also address not only the micro level of classroom interaction, but also the macro level of national curriculum policy as part of their theme of teachers' and children's agency.

Assessment is perhaps the most contentious of educational topics not only in England, but also worldwide. Pressures from statutory assessment in countries, and international surveys of assessment are part of these debates. Roberts-Holmes provides troubling evidence of the ways in which high-stakes assessment is having negative consequences for children and teachers. A practical solution he offers is the idea of learning stories that can give a much richer and more rounded picture of children's learning.

Technology, and in particular its relationship with pedagogy, is a rich area for scholarship. Examining how policy, research and practice interact in relation to new technology is enabling insight into whether we are stifling opportunities, or creating innovative ways of conceiving of pedagogy and curriculum areas such as literacy. Roberts' chapter shows the creative possibilities of new technology. She does this in a rigorously balanced account showing the importance of pedagogy, not just the technology, if children's learning is really to be advanced.

Part III: Teacher development

One of the areas where there is more agreement between educationalists and policymakers is the idea that teachers matter. However, there is still a polarity of views on how far teachers are the problem or the potential solution to improving education. Teacher development begins with initial teacher education and should be a life-long opportunity. An important aspect of teacher development is the knowledge that needs to be acquired through initial training and continuing professional development as the chapters in this part explore.

Eaude's chapter about the expertise of primary teachers addresses the themes of identity and agency, and professional development. He captures, in a way few have, the unique qualities that are required to be an early years and primary teacher. The particular knowledge that primary teachers draw upon, and that should be the emphasis of teacher education and development, is seen as a complex blend of craft knowledge, subject knowledge and pedagogical knowledge.

Ambrossi makes a powerful case for the need for teachers to address cultural heritage, including empire and invasion, as part of their teaching of foreign languages. The Spanish language is used as an example. In the chapter the history of Moorish Spain and the 'discovery' of the Americas is used to show how foreign language teaching can be brought to life.

Another area where there is societal consensus is concern for those children most in need. Mintz's chapter uses his experiences as a teacher trying to support a boy with dyspraxia. Mintz focuses on whether there should be a special pedagogy for children with specific educational needs, and the nature of knowledge required to best support children with SEN.

Part IV: Education and society

The first three parts of the book have many resonances with education and society but this final part is a more direct analysis on the basis of three examples: diversity in classrooms; parental choice of schools; and professional identity.

Perhaps nowhere is diversity more evident than in London's education settings. Hundreds of languages are spoken, and the percentages of people with origins in countries other than England continues to grow. Moving out of London, in the United Kingdom more broadly, many issues connected to gender, race, culture, class, ability and other differences are part of the daily life of schools and their communities. Ang and Flewitt show how the idea of 'habitus' can help us understand and respond constructively to diversity in their comparison of two contrasting early years contexts in England and Singapore.

Although a minority elite may only see education as what happens in private schools, the reality for the majority of people is education in state-funded institutions. There are many ways that socio-economic factors are part of education debates but a powerful example comes though Merchant's chapter and her account of the ways in which schools are selected by parents and their children, and the types of schools that are available to different groups in society.

Two of the fundamental components of education that are a constant referent through the parts and chapters of the book are children and teachers. In view of the philosophies that underpin our thinking it is quite deliberate that the first part, and the first chapter, focuses on children and childhood. It is also fitting that the last chapter is directly about the work of teachers, and specifically about teachers as professionals. Drawing on more than a decade of experience of one of the most effective approaches to helping children learn (Reading Recovery), and experiences of training teachers internationally how to adopt the approach, the authors reflect on professional identity. At a time when the idea of teaching as a postgraduate profession (learned in the context of partnerships between universities and schools) has been under threat from those who see teaching as a simple craft to be learned 'on the job', there could not be a more important reminder of the sophisticated thinking that the best teachers develop through the combination of theory, research and experience.

Finally, the last chapter of the book crystallises our thinking about future visions. We see this as a manifesto for change. We hope that you will be encouraged to think more deeply about teaching, learning and education as a result of reading the book, and that you will take up some of the visions we propose, in the hope that teaching and children's lives will be improved.

Note

1 Throughout the book we use the UK term 'primary education' (age five to 11) which is equivalent to 'elementary education' in some countries.

Part I

The foundations of childhood

Chapter 1

Childhoods and contemporary practices

Phil Jones

Chapter summary

This chapter reviews the ways in which provision in early years and primary education is driven by powerful ideas and ideals about children. It is argued that the ways contemporary theory and policy situates children needs to be critically examined in the light of problems of oversimplification and dualism. Research into how children see their experience of provision is used as a model to redress this tendency in theory, policy and practice. The chapter sets an agenda for engaging more fully with the lived experiences of children and professionals.

The children knew they were going to move to secondary school (and another phase of their childhoods was about to start). They depicted the transition as a road, from primary school to secondary school (Figure 1.1). They wanted to know what would happen to the relationships with their peers and with their teachers. The words they chose to reflect their feelings were: 'isolation', 'abandoned', 'un-loved' and 'anxious' (Figure 1.1). Anxieties included new academic challenges, new teachers and leaving friends behind.

The schools on either side were identified as full of relationships and interactions (Figures 1.2 and 1.3). These were seen as positive, negative and ambiguous. However, the importance for this chapter is that the pupils viewed their provision as dynamic, changing and complex: forming a matrix of different elements being brought into relationship with each other. Figure 1.5 illustrates this – with a range of issues from academic challenge to relationships such as new teachers or leaving friends, identifying the dynamics between pupils and their educational space and work: 'bullying', 'new teachers', 'new lessons', 'finding way around', 'getting lost' and arriving 'late', 'judged', 'being different', 'puberty' and 'fitting in'. Here the children were making meaning of their education as a space that contains interactions between subject learning, relationships between professionals and with fellow pupils, and as an emotional and social space. Their reflections addressed areas such as difference and inclusion, home life and school, dynamic changes in time and space.

The images were used to identify the most common themes identified by the words chosen, then pupils in each group voted on the issues they felt needed attention within the research – each had voting labels for 1st, 2nd and 3rd and used these (Figure 1.4).

Figure 1.1 The 'road' to transition.

These votes were tallied and then small group work was used to create sentences around the words, developing what pupils felt were important about them. These sentences were collated using Wordle to help identify phrases and terms that were foregrounded. These were discussed with the pupils in each school and used to support them in deciding upon, and forming, the questions for the research.

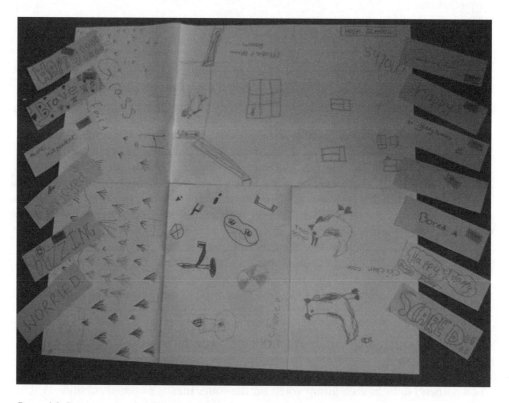

Figure 1.2 Primary school children preparing for transition.

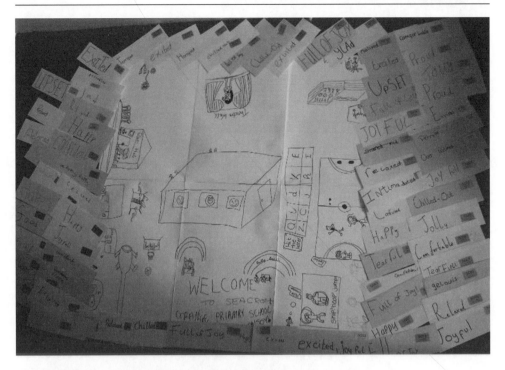

Figure 1.3 From words about transition to pictures and votes.

Figure 1.4 Voting sample.

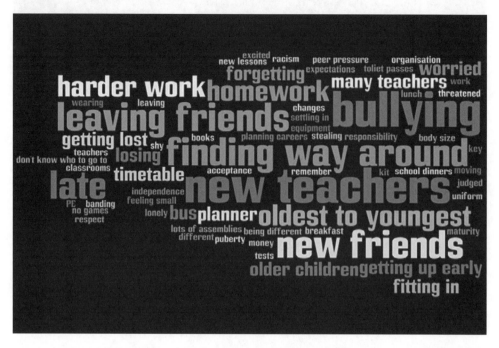

Figure 1.5 Pupils key words about transition represented as a Wordle.

Figures 1.1–1.5 are from research that aimed to explore pupil experiences of transition from primary to secondary school. The project involved designing research to establish and explore the views of children as experts in their own, and each other's, experiences of transition. Six classes from different schools co-worked with staff from the School of Education, University of Leeds (comprising Phil Jones, Mary Chambers and Emma Truelove). Class groups ranged in size from seventeen to 28 pupils and all were engaged with the process of transition. Consent was negotiated with the children, school and parents to take part and to share data. The research involved children in the design of the research project. This included participatory workshops with each class exploring areas such as the nature of research, research methodology and ethics. Sessions then engaged pupils in designing the research, and in identifying issues about transition to form research questions. Figures 1.1–1.3 are from participatory activities which pupils engaged with as part of these sessions. This involved a group drawing activity followed by the children attaching words as they discussed and identified their experiences and responses. This material reveals the ways in which pupils assemble meaning and reflect upon the dynamics and experience of their lives in education. The images and text show the complexity and richness of the children's perceptions of educational life and the relationships within it. The images and the Wordle reveal children's perceptions of life in education, and their identity there, as complex, as a living *matrix* of interactions and negotiations.

The following sections of the chapter explore the relationships between this complexity and the ways childhood has been framed by the sociology of childhood and by recent policies and practices in education. I examine whether these ideas and policies adequately reflect the lived realities of life in educational settings reflected in the pictures created by the children.

Key questions for reflection

How do children see early years and primary school life?

In what ways do early years or primary schools create spaces for children to reflect on, and make meaning of, their experiences of the setting?

In what ways do settings limit or deny spaces for children to reflect on and make meaning of their experiences?

Identify the strengths and limitations of creating such spaces?

Rethinking the sociology of childhood and educational provision

Recent attention to childhood has involved the evaluation of a particular phase of theory and related research, often described as the 'new sociology of childhood' (Prout, 2005; Tisdall, 2012; Wyse, 2004). This phase challenged traditional ways of exploring childhood, which, it argued, tended to see children through adult lenses and agendas rather than trying to understand and value children's own perspectives (Komulainen, 2007). The theory and research emphasised that childhood has changed over time, and that childhood differed for children according to their countries and contexts. The new sociology of childhood helped to examine ideas and practices that were thought to be static 'facts' about children and suggested that they were often ideas and myths constructed through powerful adult attitudes which tended to see children in negative stereotypes (Jones, 2009). An example is the assumption that children are incapable of making decisions or of having opinions of worth about what was happening in their lives. These kinds of ideas and myths, it was argued, often underestimated children's actual capabilities and hindered their true potential. Authors such as James have defined a key aspect of this approach as seeing childhood as 'socially constructed and that children are active social agents in the construction of their own childhoods' (2010, p. 486). Other connected concerns related to advocating the importance of children's perspectives or 'voice'; questioning traditional assumptions about the ways adults view children's competency; and seeing children as rights holders (James, 2010; Jones and Welch, 2010; Prout, 2011). A variety of factors had brought about these changes. The impetus to promote the participation of children in making decisions about their lives and having a say in what their services should be like, for example, had been fuelled by the United Nations Convention on the Rights of the Child (1989). Article 12 of the convention states that a child has a right 'to express an opinion and to have that opinion taken into account, in any matter or procedures that affect the child, in accordance with his or her age and maturity' (http://www.ohchr.org/en/professionalinterest/pages/crc.aspx). The new sociology of childhood has, to date, often been seen as a dialectic, offering a challenge to many 'traditional' ways of seeing and treating children by offering an 'alternative view ... often set up as a series of oppositional views' (Jones, 2009, p. 56). Table 1.1 illustrates such oppositional views. On the one hand, the 'traditional position' saw children primarily through negative stereotypes, contrasted with an 'emerging position' which identified and valued children's capacities. This can usefully be seen in terms of *dualism*: that 'for some particular domain, there are two fundamental kinds or categories of things or principles' seen in opposition to each other (Robinson, 2012, p. 1).

Table 1.1 Traditional and emerging views of children

Traditional position	Emerging position
Incapable	Capable
Not able to make valuable decisions	Active decision-makers with opinions that matter and making decisions of worth
Incomplete adults	Seen in terms of own capacities, not in terms of deficits, or as futurities based on adult set outcomes or adult functioning as a norm or goal

Source: Jones, 2009, p. 56.

Recent years have seen many shifts in the ways domains such as education think about how children are seen and treated, some influenced by seeing childhood as 'constructed', challenging negative adult stereotypes, and seeing children as capable, as rights holders and holding views of worth about their experiences of schooling. This can be understood as an *interdisciplinary* process which creates innovation, as the ideas of the new sociology of childhood are brought into dialogue with ideas and practices in domains such as health or education. For example, in 2008 such ideas are drawn on in the joint statement from the UK Children's Commissioners:

> Children are, however, still not viewed as key participants in education: discussions around improving education are often adult-based and fail to include children and their views. We are also concerned that educational inequalities persist, despite considerable investment in education across the UK. Access to sufficient, quality education remains a problem for particular groups (such as Gypsy and Traveller children, children within the juvenile justice system and children in care). (UK Children's Commissioners, 2008, p. 27)
>
> In the UK today, the gap between rich and poor is increasing, along with associated disparities in the well-being of children and respect for their rights. As Children's Commissioners, we take seriously our responsibility to ensure that the rights of children are promoted and their voices heard within the clamour of competing claims.
> (UK Children's Commissioners, 2008, p. 35)

Here children are seen as active agents in their own education in that they are described as 'participants'. This is connected to the idea that they should have a voice: meaning that their views are valuable and should be given weight in relation to what a service such as a school, or early years setting, is like. Education is also seen within a rights perspective, so children are seen as rights holders. Children rights can be used to help understand and respond to barriers in provision, such as those caused by poverty, and differences in ethnicity, health and wellbeing.

Key questions for reflection

What does it mean to you to see a child as an 'active agent' in their lives?
What other ways of thinking about children have you encountered?
How might seeing and treating a child as an active agent connect to the ways adults work with them in early years or primary settings?

However, recent commentaries have challenged some of the concepts of the construction of childhood. It has been argued that generalisations about childhood as constructed have resulted in oversimplified dualities which do not help in seeing the complex realities of children in different circumstances and contexts (Prout, 2011;Tisdall and Punch, 2012). In summary, the challenges centre on the following points:

- the need to move beyond simple dualisms – for example, that 'focusing on children and young people's perspectives, agency and participation is no longer sufficient' (Prout, 2011, p. 6);
- the need to challenge concepts which have 'typified' the new sociology of childhood, such as 'children's actorship being essentialized rather than analysed and therefore affecting the quality as well as the credibility of childhood sociological research' (Bühler-Niederberger, 2010, p. 160);
- a concern with the lack of criticality of new sociology of childhood 'givens', or, as Tisdall and Punch have described them, 'mantras' (2012, p. 251).

Revising such an approach does not abandon commitments to viewing and treating children as rights holders, nor to the view that they are capable participants rather than passive recipients of a service such as primary schooling or early years. The literature suggests there is a need is to move on from an oversimplification created by the kinds of reductive dualities illustrated in Table 1.1. Tisdall and Punch summarise a key part of this next stage of work as the need to 'reclaim and consider ideas that incorporate change, transition, contexts and relationships, moving beyond concepts that are unduly fixed and static, with unhelpful dichotomies and ignorant of cultural and contextual variations' (Tisdall and Punch, 2012, p. 254). Fielding (2007), for example, illustrates this shift when he comments on a need to respect children's rights while moving beyond a tendency to idealise or romanticise the idea of children's voice.

Interdisciplinary trouble

Interdisciplinarity has been seen to be of value in offering potentials for innovation in philosophy, theory and praxis, enabling the creation of insight in specific fields but also in the emergence and development of new ideas and ways of understanding (Alanen, 2012). Jacobs and Frickel (2009) describe a framework that positions individual disciplines as restrictive of direction and momentum, identifying them as disconnected silos that stifle innovation and restrict enquiry. The interdisciplinary is seen as active and valued as establishing a space and relations where ideas can 'flow without impediment' (Jacobs and Frickel, 2009, p. 52). They argue that 'successful' interdisciplinary endeavours can be characterised as owning the quality of being *transitional*. This concept is useful in seeing interdisciplinarity as being part of a dynamic of growth of change and insight. Within this frame, we can see the new sociology of childhood as a discipline offering a critique of the ways in which children's relationships with adults are formed in the field of education. Interdisciplinary dialogue could lead to shifts in the nature of children's involvement and participation in education. The UK Children's Commissioners statement quoted above is an example of the kinds of growth Jacobs and Frickel identify, where challenges are made to try to change established ideas and practices that do not see children as active participants in education.

However, in relation to children and adult's experiences of early years and primary education in England, a review of the interdisciplinary relationship between recent early years and primary education policies and the new sociology of childhood might see this in a different light. Central to notions such as Jacobs and Frickel's is the presence of mutuality, and that recognition is followed by exchange between disciplines resulting in change within a discipline as new ideas are assimilated and digested. Perhaps when areas of potential interdisciplinary dialogue meet resistance – areas that do not yield or do not respond to exchange – something different occurs. The basic tenets of the new sociology of childhood outlined above can be seen to be encountering problems in their 'interdisciplinary' relationship with education. What happens when interdisciplinarity meets something which is not part of Jacobs and Frickel's view of flowing without impediment? What happens when refusal, rejection and even antagonism occurs?

The next section illustrates the effects of interdisciplinarity between the new sociology of childhood and education meeting refusal and 'not flowing'. It will illustrate and contextualise this chapter's discussion of the limitations of dichotomies or oppositional dualities as a way of looking at childhood and children in early years and primary education. This will be undertaken by looking at three sets of recent material concerning educational provision for young children: Set 1 – Images of children and dualities within an early years setting's policy; Set 2 – Dualities and 'danger' in relation to Ofsted's approach to children and education; Set 3 – Dualities and oversimplification within instructions to early years inspectors.

Set 1 – Images of children and dualities

The following extract is a sample of an early years setting's policy, aims and research into early years provision, selected at random from a school judged by the Office for Standards in Education, Children's Services and Skills (Ofsted), as 'good'. Ofsted inspectors report on the achievement of pupils at the school, the quality of teaching in the school and quality of leadership in, and management of, the school and behaviour and safety of pupils.

The Early Years Foundation Stage (EYFS) Policy, revised in 2014, provided by Willowbank Primary School (http://www.willowbank.devon.sch.uk/files/8113/9093/1212/EYFS_Policy_-_January_2014.pdf) starts by outlining the four EYFS principles: 'a unique child'; 'positive relationships'; 'enabling environment'; and 'learning and development'. Regarding a 'unique child', for example, it states:

> We recognise that every child is a competent learner who can be resilient, capable, confident and self-assured. We recognise that children develop in individual ways and at varying rates. Children's attitudes and dispositions to learning are influenced by feedback from others; we use praise and encouragement as well as celebration and rewards to encourage and develop a positive attitude to learning.

The Ofsted report on the school reflects this emphasis on recognising each child as a 'competent learner', with a range of influences on their development, including teacher and child-led activity and the role of personalised learning. It noted:

> The teaching engages all pupils successfully and there is a good mix of teacher-led and child-initiated learning. This is particularly the case in the youngest classes, where all practitioners engage the children successfully in a wide range of activities.

The adapted curriculum meets the range and abilities of pupils well, resulting in all groups of pupils, including those with special educational needs and/or disabilities, making good progress. The teachers ensure individuals with specific learning difficulties have work that is personalised to their needs.

(Ofsted, 2010, pp. 4–5)

The school's aims are, in part, linked to the EYFS, and are stated as:

It is every child's right to grow up safe, healthy, enjoying and achieving, making a positive contribution and with economic well being. The overarching aim of the EYFS is to help young children achieve these five outcomes. At Willowbank Primary School, we aim to:

- provide a safe, challenging, stimulating, caring and sharing environment which is sensitive to the needs of the child including children with additional needs.
- provide a broad, balanced, relevant and creative curriculum that will set in place firm foundations for further learning and development in Key Stage 1 and beyond. (p. 3)

Willowbank's policy and aims, and its use of the EYFS, reflect particular positions on how children are 'seen': how adults and children relate to each other including approaches to the spaces and nature of the educational processes. It's possible to see reflected here the valuing of such positions from perspectives identified in research (Brooker *et al.*, 2010) undertaken into practitioners' experiences in the period following shortly on from the introduction of the EYFS:

Some of the phrases that emerged most frequently in the analysis of all the focus groups were 'child-led', 'child-focused' and 'child-centred'. All groups of practitioners reported that, despite the superficially prescriptive nature of the statutory framework, experience showed that the EYFS offered them freedom and flexibility for following children's interests and planning according to their needs.

(Brooker *et al.*, 2010, p. 25)

One manager within the research was quoted as saying, 'We observe the children then we plan and we also take ideas from the children and the parents and staff' (Brooker *et al.*, 2010, p. 26).

Key questions for reflection

How do you see the relationship between Willowbank's policies and the values identified in the quotes from the research undertaken by Brooker *et al.* (2010)?

What do you understand by 'child-centredness' and the comments about 'freedom' and 'prescription' within this section?

However, such policies and the provisions that relate to them are not neutral, and they reflect, and are in dialogue with, the kinds of dynamics discussed within this chapter. These include issues such as the nature, and effects, of the different ways children and education are seen. The material in Set 2 takes one of the themes discussed in this section – of 'child centeredness' – and looks at it in terms of the problems of dualisms and simplification identified earlier in the chapter.

Set 2 – Dualities and danger

The material in Set 1 looked at how children were seen in a school's policy, the school Ofsted report, and in related research. Right-wing think tank Civitas, in its report *Playing the Game* (Peal, 2014), attacks Ofsted's work and the way it views children and education. The report warned of 'a dangerous new situation' (Peal, 2014, p. 31) in educational settings and the need 'to curb the influence of [the] orthodoxy' of what it calls 'child-centred' learning' (Peal, 2014, p. 53). The Civitas report reflects a set of assumptions about education, stated not as assertions but as if they are facts, and these are used to paint 'child-centred learning' in particular ways. Most descriptions of Ofsted, for example, refer to it as being headed by Her Majesty's Chief Inspector (HMCI), as the non-ministerial government department reporting directly to Parliament, and as being responsible for inspecting and regulating education for learners of all ages, including early years and primary educational provision. Accounts note that Ofsted was formed under the Education (Schools) Act 1992, as part of a major overhaul and centralisation of the school system begun by the Education Reform Act 1988, which introduced the national curriculum and the publication of league tables (http://www.ofsted.gov.uk; Campbell and Husbands, 2013; Cullingford and Daniels, 1999; Shaw *et al.*, 2003). The Civitas report, however, interprets the history of Ofsted in a very particular way – saying that it was primarily created in '1992 to waylay the education establishment's preference for child-centred teaching methods'. This is accompanied by citations that set out to position Ofsted as biased and the HMCI as embattled against its perceived 'child-centredness'. One such example selected by Peal is from Sir Chris Woodhead, HMCI from 1994 until 2000, who is quoted as being 'unable to overcome' (Peal, 2014, p. 13) inspectors' preference for child-centred teaching due to the 'baggage' carried by them. This is defined by Woodhead as the 'the flotsam and jetsam of progressive education' (Woodhead, 2002, quoted in Peal, 2014, p. 13). The interpretation continues by suggesting that, over a decade later, Sir Michael Wilshaw (HMCI), head of Ofsted, takes up his post having 'inherited an inspectorate with a deeply ingrained culture in favour of child-centred teaching' (Peal, 2014, p. 13).

The Report proposes that this 'child-centred' 'preference' is still in need of purging within educational provision and identifies a series of areas classified by Peal (2014) into 'aversions' and 'preferences'. These are described as typifying a dangerous 'orthodoxy' within Ofsted inspections: 'aversion towards classes in which pupils were passive'; 'preference for pupils taking responsibility for their own learning'; 'preference for independent learning'; 'aversion towards teachers talking too much'; and 'aversion towards teachers directing lessons' (p. 19).

Peal's analysis cites what he calls a list of 'banned phrases' which has been 'circulated by independent service providers such as Serco' who manage inspections and reports 'on behalf of Ofsted' (http://www.serco.com/markets/education/ofsted/) as a guide for lead inspectors (Peal, 2014, p. 29). He argues that this is an attempt by Ofsted to redress the perceived 'bias' of its inspectors. Serco circulated the following guidance:

> There must be no writing which implies a particular style of teaching. Ofsted does not expect to see the following phrases:

- work is not matched precisely enough to the needs of individual children
- children do not have enough opportunities to be engaged in independent learning
- pupils are involved in their own learning
- teacher talk dominates too many lessons. (Serco, cited in Peal, 2014, p. 29)

The Civitas report, though, suggests that this will not be enough to 'curb' or to purge the education system of child-centredness, within an argument that if 'inspectors continue to make judgements based on their preference for child-centred teaching methods, while hiding such a judgement in the written report, we could enter a dangerous new situation' (Peal, 2014, p. 31). Peal selects two examples from Ofsted reports as diagnosis of this kind of danger with its hidden child-centred 'orthodoxy' and bias: 1.'"A key feature of learning is how students take responsibility for their own learning, working well both independently and collaboratively, and always trying their best." Maidstone Grammar School (outstanding, 26.9.2013).'"However, many lessons required improvement because teachers did most of the talking, without checking that students understood, and the pace of learning slowed as a result." Biddeham Upper School and Sports College (requires improvement, 26.9.2013)' (cited in Peal, 2014, p. 20).

It may be hard for some readers to see what the 'dangerous new situation' is that the Civitas report asserts, or that the comments made by schools about children's education are problematic. For example, what is dangerous about Maidstone Grammar School, praising children for learning in a variety ways and students 'trying their best'? Similarly, what is dangerous about teachers working at Biddeham checking whether students understood the lesson? Within the vilification found in the Civitas report such details are seen in a framework that aligns them with a danger to good education and as biased, child-centred 'orthodoxy' in need of being 'curbed'.

Wilshaw, in his role as HMCI, in a speech at a festival of education, which has been given the authority of being published on the Ofsted official website, draws a picture similar to that of the Civitas report:

> 'Informal' or 'individualized learning' is a case in point. This once-fashionable concept was based on the belief that children learn best by self-discovery, that criticism and adult supervision stifle youthful creativity. Its legacy still lingers in some schools today: academic rigour is undervalued; basic literacy and numeracy are neglected; subject specialism is relegated in favour of cross-curricula muddle.
>
> (Wilshaw, 2014a, p. 5)

Within a similar framework to Peal, Wilshaw sets a scene of contrasts based on opposites, using a religious-inflected language of exorcism and danger in education. In describing the history of UK education, he talks of how 'instruction was supplanted by indulgence' (2014a, p. 7), change is needed to 'exorcise the ghosts of the past' (2014a, p. 9) and he creates a situation where there can be no complexity: 'there is only one school model' (2014a, p. 9).

Foskett and Blackhall's (2014) response to one part of the speech identifies an aspect of the way this kind of dichotomy situates children. Wilshaw, for example, explicitly says that children do not want, or respect, teachers who consult them:

> Children, especially those who lack structure at home, want and expect teachers to give them rules. In their absence, they do not sit around politely debating the most

appropriate ones to follow. And they certainly don't think much of teachers who give them the option.

(Wilshaw, 2014a, p. 8)

Foskett and Blackhall, interpret Wilshaw's view as: 'children and young people should have absolutely no say on what they are taught, how they are taught or how the school as a whole should operate. Or in other words "done to, not done with"' (Foskett and Blackhall, 2014). This critique clearly reveals Wilshaw creating stark oppositions, and interprets his position as aligned with a particular way of seeing the relationship between children, professionals and educational practice.

Such a position of simplistic dualities, identified in my analysis of material from the Civitas report and the speech published on the Ofsted website, can be seen elsewhere in sections of educational discourse that aim to directly affect and form the nature of provision. The material in Set 3 illustrates the bridge between the kinds of thinking examined in Set 2 and material directly targeting how children are seen and treated in contemporary educational provision.

Key questions for reflection

Consider the Ofsted report material on Maidstone Grammar School and Biddeham Upper School and Sports College cited by Peal. Do you agree with his analysis?

How do you think the issues identified by Ofsted about children taking 'responsibility for their own learning, working well both independently and collaboratively' and teachers doing 'most of the talking, without checking that students understood' relate to primary and early years contexts?

Having read Peal's commentary about child-centredness, go back to Willowbank's material on the 'unique child', the quotes about their aims, and the Ofsted report. How do you see Peal's comments about child-centredness in relation to this material? Do you think it over-idealises the child as a 'competent learner', for example?

Set 3 – Dualities and oversimplification

In a letter sent in March 2014 in his role of HMCI to early years inspectors, Wilshaw states that: 'inspectors should focus on evaluating whether children are being adequately prepared for the start of their statutory schooling' (2014b, p. 1). This letter notes that:

In November 2013, Ofsted launched a revised early years inspection framework, emphasising that nothing less than good provision is acceptable. We clearly set out our expectation that adults must teach young children. How settings fulfil this is the responsibility of each provider. Therefore, I expect inspectors to apply common sense when observing how well children learn and how effectively adults teach children to develop skills, knowledge and understanding.

(2014b, p. 2)

And that:

In summary, inspectors should report on what makes teaching and assessment effective rather than on its style. I would like you to think carefully before criticising a setting because it does not conform to a particular ideological view of how young children should learn or be taught.

(2014b, p. 2)

Here the division present in the Civitas report and in Wilshaw's lecture can be seen behind and within the instruction to inspectors concerning how they should see efficacy in early years provision. The rhetorical device is to place terms and concepts together that make *assumed* connections and distinctions. We don't have the *direct statements* present in the lecture discussed in Set 3: that there 'is only one model' of education, or that 'individualised learning' and 'self-discovery' are in need of being 'exorcised' from educational provision to remove a legacy that 'lingers' and is in need of cleansing (Wilshaw, 2014a). However, the letter can be interpreted as reflecting and being driven by similar views about children and early years provision. So, for example, instructions to inspectors on the judgement of 'good provision' in the early years makes the kinds of allegiances and connections present within the lecture. The language presents the nature of early years as primarily linked to *school readiness* and *to teaching and assessment* and sees the child and the role and actions of early years professionals in a *particular way*. In one paragraph of the above extracts, the position on roles, identity and their actions is repeated within the space of three sentences: 'adults must teach young children' and 'adults teach children to develop skills, knowledge and understanding' (2014b, p. 2).

Wilshaw's wording here is less violent than in his lecture, in that it is not using images of religious exorcism and is without accusations of 'indulgence' and 'muddle', but the stance taken is the same. The letter claims to have an aim to ensure that inspectors' judgements do 'not conform to a particular ideological view of how young children should learn or be taught'. However, the document actually advocates a very particular position on how children should be seen and positioned within early years in a directly ideological way. This is a rhetorical device that claims its own position is not ideological when it is. A number of professional early years organisations argue that this is the case. For example in its response, a joint letter from TACTYC, the Association for Professional Development of Early Years Educators, the Centre for Research in Early Childhood and Early Education, the British Association for Early Childhood Education, noted that 'there are some aspects of your letter which are not in line with the current statutory EYFS Framework, and we are concerned that this gives confusing messages to inspectors' (Merrick *et al.*, 2014, p. 1). One aspect they identify says that:

You say that you 'clearly set out our expectation that adults must teach young children'. While we would, of course, agree that adult-led and adult-initiated learning has an important role to play in the early years, the use of the word 'teach' can give rise to expectations of overly formal approaches. In particular, it implies a pedagogy that is not suited to the needs of babies and very young children.

(Merrick *et al.*, 2014, p. 2)

They continue with their critique of Wilshaw's instructions:

The EYFS should not be narrowed to an instrumental focus on school readiness. Young children should be nurtured and valued in their own right as competent early learners, rather than treated as a means to a next stage. Whilst it is essential to equip young children with a love for learning, and to prepare older children for transition into primary school, early learners must be respected for who they are, rather than viewed simplistically and judgmentally in terms of who they might one day become.

(Merrick *et al.*, 2014, p. 3)

The criticism launched by the organisations uses language similar to that of the analysis within this chapter. They express concern with oversimplification and the creation of an agenda which is led by the creation of opposition and duality between teaching, seen primarily as 'adult-initiated learning' and young children being 'nurtured and valued' in their own right.

Key question for reflection

Consider the perspectives reflected in the letter from Wilshaw (2014b) and from the professional early years organisations (Merrick *et al.*, 2014): what are your opinions about the ideas and debates they contain and represent?

Connections can be seen between the attitudes underlying the Civitas report, Wilshaw's lecture and his letter. The complicated realities and nature of education are ignored. The focus is not on seeing education in spaces such as early years settings as complex, nor on rigorous understanding of space, relationships and of the tasks involved in education. Documents such as Peal (2014) and Wilshaw (2014a, 2014b) reflect a simplified, exaggerated dichotomy being used for political ends. Table 1.2 presents the quotes cited in sets 2 and 3 in clusters.

In Table 1.2 the simplistic duality is illustrated. A position is created whereby particular terms are associated together and then set against each other as if they are in opposition. The kind of rhetoric involved relies on vilification of a position, attacking terms such as 'child-centred', 'individualised' or 'independent learning', and positioning these as if they were opposite to teacher-initiated academic rigour and rules. The ways children are seen are represented primarily in stark contrasts. The concept of children as active meaning-makers and learning independently or as capable of having a voice in their provision is undermined and rejected, and adults who respond to them in this way are seen as not worthy of the respect of Ofsted or of the children they work with, as reflected in Wilshaw's comment, cited earlier, that pupils 'don't think much' of such professionals (2014a, p. 8).

The analysis of the three sets creates powerful examples and illustrations that children in early years and primary education are seen in ways:

Table 1.2 Clusters placed in opposition within the texts

'Child-centredness'	'There is only one model'
'Self-discovery' as learning	'Basic literacy and numeracy'
'Active learner'/pupils 'taking responsibility for their own learning'	Academic rigour
'Indulgence'	'Instruction'
	'Teacher talk'
	'Rules'
	'Teachers directing lessons'

- that are not neutral
- that represent debates about how society sees children and the role of education
- that represent choices and are changeable
- that affect how the purpose and nature of provision is formed and delivered.

I have argued that children and their experiences in education are reduced to simplified dualities. These are then used to make decisions about areas such as policies, which have serious consequences for the children and adults involved in education.

The examples in the sets show that this dualism and oppositional dynamic can result in oversimplification and an inaccurate way of representing lived experience, decision-making and what is effective in early years settings and primary schools. The creation of these dualities represent, or can result in, a way of seeing and treating children that creates splitting, opposition and actions that are rooted in reactions rather than effective understanding and a recognition that childhood itself, and that the position of children in education, is complex.

Future visions: childhood and children in education

The following material re-examines the nature of the 'dualism' identified in the analysis of these three sets and its relationship to policies and practice in early years and primary education. Contemporary scholarship on childhood advocates for the need to 'forge a line of flight' away from 'dichotomies through which modern western childhood has been forged' (Ryan, 2012, p. 440). Ryan argues for the need to 'break the grip' of this dualism with the purpose 'to clear the way for new ways of thinking about childhood' (2012, p. 440). He creates a contrast between a 'divided childhood' and 'representation of childhood' as a 'mixing site', referencing the language of Lee and Motzkau, who describe a 'test tube' (2011, p. 8) as typifying 'a blend that shapes the growing child' (2012, p. 441). We can replace simple dualities with a more finely grained set of understandings that can engage with material that deserves and needs a more complex interrogation. The goal is a different agenda for the relationships between policies and practice, adults and children.

The idea of a matrix is useful to further understand and respond to the ways in which essentialism creates oversimplified dualities through rhetoric. The term 'matrix' here is used in the sense of a number of elements which form a situation or set of elements which are brought into relationship with each other 'in which something else develops or forms' or 'from which a person or society can grow and develop' (*Oxford English Dictionary*, 2010). A 'matrix' can be used as a more effective concept to reflect and understand the complex negotiations of adults and children in early years and primary education. It represents a redress to oversimplification. The educational space, as a dynamic created by roles and relationships in complex interaction, is illustrated in Figure 1.6.

How individuals and groups work together to create practice in their own setting is best understood and responded to not through oversimplified duality, but by a matrix of dialogues between child, educational professional, political, social and cultural contexts, national and setting-specific policies. The matrix in Figure 1.7 illustrates this.

This matrix can be used to form an agenda for resisting the essentialising of children as active meaning-makers through romanticised images in ways that do not reflect the

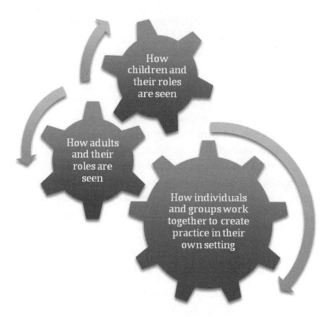

Figure 1.6 Children and adults in relation.

complexities of children's lives and their relationships with professionals in early years and primary education. The matrix view can also help respond to the kinds of simplistic divisions and oppositions seen within the earlier analysis of the material by Civitas and Wilshaw. The rhetoric of the sets within this chapter attempted to underpin a set of policy assumptions reflecting a simplistic ideology that does not match the matrix of children's

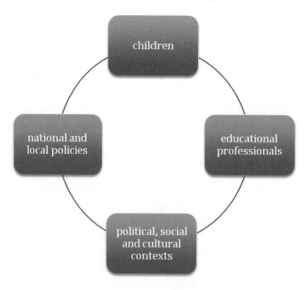

Figure 1.7 Matrix not duality.

and professionals lives together. It is inevitable that policy based on simplistic ideology will only fracture when it attempts to control and bind the living, dynamic complexity of the real world of early years and primary education.

Conclusion

In summary, the shift needed to avoid oversimplified dualities is as follows:

- Being in educational settings must be seen as a complex act with children and adults engaging with this in a variety of ways.
- Attempts to oversimplify education and childhood do not serve children and those living and working with them.
- Oversimplified dualisms present in contemporary thinking and policy can create false representations and unhelpful engagement with early years and primary provision – and those involved in education should view them critically.
- Research and development into the future place and role of adults and children in education is best represented by a matrix of interactive elements.

My recommendations above are built on the complex and interactive view of education reflected by the children's images and analysis that began this chapter. In contrast to the material reviewed within the three sets above, I position early years and primary education as a matrix, of interactions between subject learning, relationships between children, professionals and their fellow pupils. Education is an emotional and social space, reflecting areas such as difference and inclusion, home life and interactive changes in time and space. This will allow thinking, research and policy in early years and primary education to see children, their lives and their engagement with their provision as complex and not in a reductive and oversimplified way. This avoids an unhelpful view that there is 'only one model' pushed by the creation of simplified dualism and helps to explore in a way that better reflects the lived realities of how adults and children can best work together. In this way it will help to work with the complexity of changing lives and the dynamic matrix which the children's pictures and Wordle of transition depicted.

Further reading

Brooker, L., Rogers, S., Ellis, D., Hallet, E. and Roberts-Holmes, G. (2010). *Practitioners' Experiences of the Early Years Foundation Stage, Department for Education.* Research report DFE-RR029, London: Department for Education.
A useful review of early years practitioners' experiences and thoughts.

Jones, P. and Welch, S. (2010). *Rethinking Children's Rights*, London: Bloomsbury.
Reviews how children's rights are responded to within a range of educational contexts and explores research on barriers and problems to realising children's rights.

Kellett, M. (2011). *Children's Perspectives on Integrated Services.* Basingstoke: Palgrave Macmillan.
A book including and examining children's perspectives on provision.

References

Alanen, L. (2012). Disciplinarity, Interdisciplinarity and Childhood Studies. *Childhood: A Global Journal of Child Research.* 19 (4), 419–22.

Brooker, L., Rogers, S., Ellis, D., Hallet, E. and Roberts-Holmes, G. (2010). *Practitioners' Experiences of the Early Years Foundation Stage, Department for Education.* Research report DFE-RR029, London: Department for Education.

Bühler-Niederberger, D. (2010). Introduction: Childhood Sociology – Defining the State of the Art and Ensuring Reflection. *Current Sociology.* 58 (2), 155–64.

Campbell, J. and Husbands, C. (2013). On the Reliability of OFSTED Inspection of Initial Teacher Training: A Case Study. *British Educational Research Journal.* 26 (1), 39–48.

Cullingford, C. and Daniels, S. (1999). Effects of OFSTED Inspections on School Performance, in C. Cullingford (ed.), *An Inspector Calls.* London: Kogan Page.

Department for Education (2013). *Open Consultation: New National Curriculum: Primary Assessment and Accountability.* Available from: https://www.gov.uk/government/consultations/new-national-curriculum-primary-assessment-and-accountability. Accessed 25 August 2013.

Fielding, M. (2007). Beyond 'Voice': New Roles, Relations and Contexts in Researching with Young People. *Discourse: Studies in Cultural Politics of Education.* 28 (3), 301–10.

Foskett, G. and Blackhall, C. (2014). 'Sir Michael Wilshaw's Comprehension of the Comprehensive System' 3D Eye. Available at: http://3diassociates.wordpress.com/2014/06/27/sir-michael-wilshaws-comprehension-of-the-comprehensive-system/. Accessed 15 July 2014.

Jacobs, J. and Frickel, S. (2009). Interdisciplinarity: A Critical Assessment. *Annual Review of Sociology.* 35 (1), 43–65.

James, A. L. (2010). Competition or Integration? The Next Step in Childhood Studies? *Childhood: A Global Journal of Child Research.* 17 (4), 485–99.

Jones, P. (2009). *Rethinking Childhood.* London: Continuum.

Komulainen, S. (2007). The Ambiguity of the Child's 'Voice' in Social Research. *Childhood: A Global Journal of Child Research.* 14 (1), 11–28.

Lee, N. and Motzkau, J. (2011). Navigating the Bio-politics of Childhood. *Childhood: A Global Journal of Child Research.* 18 (1), 7–19.

Merrick, B., Payler, J., Pascal, C. and Bertram, T. (2014). *Your Letter to Early Years Inspectors: Joint Letter from TACTYC, the Association for Professional Development of Early Years Educators; the Centre for Research in Early Childhood and Early Education and the British Association for Early Childhood Education.* Available at: http://www.crec.co.uk/Letter%20to%20Sir%20Michael%20Wilshaw%2028%20March%202014.pdf. Accessed 15 July 2014.

Office of the Children's Commissioner (2013). *'Always Someone Else's Problem': Office of the Children's Commissioner's Report on Illegal Exclusions.* London: Children's Commissioner.

Ofsted (2010). *Willowbank Primary School Inspection Report.* 113119. Available at: http://www.willowbank.devon.sch.uk/files/2713/8516/4495/Ofsted-report.pdf. Accessed 24 July 2014.

Oxford English Dictionary (2010). *Oxford English Dictionary*, Oxford: Oxford University Press. Available at: http://www.oxforddictionaries.com/definition/english/matrix. Accessed 19 July 2014.

Peal, R. (2014). *Playing the Game: The Enduring Influence of the Preferred Ofsted Teaching Style.* London: Civitas, Institute for the Study of Civil Society.

Prout, A. (2005). *The Future of Childhood: Towards the Interdisciplinary Study of Children.* London: Falmer Press.

Prout, A. (2011). Taking a Step Away from Modernity: Reconsidering the New Sociology of Childhood. *Global Studies of Childhood.* 1 (1), 4–14.

Robinson, H. (2012). Dualism. *The Stanford Encyclopedia of Philosophy.* Available at: http://plato.stanford.edu/archives/win2012/entries/dualism/. Accessed 19 July 2014.

Ryan, K. (2012). The New Wave of Childhood Studies: Breaking the Grip of Bio-social Dualism? *Childhood: A Global Journal of Child Research.* 19 (4), 439–52.

Ryan, P. J. (2008). How New Is the 'New' Social Study of Childhood? The Myth of a Paradigm Shift. *Journal of Interdisciplinary History.* 38 (4), 553–76.

Serco (2014). *Serco, Bringing Service to Life: Ofsted Inspections.* Available at: http://www.serco.com/markets/education/ofsted/. Accessed 19 July 2014.

Shaw, I., Newton, D. P., Aitkin, M. and Darnell, R. (2003). Do Ofsted Inspections of Secondary Schools Make a Difference to GCSE Results? *British Educational Research Journal*. 29 (1), 63–75.

Tisdall, E. K. M. (2012). The Challenge and Challenging of Childhood Studies? Learning from Disability Studies and Research with Disabled Children. *Children and Society*. 26 (3), 181–91.

Tisdall, E. K. M. and Punch, S. (2012). Not So 'New'? Looking Critically at Childhood Studies. *Children's Geographies*. 10 (3), 249–64.

UK Children's Commissioners (2008). *UK Children's Commissioners' Report to UN Committee on the Rights of the Child*. Available at: www.childrenscommissioner.gov.uk. Accessed 27 January 2014.

Wilshaw, M. (2014a). *Reclaiming Comprehensives*. Sunday Times Festival of Education, Wellington College, HMCI's speech. Available at: https://www.gov.uk/government/speeches/reclaiming-comprehensives

Wilshaw, M. (2014b). *Letter from HMCI to Early Years Inspectors – March 2014*, Ref. 20140005. Available at: http://webarchive.nationalarchives.gov.uk/20141124154759/http://www.ofsted.gov.uk/sites/default/files/documents/other-forms-and-guides/l/Letter%20to%20early%20years%20inspectors%20March%202014.pdf. Accessed 15 July 2014.

Woodhead, C. (2002). *Class War: The State of British Education*. London: Little, Brown.

Wyse, D. (ed.) (2004). *Childhood Studies: An Introduction*. Oxford: Blackwell.

Chapter 2

The child's voice

Rosemary Davis

Chapter summary

This chapter focuses on the issue of the child's voice which is considered in a framework of the needs and rights of the child. It is shown that legislation and declarations of human rights provide for the child's voice to be heard. However, the diversity of childhoods, multifaceted within and across cultures, poses challenges for the reality. Voice and how it may be expressed is discussed in the first section of this chapter. Conceiving education as entitlement, it is argued, provides a means for children to reach their full potential and enable their voices to be heard.

A sixteen-year-old girl from a poor area of Gaborone, the capital of Botswana, was asked about her aspirations. She wrote,

> If you not educated you go to the cow. Again if you not education you go to cattle post at the cow. So I dont want there people go to cattle post they do not nothing. I want to teach people they must be educated.
>
> (Davis, 1987, p. 43)

In Botswana, and many countries of the world, the ownership of cattle represents significant wealth. People in Botswana aspire to have a *cattle post* which is a place where they can rear cattle, often a considerable distance from the main home.

The quote shows that the girl was already aware of the importance of education, and what life would be like without a good education; a life that for a woman would be much more restricted than for a man. Looking after the cows at the cattle post was often the future for such children. This sixteen-year-old girl was in Standard 7, the class for twelve-year-olds in Botswana at the end of primary school. The difficulty for many children, particularly girls, or in rural areas, is to get access to a school at all. Added to this is the problem with having to repeat primary school years if end of year exam results are not good enough, meaning that some older children attend classes aimed for younger children. Officially, children in Botswana were allowed to repeat once at Standard 4 (age eight to nine, when English becomes the medium of instruction) and again, once at Standard 7, the end of primary education and the year in which the Primary School Leaving Certificate examination was taken. The reality was that many children repeated more than the permitted number of times.

The quote from the girl from Botswana was part of a research project that I carried out that put the 'voice' of children, and their views, at its centre. Over 1,000 children participated, including children from Swaziland and Lesotho. In Lesotho, many primary school-aged children walked up to ten kilometres across mountainous terrain outside the capital, Roma, in order to reach a school. Lengthy journeys to school are commonplace around the world. This is a phenomenon that demonstrates a strong desire for education by children and their families: '[many children] demonstrate an outstanding resolve to get to school. They show that it is still possible to get an education despite the obstacles of poverty, gender inequality, social exclusion, urban insecurity, natural hazards or conflict' (UNESCO, 2013b, p. 1).

Different cultures not only have different practical opportunities and obstacles to education, such as very long walks to school in some rural areas in economically poor countries, but different cultures also evolve their thinking about education in different ways. The ways that we think about education in the West, and that perhaps you take for granted, have some elements that are intrinsically part of a particular western culture and its thinking. For example, the idea of child-centred learning evolved historically from changing philosophical and psychological perspectives on the nature of childhood. Connected to child-centred learning, but with a subtly different emphasis, the 'developmental tradition' is based on education processes that take the child's existing cognitive and social state as the starting points for learning.

A trend in western thinking has been the idea that there is no simple and absolute definition of childhood because childhood is itself a *social construction*. This means that the way we define childhood is dependent on our cultural background. One striking example of this is the way that the age of consent to have sex varies in different countries of the world, ranging from age twelve in some countries to age 21 in other countries. These laws are established based on conceptions of childhood and children in the different societies. If you accept the idea that childhood is a construct that differs according to culture and society, then Burman's advice is applicable: 'Study not only the child but also the context (that is the inter-personal, cultural, historical and political situation) that produces her' (Burman, 2008, p. 9). They may be thought of as 'producers of knowledge' (as Porter *et al.*, 2012, term it), an important concept for the issue of voice.

In this chapter I explore the concept of *voice*. In simple terms, 'voice' refers to a child expressing their needs, wishes and desires. But in order to express in this way, they need to be supported and encouraged to enact the sense of voice. My experience working in countries around the world, including Africa, leads me to consider voice not only in relation to the UK context, but also in wider cultural contexts. The chapter raises a series of issues about childhood and voice. For example, I consider to what extent voice genuinely reflects children's views and/or is filtered through adult mediations and representations. The chapter begins by showing how voice may be reflected in play and how sensitive teachers can support children's overall development. Children's own views on their education are discussed in the section which follows, drawing from research undertaken in the UK. Some of the ideas of play and children's voices are extended in the section on children's rights. The central part of the chapter focuses on international perspectives. The chapter concludes with setting out a vision for the future which would empower the child through education, providing for choice; the essence of voice.

Key question for reflection

What does the term 'voice' mean to you?

Voice and play

A universally important aspect of human learning (and animal learning) is play, something that is also closely connected to the idea of child-centred education. Rogers (2008, 2010) showed powerfully how children build their knowledge of their world, drawing on her studies of role-play in early childhood settings. She used a variety of multimodal methods and elicited children's understanding of roles, together with their likes and dislikes within the role-play. In her study, through the role-play, children modelled much of their language and activities on their perceptions of adults. This is not dissimilar to the responses of children in Botswana, Lesotho and Swaziland. When asked to write about 'what they wanted to be when they grew up' (Davis, 1987), the children I spoke to demonstrated how their aspirations, whether teacher, nurse, doctor or lawyer, were modelled on their perceptions of adult roles. Their play also reflected this.

Play is not only a natural part of development, and an important vehicle for learning, it is also an important vehicle for 'hearing' the voice of the child as shown by Rogers (2008). Brock et al. (2009) explore this in detail in a chapter entitled Three Perspectives on Play (pp. 9–40). In the same edited book, Jones (2009) shows how play may be used for therapeutic purposes as part of drama therapy. My informal observation of a child hints at the ways teachers can attend to voice through sensitive observation and interaction:

> Colin, a four-year-old in a nursery class in England, came from a comfortable professional home, with caring parents who wanted the best for their only child. However, Colin was not allowed to get muddy or engage in messy play at home. His teachers found that, on entering the class in the morning, Colin would not join in until he had up to an hour on the rocking horse. He was then happy to join in other class activities. Colin's voice was expressed in non-verbal ways, and was understood by his teachers as communicating his needs; hence his teachers supported his need to play on the rocking horse before other activities.

Teachers sensitive to how young children express their hopes, fears and reflect their lives and knowledge of their worlds, will be aware that play is one important medium through which they can interpret children's voices.

The examples given of voice expressed in play are taken from UK school contexts, but the principle of observing children in their play can be seen in other countries as well. However, just as concepts about children and childhood are culturally based, some also argue that play itself differs according to its context, something that Marfo and Bierstekker (2011, p. 74) call a 'culturally embedded concept'. The distinction between play and work that we make in the West is not necessarily the same in other contexts.

For example, Marfo and Biersteker (2011, p. 74) describe Ghanaian children turning the chore of fetching water into play, using a home-made wheeled vehicle, which served both the task in hand and as a racing vehicle. I have observed Batswana boys constructing toy 'bicycles' and 'cars', using old wire, acting both as playthings and as sale items, especially to tourists.

Key question for reflection

Think about a child that you teach who, in play, is expressing voice. How would you try to interpret what is not said and how would you respond?

Children's views of their education

The *Guardian* newspaper ran a project called 'The School I'd Like' (*Guardian*, 2011). The children who responded expressed strong views on what their schools should be like. The project's results became a Children's Manifesto, for which the essential features were that every child's education should be productive and happy. Flexible timetables including the opportunity to undertake school trips were seen as important by the children. A Year 4 (age eight to nine) pupil wrote,

> I think it's important to listen to children since we have a really big imagination, and we could have ideas on how to make lessons fun. Also the teachers may be able to learn something from us since they don't know everything.

A Year 1 boy (age five to six) said, 'Children sometimes have better ideas than adults. That is because children's brains are new and not old' (*Guardian*, 2011, p. 2). The *Guardian* project provided a national and international media platform for the voices of children to be heard.

In addition to media representation of children's views, there is also a tradition of educational research that has sought to hear children's voices. In the research surveys of the *Cambridge Primary Review* (Alexander *et al.*, 2010), there is reference to the increase in the literature which focuses on the voices of children in their schools. Robinson and Fielding, in chapter 2 of the surveys, focus specifically on primary school children's voices in the UK. The nine sections of their chapter reflect children's views on the purposes of education, the culture of schooling, school organisation, learning, teaching, the curriculum, and assessment within primary schools. The transfer from primary to secondary school is also addressed (also see Chapter 1 in this book for children's views about transfer) and pupils' aspirations and preferences in respect of children's own futures. The main purpose of primary school was seen by the children as preparation for a job in the future:

> If I didn't go to school I'd know nothing and wouldn't be able to get a job or nothing … it's really for people to learn things you didn't know before and when you are older you'll have so many 'O' levels you can get what you want … If you didn't go to school you wouldn't have no 'O' levels and you wouldn't ever get a job nowhere.
> (Cullingford, 1986, p. 43, cited in Robinson and Fielding, 2010, p. 19)

In different words and from a very different culture, you will have recognised the close similarity to the views of the Botswana girl at the beginning of this chapter.

The children's perceptions about disempowerment were apparent in their concerns about assessment. The studies cited by Robinson and Fielding (2010) concluded that children felt uneasy about their SATs results and what these might mean for their future.

The assessment regime in England has produced intense pressures that ultimately are funnelled down to children. In the memorable and troubling idea expressed by a child that, as a result of his likely test results, 'I'll be a nothing' (Reay and Wiliam, 1999, p. 343) it is important to remember that identity and voice are closely related. Children who feel like 'nothing' are very unlikely to feel confident to express their voice.

One strength of the data provided by Robinson and Fielding (2010) is that it drew only on children's views directly expressed by them, and excluded those of teachers and others adults. Attention has elsewhere been drawn to the problems of hearing and responding to children's voices when these are filtered through adult interpretations (James, 2007). However, teachers and adults who are perceptive about voice may be able to act as advocates for children's voice, a 'third way' that Jones discusses in the first chapter of this book.

Research undertaken for the NFER (Chamberlain *et al.*, 2011) concluded that children are not often asked for their opinions, with education debates dominated by adults. Yet the views of the Year 5 and 6 pupils (age nine to eleven), who constituted 28 per cent of the primary- and secondary-aged sample of approximately 2,000 children, were clear in what they thought of their school lives, what made for a good teacher and their desire to become more involved.

Overall, the children felt it very important that teachers should know what they were teaching, prevent bullying, help pupils who have difficulties with their work, help all pupils and listen to pupils' ideas. A theme identified in the *Cambridge Research Survey* and echoed by the children surveyed by Chamberlain *et al.* (2011) was the importance of being able to learn well at a good school and able to get a good job or opportunities for the future. As a primary school Year 5 girl said, 'If you don't get into good secondary schools you won't have a good job, as teachers might be poor, and if the teachers are poor then we don't learn much like we should' (Chamberlain *et al.*, 2011, p. 38).

Key question for reflection

Should play be part of the school curriculum or is it only suitable for out of school? Consider what needs play might serve for children aged i) three to five years; ii) five to seven years; iii) eight to eleven years.

Children's rights and voice

Another way to think about the voice of the child is as something that is one of their rights. The idea that children have rights has been endorsed by nearly every country in the world as signatories to the United Nations Convention on the Rights of the Child (UNCRC). Like all such conventions, the UNCRC is organised into 'articles' that itemise children's rights. One of these has a very direct relevance to my consideration of voice. Article 12 says:

Article 12
1. States Parties shall assure to the child who is capable of forming his or her own views the right to express those views freely in all matters affecting the child, the

views of the child being given due weight in accordance with the age and maturity of the child.

2. For this purpose, the child shall in particular be provided the opportunity to be heard in any judicial and administrative proceedings affecting the child, either directly, or through a representative or an appropriate body, in a manner consistent with the procedural rules of national law. (UNCRC, online, http://www.ohchr.org/EN/ProfessionalInterest/Pages/CRC.aspx)

The idea that children's right to express their views freely in all matters affecting them, including all aspects of their education, is established in law should, in theory, provide powerful justification for teachers to ensure that children voices are heard and acted upon. The reality is, however, rather more complicated (see Tisdall, 2012).

Before children can have the confidence to make their voice heard there are a range of basic needs that have to be in place. For example, it is almost impossible for children to make their voice heard if they are frightened of being beaten or coming to some other harm. The UNCRC includes legal obligations to protect children. For example, Article 2: the right to non-discrimination; Article 3: the best interests of the child should be paramount; Article 6: that children have a right to life, survival and development. And importantly, for the purpose of this book, Article 30 gives a right to free and compulsory education, at least for the elementary (primary) phase.

This chapter began with an example of how a girl in Botswana saw the vital importance of education. I have also shown the importance of education to all societies by its inclusion as a right in the UNCRC. Children have a right to education. But education is regarded as very important for another reason. It is seen as a vehicle to improve the conditions of all members of a society, including children. So important is education that it has even been used to promote a country's democracy as the following example shows.

Until 1989, Namibia was under South African rule and therefore subject to apartheid, the policy that systematically discriminated between white people and black people. Peace, brokered by the United Nations, ended 25 years of war, and elections in November 1989 resulted in the South West African Peoples' Organisation (SWAPO) forming a government and a new democratic constitution. The constitution provided for equality and outlawed discrimination by race, gender or religion. Through the introduction of 'learner-centred' education (LCE), schools were to be the medium for the creation of a democracy and, by implication, enable previously disempowered peoples to express their voice.

The article in the UNCRC that deals directly with protection from abuse is Article 19:

Article 19

1. States Parties shall take all appropriate legislative, administrative, social and educational measures to protect the child from all forms of physical or mental violence, injury or abuse, neglect or negligent treatment, maltreatment or exploitation, including sexual abuse, while in the care of parent(s), legal guardian(s) or any other person who has the care of the child.

One form of physical violence that happens in schools is corporal punishment, which is the use of the hand, a cane, or other implement to punish children. This was only banned in British state schools in 1987. I found similar challenges in eradicating corporal punishment when I worked in Namibia in 1993. During my four years, from the beginning of 1992 until the end of 1995, of providing training for all primary head teachers there was evidence that the head teachers were divided on the issue of corporal punishment. However, when asked for suggestions for 'alternatives to corporal punishment' these included ideas such as 'sit on knees 30+ minutes'; 'fetching water from the river 800 metres';'tie to fence';'dig out tree stump'. But there were also suggestions that seemed to be more consistent with the new democratic constitution of the country, for example: 'speak to parents';'reprimand';'remind of rules of conduct';'restitution by pay for damage'; 'refer to pupils' council' (Ministry of Basic Education and Culture, 1993). Although pupil councils provide a means for children's voices to be expressed, emotions, feelings and needs need to be heard in a variety of ways. My experiences in Namibian primary schools showed that the stick was often much in evidence in classrooms and children showed fear even where the stick was not actually used. A paradigm shift in attitudes was needed for reality to match intention, a shift that applied to teachers, parents and other adults. Namibia, however, was not alone in this. An example from Botswana demonstrates the damaging effects of corporal punishment, and how children's attitudes and aspirations are modelled on their perceptions of the teacher's role. As this Standard 7 girl from a rural school, wrote:

> when I grow up I want to be a teacher to be a teacher is very nice, because I want to hit naughty children boys are very naughty sometimes they do not do classwork they always play outside playing football. I want to be a teacher to hit boys if they are naughty because teachers hit children.
>
> (Grammar as written by child. Davis, 1987, p. 43.)

Botswana is one of many countries in which, with or without a ban on corporal punishment, serious abuses occur; others include Japan and Nepal (Stewart, 2013). Article 19 of the UNCRC (1990) provides for 'protection from all forms of violence', but nowhere is this a reality. Legislation in the UK, however well intentioned, has been unable to provide protection from physical or emotional abuse. An extreme example, which became public news in 2013, was of Daniel Pelka, a five-year-old, starved, beaten and tortured to death. Teachers and others involved with Daniel failed to recognise and act upon the evidence of bruising and scavenging for food. His actions and face signalled his need to be heard by the adults around him. He was not. Abuse is a global problem, as demonstrated also by the UNESCO exhibition on *Journeys to School – Against All the Odds* (2013b).

> Six-year-old Elizabeth Atenio lives in Kibera, East Africa's largest slum near Nairobi, Kenya. Each day, dressed in a clean uniform, she sets out on the hazardous hour-long walk to school. At least 20 per cent of Elizabeth's school have been raped, according to her teachers.
>
> (UNESCO 2013b)

For Elizabeth, her right to protection had no standing in practice, nor does it for the many children, especially girls, who are preyed upon by teachers or those who should ensure a child's right to health, safety and protection.

For some children the idea of having voice is so far from their lives that they appear almost invisible, an idea highlighted in the most recent report by UNICEF (2014).

This gives data sampled from 196 countries across a range of indicators. A particularly important idea for this chapter is that if children are not officially recognised by nation states then they cannot have a voice:

> But not all children are being counted, and not to be counted only perpetuates invisibility and voicelessness. Groups commonly undercounted or overlooked include children living in institutions or temporary housing, children in detention, children living and working on the street, children with disabilities, trafficked children, migrant children, internally displaced and refugee children, and children from ethnic minorities living in remote areas or following a nomadic or pastoralist way of life.
> (UNICEF, 2014, pp.11–12)

The report also notes the importance of their monitoring of the reality for children, and of 'telling the untold stories': 'Being counted makes children visible and this act of recognition makes it possible to address their needs and advance their rights' (UNICEF, 2014, p. 10).

The problems with lack of being counted and lack of voice have occurred in the UK, and have resulted in repeated attempts to improve matters. For example, the Children and Families Act became law on 13 March 2014 (DfE, 2014). Its wide-ranging provisions for the protection of children superseded earlier legislation affecting education, health and care (EHC), and the act upholds the articles of the UNCRC (1990). The Act's provisions include the appointment of a Children's Commissioner with the primary function of upholding children's rights together with taking their views and interests into account in any decision-making. Children should be made aware of this important primary function. Elsewhere, Iceland, Norway and Sweden appointed ombudsmen for this purpose (Einarsdottir, 2007).

Non-government organisations (NGOs) play their part in giving children voice. There are many such, one being BRAC, originally the Bangladesh Rural Advancement Committee, which supports initiatives aimed at empowering children and communities in a number of countries, including the UK (BRAC, 2013). Their work, aimed at reducing poverty and promoting culturally acceptable education, helps to raise consciousness, with potential to enable children to express voices, an underlying goal of Education for All (UNESCO, 2000). Another important example is the Child to Child Trust which works in a number of countries throughout the world to empower children, promoting their rights by encouraging children to work together. Through the Trust's work, children help others learn in an informal manner, often using books on life and health issues for the text. An Ethiopian girl is quoted as saying, 'When I teach others it helps my own learning' (Child to Child Trust, 2009, p. 1).

However, 57 million children are reported by UNESCO as being out of school, 31 million of whom are girls. Poverty, distance, discrimination and conflict are among the reasons for this (Davis et al., 2005; UNESCO, 2013a). These risk factors are given prominence not just by United Nations documentation; they are explored in data from the Millennium Cohort Studies in the UK, for example, Kieran and Mensah (2009). Risk factors in child development on cognitive development and behaviour are highlighted and apply across the world. The multiplicity of cultural influences, together with, for example, strengths or weaknesses in family structures, all affect outcomes for children. Whether they survive or have access to education is shown to be uncertain, judged by reports such as those of UNICEF (2014). In global terms, access to education is limited. Inequities, especially for poorer children, are not easily overcome (Lewin and Sabates, 2012)

Key questions for reflection

1. What could an individual teacher do to promote children's rights within the school?
2. How far do you think children's rights, especially to voice, balance with the teacher's responsibilities for children's learning?

Future visions

A vision for the future whereby children will be empowered to use their voices and make them heard has been implicit throughout this chapter. The starting points have been the legislative frameworks in the UK, and throughout the world, to promote the rights of the child, including through education. An utmost priority is that children have a right to be protected from harm, whether from within school or from outside. Too many children do not have access to education, and where they do the conditions in which they find themselves often militate against learning opportunities. Once in school (access to schooling is still not universal across the world) children have a right to a good education from well-educated and trained teachers.

In the UK, teacher development needs to address the importance of voice and ways to listen to children, both to attend to children's learning needs and in the serious circumstances where abuse is suspected. The state, parents, teachers and welfare services (the guardians of the child's rights) all have a responsibility to ensure that these issues are not simply rhetoric, and that their right to voice is upheld.

A major point made by the children studied in the UK is that they want good teachers who help them when needed and who listen to their points of view. It is also important to find varied opportunities for children to express their views in non-verbal ways. Observation of children and the way they enact adult roles in play reflect their perceptions of their worlds, and can give important clues to children's views.

Children state that they want their education to be 'fit for purpose', to equip them with the knowledge and skills they will need for their futures. They see this as empowering them through the ability to choose their future, the essence of ensuring voice. Part of being 'fit for purpose' would take account of children's desires for an orderly learning environment and for their anxieties concerning assessments to be taken seriously. Putting this into practice would need to recognise the child as co-constructor of knowledge, not as passive recipient. All of the points made in this section have implications for policy and practice. If the voices of children are to become reality, as is their right and entitlement, this implies reciprocity and a democratic relationship between children and their educational experiences.

Further reading

Alexander, R. (ed.) (2010). *Children, their World, their Education: Final Report of the Cambridge Primary Review*. London: Routledge.

A large-scale review of primary education that includes significant attention to children and their voices.

Brock, A., Dodds, S., Jarvis, P. and Olusoga, Y. (eds) (2009). *Perspectives on Play: Learning for Life.* Harlow: Pearson Education. 9–40.
Broad research-based overview on play.

Jones, P. and Walker, G. (eds) (2011) *Children's Rights in Practice.* London: Sage.
Useful text on legislation and issues on children's rights.

Kanyal, M. and Cooper, L. (2012). Young Children's Perceptions of their Classroom Environment: Perspectives from England and India. In T. Papatheodorou and J. Moyles (eds), *Cross-Cultural Perspectives on Early Childhood.* London: Sage. 58–72.
Interesting cross-cultural comparison of children's perceptions; an aspect of voice.

Palaiologou, I. (ed.) (2013). *The Early Years Foundation Stage: Theory and Practice.* London: Sage.
Covers a wide range of EYFS issues from child development, welfare and pedagogy.

References

Alexander, R., Doddington, C., Gray, J. and Kershner, R. (eds) (2010). *The Cambridge Primary Review Research Surveys.* London: Routledge.

Bangladesh Rural Advancement Committee (BRAC) (2013). BRAC UK *Annual Report and Financial Statement.* London: BRAC/UK.

Birkett, D. (2011). *The School that I'd Like: Who Made the Grade?* Theguardian.com Thursday, 20 October 2011. Available at: http://www.theguardian.com/education/2011/oct/20/school-id-like-childrens-imagination

Burman, E. (2008). *Deconstructing Developmental Psychology 2nd ed.* London: Routledge.

Chamberlain, T., Golden, S. and Bergeren, C. (2011). Children and Young People's Views of Education Policy. Office of the Children's Commissioner. NFER. March.

Child to Child Trust (2009). *Annual Report.* Institute of Education, University of London. 1.

Clark, A. (2005). Ways of Seeing: Using the Mosaic Approach to Listen to Young Children's Perspectives, in A. Clark, A. T. Kjorholt and P. Moss (eds), *Beyond Listening: Children's Perspectives on Early Childhood Services.* Bristol: Policy Press. 29–49.

Davis, R. (1987). The Influence of Social Context on Aspirations of Primary School Children in Botswana. *BOLESWA Education Research Journal.* 5. 46–59.

Davis, R. (with Lloyd, E., Penn, H., Bareau, S., Burton, V., Potter, S. and Sayeed, Z.) (2005). *How Effective are Measures Taken to Mitigate the Impact of Direct Experience of Armed Conflict on the Psychosocial and Cognitive Development of Children aged 0-8?* Available at: http://eppi.ioe.ac.uk/cms/LinkClick.aspx?fileticket=cJ4-QD3CSRE%3D&tabid=166&mid=980

Department for Education (2014). The Children and Families Act. Available at: www.legislation.gov.uk?ukpga/2014/6contents/enacted

Eaude, T. (2012). *How do Expert Primary Classteachers Really Work?* Critical Publishing. Available at: www.criticalpublishing.com

Einarsdottir, J. (2007). Children's Voices on the Transition from Pre-school to Primary School. In A. W. Dunlop and H. Fabian (eds), *Informing Transitions in the Early Years: Research, Policy and Practice.* Maidenhead: McGraw Hill, Open University Press. Ch 6. 74–91.

James, A. J. (2007) Giving Voice to Children's Voices: Practices and Problems, Pitfalls and Potentials. *American Anthropologist.* 9 (10). 261–72.

Jones, P. (2009). Opening Play: Research into Play and Dramatherapy. In A. Brock, S. Dodds, P. Jarvis and Y. Olusoga (eds), *Perspectives on Play. Learning for Life.* Harlow: Pearson Education. Ch. 10. 231–50.

Kieran, K. and Mensah, F. F. (2009). Poverty, Maternal Depression, Family Status and Children's Cognitive and Behavioural Development in Early Childhood: Longitudinal Study. *Journal of Social Policy*. 4. 569–88.

Lewin, K. M. and Sabates, R. (2012). Who Gets What? Is Improved Access to Basic Education Pro-poor in Sub-Saharan Africa? *International Journal of Educational Development*. 32. 517–28.

Marfo, K. and Biersteker, L. (2011). Exploring Culture, Play and Early Childhood Education in African Contexts. In S. Rogers (ed.), *Rethinking Play and Pedagogy in Early Childhood Education: Concepts, Contexts and Cultures*. Oxford and New York: Routledge. 73–85.

Ministry of Basic Education and Culture/Florida State University (1993). *Basic Education Reform Project: Training Workshop for Head Teachers*. Arandis, Republic of Namibia.

Porter, G., Townsend, J. and Hampshire, K. (2012). Children and Young People as Producers of Knowledge. *Children's Geographies*. 10 (2). 131–4.

Reay, D. and Wiliam, D. (1999). 'I'll be a nothing': Structure, Agency and the Construction of Identity Through Assessment. *British Journal of Educational Research*. 25 (3). 343–64.

Robinson, C. and Fielding, M. (2010). Children and their Primary School. In R. Alexander, C. Doddington, J. Gray and R. Kershner (eds), *The Cambridge Primary Review Research Surveys*. London: Routledge.

Rogers, S. (2008) Researching Young Childrens' Perspectives: A Multi-method Approach. In S. Rogers and J. Evans (eds), *Inside Role-Play in Early Childhood Education: Researching Young Children's Perspectives*. London and New York: Routledge. 39–51.

Rogers, S. (2010). Powerful Pedagogies and Playful Resistance. In L. Brooker and S. Edward (eds), *Engaging Play*. Maidenhead: McGraw Hill, Open University Press. Ch 11. 152–65.

Stewart, W. (2013) Discipline – Soul Searching as Survey Reveals Japan's Dark Side. *Times Educational Supplement* 13 September. Available at: https://www.tes.co.uk/article.aspx?storycode=6356577. Accessed 21 June 2014.

Tisdall, E. K. M. (2012). The Challenge and Challenging of Childhood Studies? Learning from Disability Studies and Research with Disabled Children. *Children and Society*. *26:181-191* DOI:10.1111/j.1099-0860.2012.00431.x

United Nations Convention of the Rights of the Child (UNHCR) (1990). United Nations General Assembly.

UNESCO (2000). *Education for All: Framework for Action*. The World Education Forum. 26–28 April. Dakar, Senegal.

UNESCO (2013a). *Education for All. Out of School Children*. Global Monitoring Report. Paris: UNESCO. 1.

UNESCO (2013b). *Journeys to School – Against All the Odds*. Exhibition. Paris: UNESCO.

UNESCO/UNICEF (2013). *Making Education a Priority in the Post-2015 Development Agenda*. Paris: UNESCO.

UNICEF (2014). *Every Child Counts*. New York: UNICEF. 7 January. 11–12.

Chapter 3

Children's thinking

Anne Robertson

Chapter summary

This chapter considers children's thinking about their thinking, which is known as meta-cognition. In particular it examines children's use of metacognitive strategies within a cognitive acceleration (CA) programme. The central part of the chapter reports a research study that examined metacognition and CA. It is proposed in the chapter that developing a dialogic pedagogy that supports young children's metacognitive skills is beneficial to learning across the curriculum and should be fostered more widely in early years and primary settings.

> You use your brain and think in it and then you could work out the kind of thinking you need and if you do that it means that you get the puzzle right but if you don't think in your head to let your brain tell you the thinking, you won't.
>
> (Abdul, aged six)

Abdul clearly demonstrated his understanding of the thinking process. He described thinking as utilising two separate activities: using his brain and working out the type of thinking he needs. The process he described may characterise metacognitive aware-ness for Abdul, in that he appeared to be 'looking' at his thinking through using his brain, standing back from the task to use his brain at another level. In many ways this example shows how sophisticated young children's thinking can be if we encourage them to reflect on and express their experiences. Abdul's teacher, concerned about how to facilitate metacognition in young children, was reassured by examples of this kind and was inspired to value activities that develop metacognitive strategies in the classroom.

'Metacognition' means the ability to reflect upon our thinking and the processes of thinking (Flavell, 1979). Metacognition (and related self-regulatory abilities) is one of the most powerful determinants of children's academic success (see, for example, Whitebread *et al.*, 2009). However, it is also clear that metacognition is significantly influenced by its social context, and in particular the ways in which children view themselves as learners. As metacogition is beneficial, consideration has turned to whether and how we might help children develop better metacognitive thinking. One potential way of doing this is through an approach called cognitive acceleration (CA). CA programmes are based on the idea that if children are given the necessary experiences and environment to understand the processes of thinking and learning, they develop not only better reasoning, but also an increased awareness of the process of learning through metacognition. By becoming increasingly aware of the process by which they learn, children, in turn, may take more control over their learning.

Barnes and Todd (1978) argue that we learn only by making sense of what happens to us through actively constructing a world for ourselves. In CA lessons the children and teacher talk together while manipulating equipment and artefacts in an effort to solve challenges through discussion and by coming to agreed conclusions. In this way CA brings together both the Piagetian constructivist and the Vygotskian social constructionist perspectives. Teachers are encouraged to consider how to facilitate children's developing ability in using language to learn and to think as they construct knowledge through their interactions with and explorations of the environment and objects.

Mercer *et al.* (1999) maintain that teachers rarely induct children into how best to use language for constructing knowledge. It has been noted that where teachers provide instruction in the use of talk children benefit more fully from shared group activities (Howe and Mercer, 2007). Mercer *et al.* (1999) use the concept of exploratory talk originally suggested by Barnes and Todd (1978), defined as:

> Statements and suggestions are sought and offered for joint consideration. These may be challenged and counter-challenged. But challenges are justified and alternative hypotheses are offered. In exploratory talk, knowledge is made publicly accountable and reasoning is visible in the talk.
>
> (Mercer *et al.*, 1999, p. 97)

Drawing on Vygotsky, Mercer endorses the view that language is a cultural tool vital in the development of thinking. It is 'a means for transforming experience into cultural knowledge and understanding' (Mercer *et al.*, 1999, p. 97). Vygotsky argued that the true direction of the development of thinking is from the interpersonal social context to the intrapersonal or individual. Mercer also argues that language is a means for people to think and to learn together. Wells (1999), updating Vygotsky's ideas, called this 'dialogic inquiry' and promoted 'a community of inquiry' which has similarities with Mercer's 'interthinking' (Mercer, 2000). Talking in learning is, therefore, a reciprocal process where ideas bounce back and forth as children advance their ideas and thinking skills.

Key questions for reflection

How might you plan lessons which encourage children to engage in exploratory talk?
What kinds of questions could you use to encourage children's metacognition?

Personal Construct Theory (PCT) is a recognised and well-established framework for enabling and understanding dialogue. PCT was originally developed by Kelly (1955), whose view was that although reality exists nobody has direct access to it. On the contrary, each person looks at their world through their system of personal constructs thus enabling them to place unique interpretations upon events and circumstances.

This process results in being able to predict likely outcomes within a range of familiar circumstances. Many alternatives are available with which to make sense of self, relationships and the world. To some extent these alternatives are limited, for example, by the person's social context, but in some ways people's minds can be opened to the wider horizons of further possible constructs.

According to Kelly, constructing is a process by which we anticipate and experience events. In this context, 'construct' is the word used for the basis on which a prediction is made and, therefore, involves action on the part of the person. Kelly also argues that constructs are dichotomous or bi-polar in that to understand a construct, the individual must recognise both similarities and differences between people, objects and experiences (Kelly, 1955). For each person the meaning of each construct will be different. This approach offers a useful way to make sense of the children's understanding of their classrooms experiences. For example, a child named 'patience' as a quality of a teacher helpful to their learning and named the opposite pole as 'noisy'. Another child named 'patience' as helpful, but for her the opposite pole was articulated as 'gets angry quickly'. In discussion with each of these children it transpired that the first child sometimes found her teacher's style daunting. The teacher sometimes spoke forcefully when she encouraged children to actively engage in drama activities. The second child enjoyed the same drama activities but described how she felt scared by the teacher when she lost her temper; it was that this made her reluctant to learn.

According to Kelly's theory a child constructs the story of their reality based on their experience. In expressing constructs children are sharing their individual view of their experience. By listening to children's constructs the teacher can understand the sense they are making of their experiences.

My argument in this chapter is that, inevitably, each child's personal perspective on their experiences will impact on their learning. Using PCT to discuss the learning process with children can surface these experiences and reveal a wealth of information useful to teachers in developing their pedagogy.

Listening to children to understand their thinking

A research study was conducted over a two-year period in collaboration with four teachers, each of whom taught classes of Year 1 children (Robertson, 2014). This part of the chapter focuses on data from the second year of the study where differences in children's participation during CA lessons and in their personal constructs were explored. Additionally, by the second year the teachers had participated in intervention activities to help raise their awareness of the children's developing understanding of their thinking.

The methods for the research included individual interviews with the children that encouraged them to express their unique experience of the CA programme and of learning in the classroom. It allowed the children's voices to be heard and valued without judgement. Interviews were initially sought at three points in each of the two years: in September, March and July. Eight CA groups were established. At the start of each interview, name cards for each child in the group were placed on the table. Participating children were then asked: 'Can you say what you think helps your learning in CA?' In order to obtain the opposite pole of a construct children were asked: 'Do you all do this in the same way?' The children then looked at the name cards and chose children whom they thought were in some way the same and then identified the opposite pole by choosing names of children that were in some way different. Following this, the children were asked to say how each construct helped their learning (Table 3.1 shows the constructs and their definitions).

At each point in the year, all of the children were able to articulate personal constructs in answer to the question: what helps you to learn? They were also able to produce each opposite pole. For example, many children mentioned the construct 'have to work' in September. When the children looked at the name cards, they could separate them and say of other children in the group 'these ones work like me but these ones play or chat all the time'. Children had neither difficulty in producing constructs nor in identifying differences between themselves and others in their group. The opposite poles were always expressed in a coherent way implying that the children understood the task and could identify, without difficulty, similarities and differences between children in the group. These constructs gave teachers important insights into how the children viewed themselves and some of their peers at this early stage in their schooling.

Observation of CA lessons illuminated how children's verbal constructs reflected their actions and behaviours during CA lessons. Listening to children as they worked through CA activities revealed something of their reasoning processes to the teachers. Children were heard describing their ideas, explaining their reasons and asking questions within the social context of the learning group. This is an essential aspect of the CA pedagogy.

The children's views on what helped their learning

At the start of the year in September, there was little evidence of progression or variety in the children's responses. However, six months later in March, the constructs expressed by children were very different. Many were expressed by the children as active verbs, suggesting a more developed understanding of their participation in the learning process. To give an example, many children distinguished between *not* doing something and being *unable* to do something. Some children said that they needed to 'understand' the problem in order to learn but that sometimes children could 'not understand'. This is illustrated that children were aware of times when they were able to do things and times when they tried, but were unable to succeed. This could imply that children were developing their understanding of their personal part in the learning process, while experiencing some aspects as difficult. It would seem that these children were already constructing a world where some aspects were too difficult or complex. Some children were unable to provide an alternative solution or way forward, thinking instead that they were simply incapable of undertaking the task. For example, Tiffany said 'I can't understand the problems sometimes so I can't help get them right. You can't do it if you don't understand, can you?' This is an important point for teachers in developing a pedagogy that recognises and supports young children to become competent and confident learners.

In March some of the constructs expressed by the children still related strongly to externally imposed behaviours on the part of adults. For example, 'Hands up, keep tidy' related to classroom management strategies used by the teacher which if not adhered to would lead to some form of admonishment. The children could not explain how putting their hands up helped their learning but they could easily describe their teachers' reactions to their non-cooperation. In these cases children were constructing a world where management strategies and keeping the teacher happy were interwoven with what it meant to be a learner.

It was expected that, by July, children's constructs regarding their learning would have become more complex as a result of the normal development that takes place during an academic year as children mature and gain new experiences. At this point, children indicated the difference between engaging in something (listening), not being able to do something (can't make sense) and choosing not to do something (won't talk). This may indicate that the children were more aware of their part in learning and also their capacity to choose how to be involved in the learning process. Children were able to discuss their constructs in a way that indicated understanding of them as skills that helped them to learn. For example, Weena explained that 'You think in your head. It gives you ideas because your brain tells you answers.' Weena's comment showed that she had developed and integrated her understanding of 'thinking', a process that she may first have heard in her CA group. This illustrates Vygotsky's (1978) notion that children develop understanding of concepts as they integrate language that they hear in the social context. If children integrate concepts in this way it is a reasonable assumption that they integrate skills that facilitate learning. In this case, because Weena can explain her constructs it can be assumed that she integrated this skill and used it during lessons. As the constructs from each group were very similar in September, it is possible to attribute the substantial differences in children's responses during the year to differing classroom experiences.

Having completed a programme designed to develop children's thinking abilities it might be assumed that the CA children should have developed a strong understanding of what helps their learning since they were given a weekly opportunity to articulate their thinking while being challenged in a collaborative context. This appeared to be the case. At the end of the school year, all participating children were able to explain their constructs and provide examples of when and how these constructs had helped them to learn. For example, Margarite explained why listening helped.

> When I *listen* to John and Abdul, I hear their ideas in my head. They get sort of mixed up with my ideas and then I can say new ideas what help sometimes. If I didn't listen, I wouldn't get them new ideas, I don't think.

To illustrate the interactions that focused on children's metacognitive activity, it is useful to compare the constructs from March and July across the two years of the study, remembering that in the second year the teachers had actively encouraged these skills in regular CA teaching sessions.

As Table 3.2 shows, in the first year metacognition did not figure very much in the March constructs but appeared more in July when, for example, one construct in particular 'work out what thinking you need' was mentioned eleven times. The children had various ways of describing how helpful this construct was to their learning. Grace explained that if:

> you knew how to think about the problem that would help you, like if you have to work out groups of things, or sorting in order or looking for reasons [the] others were not good at thinking first about what kind of thinking to do and that didn't help them.

Table 3.1 Constructs provided by the CA children in March of the first and second year of the study

| Constructs | March – Years 1 and 2 | | | | | | | |
| | Pine School | | | | Larch School | | | |
	A1	A2	B1	B2	C1	C2	D1	D2
Listen	4	6	5	6	5	6	6	6
Talk	2	5	6	5	1	5	6	4
Explain	1	4	5	5	1	5	3	5
Share things	2	4	5	4	2	3	4	4
Share ideas	0	4	0	3	0	4	0	6
Solve a problem	1	0	2	0	2	0	3	0
Solve challenges	0	4	0	5	0	5	0	4
Look	1	3	2	3	2	4	5	3
Think	0	6	1	6	2	6	4	6
Ask	0	4	2	5	0	6	1	5
Sort	2	0	1	0	1	0	0	0
Discuss	1	5	2	6	0	5	1	0
Work hard/sensibly	5	0	3	0	1	0	1	0
Understand	1	0	2	0	0	0	0	0
Remember	0	0	0	0	0	0	3	0
Kind	1	0	1	0	0	0	1	0
Not argue	1	0	0	0	1	0	0	0
Helpful	1	0	0	0	0	0	1	0
Get right	0	0	0	0	0	0	1	0
Confused	1	0	0	0	0	0	0	0
Play	0	0	1	0	0	0	1	0
Order	1	0	0	0	0	0	0	0
Feel objects	1	0	0	0	0	0	0	0
Difficult	1	0	0	0	0	0	0	0
Try	1	5	0	4	0	1	0	5
Put things in groups	0	5	0	4	0	2	0	5
See other ways of doing things	0	2	0	4	0	5	0	3
Agree/disagree	0	5	0	6	0	4	0	4
Use your brain	0	5	0	6	0	4	0	3
Work as a team	0	3	0	4	0	3	0	5
Show what to do	0	4	0	2	0	3	0	4
Total	**28**	**74**	**38**	**78**	**18**	**71**	**47**	**72**

Grace had clearly begun to consider how to go about a task and reflect upon how to solve challenges. Other children discussed the importance of considering which schema to use before embarking on the task. For example, in one group Sacha, Abdul, John and Margarite all expressed the construct 'work out what kind of thinking you need'. Sacha found it difficult to explain how this helped her to learn, but said 'like if you know if you are to think of groups or lines of things then it helps you so you do the right thing and the right thinking'. Margarite also tried to explain this:

> when you look at the game, you should think in your head what kind of game is it and what kind of thinking you need so you can work out if it's groups or rules or orders of things, If you don't not do that you won't get it right really 'cos your head'll be all wrong, like Sacha's.

Table 3.2 Constructs provided by the CA children in July of the first and second year of the study

| | July – Years 1 and 2 | | | | | | | |
| | Pine School | | | | Larch School | | | |
Constructs	A1	A2	B1	B2	C1	C2	D1	D2
Listen	6	6	6	6	6	6	6	6
Talk	2	6	5	6	5	5	6	6
Explain	1	5	4	6	5	6	6	5
Share	4	5	4	5	5	5	6	4
Discuss	3	6	6	6	4	6	6	6
Solve a problem	1	0	4	0	5	0	5	0
Solve challenges	0	5	0	5	0	5	0	6
Look	3	5	2	4	2	5	3	3
Think	3	6	6	6	6	6	6	6
Ask	1	6	3	5	3	4	5	5
Describe things	2	0	1	0	4	0	3	0
Put things in order	4	0	4	0	4	0	5	0
Make sense	2	0	5	0	3	0	4	0
Agree and disagree	3	6	6	6	3	5	5	4
Use your brain	3	6	6	6	4	4	6	6
Work out what thinking you need	1	0	4	0	1	0	5	0
Try	2	5	3	4	3	4	5	4
Share ideas	0	5	0	6	0	6	0	6
Make stories right	0	2	0	3	0	2	0	3
Think of other views	0	4	0	4	0	2	0	3
Work as a team	0	3	0	4	0	5	0	3
Show what to do	0	4	0	2	0	3	0	2
Think of how to think	0	3	0	4	0	2	0	3
Say how you are thinking	0	4	0	4	0	1	0	3
Ask how people think	0	2	0	1	0	1	0	1
Challenge someone	0	1	0	1	0	0	0	2
Say if you remember something like it	0	1	0	1	0	0	0	0
Total	**41**	**96**	**69**	**95**	**63**	**83**	**82**	**87**

My understanding of this explanation is that Margarite had experienced the value of thinking about what was required to solve the task and that when the group gave consideration to this activity they were successful. Tamu also showed some insight into this construct when he explained:

> If you think in your brain what you have to do like groups or orders or getting things right then you'll know what kind of thinking to start and then you can go and maybe get it right or you can change your mind and maybe try another kind of thinking and see if that helps you.

Tamu demonstrates here that he also understood an evaluative aspect of metacognition.

In March, Weena stated that 'if you think in your head it gives you ideas because your brain tells you answers'. In July this idea had developed to 'if you listen and then think hard in your brain, ideas come into your mind and if you can use them they help to solve the puzzles'. When asked to say more she added:

Once you have thinked it helps you to make sense and then people can agree or disagree if they talk and explain. I use my brain to work out what kind of thinking you need and then I work it out and then I know the answer.

Weena showed that she was reflecting on the thinking process and how it helped her to solve the challenges.

In the second year of the project, further evidence of metacognitive activity could be seen in the construct 'see other ways of doing things'. To try to understand whether this referred to metacognitive functions children were asked to say more about this construct. Aurora explained, 'Well, if you think about a problem one way you might try to do it the wrong way but if you think of lots of ways of doing it then you can maybe choose the right one.' By July, Aurora said that she liked to 'think of other views' and this seemed to replace the March construct 'see other ways of doing things'. When asked how this helped her to learn she said:

If you look at things from different ways you'll probably find a best way of looking at it. Then if you tell the others like what you're thinking then that helps too 'cos they share and you see lots of different ideas then. When we do that we always sort our puzzles out.

From this I understood Aurora to have had positive experiences of sharing at a metacognitive level in her group, so not only did she experience metacognition as helpful to herself, but also she saw it as helpful to the whole group. This observation has important implications for classroom pedagogy as children in the early stages of schooling become more socially aware and benefit from working collaboratively on tasks.

Joshua also showed that he was learning to collaborate.

When I think about a puzzle, I look and see which way will I do it and I listen to Aurora and she says something else and I think Oh that's another way but I don't think it will work and I tell them and then we say all the ways what might work that we can see in our brains.

When asked how that helped him to learn he said, 'Well you can *think* about all the ways the next time you have a puzzle and one of them other ways might be the one to go.' By this I understood that he was aware that he was developing a repertoire of strategies to solve challenges and that this repertoire could be 'dipped into' on subsequent occasions. Different strategies suit different challenges so by building his repertoire he was enabling himself, and others, to be able to solve a range of problems.

In July Group A2 gave several insights into how they were working together and actively using metacognition in the CA lessons. Anna, for example, explained how metacognition helped her to learn.

ANNA: You need to get like inside your head, you know, and think and say what you are thinking and then you need to like get inside the others' heads too and think what they think and that helps you to understand.
R: I wonder how that helps?

ANNA: Well, if you can sort of think what they might think then you can ask them or like a question 'cos sometimes they don't say what they think so you get their ideas if you like tell them you want to know 'cos it helps. If you just try to solve the puzzle without thinking you're thinking then you probably won't get it.

In this example, we can see that Anna was clearly grappling with considering how to work out her own thinking. But she was also aware of the importance of understanding or trying to work out other children's thinking. Working as a team to solve a challenge featured strongly for the children in the project, so alongside the cognitive benefits of CA it would seem that social skills were also enhanced and made explicit. Not only did the children appear to grasp some of the usefulness of metacognition, but also the value of collaborative learning.

At times, the children came up with images to express how they understood metacognition. For example, Aurora said:

When you want to learn something like new like you don't know before you need to think, like go inside your brain and then it tells you like a voice like new ideas. My brain listens and looks at the things on the table and people's ideas and then it whizzes about to make sense of everything. When it's made sense it puts words in my mouth and then I say ideas what help to solve the problems. Then the others can agree or disagree and we keep going until we get to the end of the puzzles.

Similarly, Joshua reported that his brain helped him to think about all he heard and saw and tried to work out because 'that's what brains are supposed to do – think, you know'. He also had his own image, 'You see, if you *think*, well, you can do anything 'cos you have a brain and it thinks you know like it goes bzzzz in your head and all the ideas go bzzz and move around until they get the ideas sorted out and then your brain tells you what to do or say next. It's clever my brain and that means I'm clever.'

Joshua also experienced metacognition as helpful:

If you think how am I thinking oh yeah I know it's like rules and then say how are you thinking and they say well it's tricky but I think it's rules then you say oh yeah let's follow rules and we'll find out the answer. If you do that and it works it means that asking about how they were thinking has helped you but if it's wrong then you have to ask another people how are you thinking and they'll say groups and then that'll help you maybe. Aurora and Bernie help me 'cos they say what are you thinking too and we all say. But Rakhmi and Keendi don't say much ideas so we tell them our ideas and that helps them and they can get the puzzle too.

In this example, Joshua demonstrates that he has had positive experiences of metacognition in a collaborative approach. He was also confident to explain that when the group did not get the method right first time they were prepared to discuss their ideas again. These expressions of children's thinking provided rich and valuable insights into how and what children were learning which in turn supported the teachers in planning an appropriately challenging and stimulating curriculum and pedagogy. What is also striking is the way in which children such as Joshua showed empathy in the learning context, identifying that some children required more help than others. There was no negative judgement made of children but the situation was acknowledged as a matter of fact.

It is clear from the children's explanations at this point that they had integrated an understanding of how thinking about their thinking affects how they set about a task. Discussing their ideas involved reflection and evaluation of how they are more successful in solving tasks when they engage each other by sharing ideas and agreeing on the best strategies. In these examples, the children show that they have engaged fully in the meta-cognitive process (see for example, Hartman, 1998). Research has shown that children who were strong at processing metacognitively performed better than children who did not engage in metacognition so effectively (Whitebread et al., 2009). So, these children have every possible chance to become highly successful learners.

New visions

During the intervention meetings, all four teachers on the project had expressed a lack of confidence in working to support metacognition, which suggests there is a case for initial and continuing professional development in this area. Following the intervention to support teachers' use of CA to enhance metacognitive activity, there was a consistent effort in each lesson to use a range of questions to encourage children to think about their thinking. As the teachers grew in confidence, opportunities for metacognition were substantially increased and evident in their pedagogy. The teachers became more adept at reminding children to think about their thinking and to raise their awareness of the ways in which they were learning as well as what they were learning in each of the CA lessons.

As shown in the children's data, children were not only aware of their own thinking but that of other children in the group. The children often spoke of other people's thinking and how this impacted upon them in terms of their success or failure to solve a puzzle. This awareness of others, described in the literature as 'theory of mind' (Piaget, 1955), is an indication of a child's ability and readiness to engage with metacognitive thinking. The findings of this study correspond to those of Larkin (2005). She concluded that most Year 1 children naturally develop a theory of mind and that, critically for this chapter, that metacognition can be developed through nurturing this within a classroom environment where thinking about thinking is a valued part of pedagogy. Children also developed an awareness of 'thinking behaviours' that they could use but chose not to at particular times. As Margarite explains:

> Sometimes I listen to the others and that helps me 'cos it gives me ideas and then I say my ideas too but sometimes I don't listen. I just look around at the rest of the class sometimes to see what things they are doing 'cos I like to see that.'

Such insights are important in shaping a pedagogy that listens to children acknowledging them as active agents in the teaching and learning process. Evidence that the children had become aware not only of behaviours and attributes which helped them to learn but also of their willingness or not to engage with the tasks and/or the groups was also indicative of metacognitive skills. To some extent this point echoes the work of Flavell, who discussed one aspect of metacognitive behaviour as including 'intentionality' (Flavell, 1979). In the extract above, Margarite declared that she knew that listening helped her to learn as she heard ideas that she had not thought about. According to Flavell, intentionality presupposes thinking which is deliberate and goal directed. In this example, Margarite was aware that listening to others helped her towards the goal of solving a puzzle. However, she was also aware that she was not always willing or able to attend and concentrate on what was going on in the group as the rest of the class attracted her attention.

According to Flavell (1976) there are three aspects that children learn and acquire over time in the context of storing and retrieving information helpful to learning. They learn to:

- identify situations in which intentional, conscious storage of information is important and may be useful later;
- keep current information related to problem-solving and are able to retrieve it when necessary;
- make systematic searches for information helpful in problem-solving.

Children provided evidence that they could recall what kind of thinking to use when solving challenges. They were able to explain why using the right kind of thinking helped them. However, they did not provide evidence that they understood or were aware that their method of storing information was important. The children provided evidence that they were learning to use current information, particularly ideas from other children in their group but there is no evidence to suggest that they were at the stage of being able to make systematic searches for relevant information. It could be that children had not yet acquired the necessary skills and cognitive capacity to work in this way. Knowing what impacted most upon the children in the first year of the study supported the teachers in the second year to focus their pedagogical skills more acutely on aspects of CA pedagogy. They were alert to creating occasions for raising the conversation to a metacognitive level and increasing the number of opportunities for children to engage in metacognitive activity. As teacher confidence grew in the second year of the study so the children's ability to describe and explain developed earlier. In the second year the teachers reported that they began to allow these same 'thinking behaviours' to spill over into other lessons and gradually over the course of that year more and more lessons were taught in a collaborative, supportive environment that encourage talk. In a primary classroom this is important because the teachers are with the children all day and teach all subjects so opportunities to enable children to develop 'thinking behaviours' in a range of lessons arise.

The current policy climate places increasing demands on teachers to achieve improved outcomes for children in early years and primary settings, particularly those from the most disadvantaged backgrounds. With this in mind, it is argued here that there is compelling evidence of the benefits of pedagogies that are dialogic and allow for children to articulate their perspectives on the learning process. It is also the case that teachers need to be supported through initial and continuing professional development to acquire the requisite skills and confidence to work with children in ways which support metacognitive activity. Raising teachers' awareness of metacognition and the importance of understanding children's experiences of learning can make a significant difference to the ways in which they enact pedagogy, and in turn can impact positively on children's ability to think critically and creatively. Several authors in this book make reference to the dangers of focusing too narrowly on subject knowledge delivered via 'chalk and talk' pedagogies. A future vision of education which can meet the complex learning needs of children in the twenty-first century needs to emphasise children's capacities to reflect on their own thinking and learning. An emphasis on space for reflection could usefully be applied to teachers too.

Further reading

Adey, P. (ed.) (2008). *Let's Think Handbook: A Guide to Cognitive Acceleration in the Primary School.* London: G. L. Assessment.
An accessible text, which explores the meaning of cognitive acceleration.

Flavell, J. H. (1979) Metacognition and Cognitive Monitoring. *American Psychologist*. 34 (10). 906–11.
Flavell has researched and written extensively about metacognition. You may find it interesting to look at this work in relation to more recent applications mentioned below.

Larkin, S. (2012) *Metacognition in Young Children*, London: Routledge.
An accessible text, which addresses how metacognition can be fostered in young children in primary schools through a review of evidence from psychology and education and through the author's own empirical work.

Whitebread, D., Coltman, P., Pino Pasternak, D., Sangster, C., Grau, V., Bingham, S., Almeqdad, Q. and Demetriou, D. (2009) The Development of Two Observational Tools for Assessing Metacognition and Self-regulated Learning in Young Children. *Metacognition and Learning*. 4 (1). 63–85.
This paper describes tools for assessing metacognition in the classroom and can help you to think about your approach to pedagogy.

References

Adey, P. (ed.) (2008). *Let's Think Handbook: A Guide to Cognitive Acceleration in the Primary School.* London: G. L. Assessment.
Barnes, D. and Todd, F. (1978). *Discussion and Learning in Small Groups*. London: Routledge and Kegan Paul.
Barnes, D. and Todd, F. (1995). *Communication and Learning Revisited: Making Meaning Through Talk*. Oxford: Heinemann.
Butler, R. J. and Green, D. (2007). *The Child Within: Taking the Young Person's Perspective by Applying Personal Construct Psychology*. Chichester: Wiley.
Flavell, J. H. (1976). Metacognitive Aspects of Problem Solving. In L. B. Resnick (ed.), *The Nature of Intelligence*. Hillsdale, NJ: Erlbaum. 231–6.
Flavell, J. H. (1979). Metacognition and Cognitive Monitoring. *American Psychologist*. 34 (10). 906–11.
Hartman, H. J. (1998). Metacognition in Teaching and Learning: An Introduction. *Instructional Science*. 26 (1–2). 1–3.
Howe, C. and Mercer, N. (2007) Children's Social Development, Peer Interaction and Classroom Learning. *Primary Review*. Cambridge: University of Cambridge.
Johnson, K. (2004). *Children's Voices: Pupil Leadership in Primary Schools*. National College for School Leadership, International Research Associate Perspectives, Australia, Summer.
Kelly, G. A. (1955). *A Theory of Personality: The Psychology of Personal Constructs*. New York: Norton Library.
Larkin, S. (2005). Metacognition in Year 1: An Exploration of Metacognition in Five and Six Year Old Children During a Cognitive Acceleration Programme. PhD thesis. London, King's College.

Mercer, N. (2000). *Words and Minds: How we use Language to think together.* London: Routledge.

Mercer, N., Wegerif, R. and Dawes, L. (1999). Children's Talk and the Development of Reasoning in the Classroom. *British Educational Research Journal.* 25 (1).

Piaget, J. (1955). *The Origins of Intelligence in Children.* New York: International Universities Press.

Robertson, A. (2014). Let the Children Speak. Unpublished PhD thesis, Institute of Education, University of London.

Swanson, H. L. (1990). Influence of Metacognitive Knowledge and Aptitude on Problem Solving. *Educational Psychology.* 82 (2). 306–14.

Vygotsky, L. S. (1978). *Mind in Society.* Cambridge, MA: Harvard University Press.

Wells, G. (1999). Dialogic Inquiry: Towards a Socio-cultural Practice and Theory of Education. Cambridge: Cambridge University Press.

Whitebread, D., Coltman, P., Pino Pasternak, D., Sangster, C., Grau, V., Bingham, S., Almeqdad, Q. and Demetriou, D. (2009) The Development of Two Observational Tools for Assessing Metacognition and Self-regulated Learning in Young Children. *Metacognition and Learning.* 4 (1). 63–85.

Part II

Curriculum, pedagogy and assessment

Chapter 4

Agency, pedagogy and the curriculum

Sue Rogers and Dominic Wyse

Chapter summary

The curriculum is one of the most important elements of education. Not only does the curriculum determine the majority of the activities that children and young people encounter each day at school, but it is also central to a great deal of education research, and to governments' education policies. Curriculum is also bound up with pedagogy because pedagogy is the means by which the curriculum is enacted. This chapter focuses on curriculum and pedagogy through an examination of teachers' agency and pupils' agency. Agency is understood in the chapter as the extent to which children and teachers have control over the curriculum, and the way this links with classroom interaction. The chapter proposes that greater agency on the part of teachers will allow for opportunities to recognise and nurture children's agency through particular pedagogies.

TEACHER: Legs crossed, like this … everybody listen … well done, Kieran for being ready. Well done, Sophie for being ready … What I would like you to do, is to turn to the person next to you, and have a think of as many words as you can that begin with the sound /ch/
The children call out
CHILD 1: Chocolate creams
CHILD 2: Chair
Kieran appears to be experiencing difficulties and is fidgeting.
CHILD 3: Chowder … Cheese … Mouse … Sheep
After a few seconds, an adult asks Kieran whether he has found any words beginning with /ch/. Drawing on what he has heard other children say, he enthusiastically replies:
KIERAN: Yeah! Chowder … cheese … mouse … tree
TEACHER: 'Tree' begins with /t/ not /ch/
CHILD 4: [*shouts loudly*]: Chocolate bread, chocolate cream
KIERAN: [*That's wrong because*] everything begins with 'chocolate'.
The noise level increases. The teacher begins to clap to gain the children's attention. The children clap in response to the teacher's clap pattern. The teacher praises a child for 'good stopping', then another child for 'good sitting'.

After the school's summer vacation Kieran (aged five) had moved from the 'reception class'[1] to Year 1 (an important transition for the purpose of this book because it is the move from early years education into primary education). When the extract was recorded it was early October, and Kieran had been in statutory schooling for just four weeks. The example took place in a whole class phonics session, a lesson that has become common in many countries.[2] Kieran was trying to exercise agency by actively seeking to understand the task, to understand the routines and rituals of the lesson, and the expectations of the teacher, but his opportunity for agency was very limited as a result of the nature of the lesson and the teacher's interaction. For example, the teacher could have encouraged Kieran's agency more by responding to his suggestion like this: 'Chowder does begin with the /ch/ sound, and its an interesting word, what made you think of 'chowder' Kieran?' There would then be the option to more supportively explain that the sound at the beginning of the word 'tree' sounds a bit like /ch/ (particularly the way some children articulate it) but is in fact /t/.

To continue the focus on the curriculum and pedagogy of the teaching of reading we now compare the first example of learning and teaching with another.

A nursery teacher had organised a 'writing area' in her classroom, with a range of resources to support children's mark-making. A child called Mark had opted to work in the writing area. He had been folding a piece of sugar paper into an irregular structure to which he added some marks with felt pen. He turned to show the researcher what he had done: a parcel for his friend Ben.

In seeking to ensure that a photograph of Mark's writing was appropriately oriented the researcher was drawn into a pedagogic role that centred on the children's good-natured disagreement about letters and phonemes.

RESEARCHER: Oh that's good, a parcel for Ben [*Mark's friend who did not attend the same early years centre*], I like that. I'll take a picture of it like that.

MARK: I want to hold it like that.

RESEARCHER: Do you, that makes the writing upside down, is that all right? OK. You want to hold it. Well tip it back a bit so that I can get the writing. Look at the camera, you can see it … That looks like a letter M.

MICHAEL: No it's a /m/ [*Michael, who had come to the writing area and joined the conversation, voiced the sound*].

RESEARCHER: It's a /m/ is it?

MICHAEL: /m/ for mummy. It's for my mummy.

NEIL: [*who also came to the writing area and joined the conversation*] No it's M for mummy.

RESEARCHER: That's right, M is the name of the letter isn't it, and /m/ is the sound.

NEIL: No M! [*spoken very firmly*]

RESEARCHER: M's the name yes. They're both right … Is that mummy?

NEIL: Yes.

The transcript of dialogue was part of a project carried out in an early years centre in England. Taking an ethnographic approach the research analysed the ways that the children engaged with print and texts, and the implications of this for curriculum and pedagogy. Although the spontaneous learning and teaching that took place in the extract is significant from the perspective of children learning to read (see Wyse, 2010), perhaps equally important is what this example shows about agency, particularly in comparison with the first example in this chapter. The children's agency was enacted in the choices they made over their learning, and in their initiation of conversations of interest to them.

However, the extent to which the teacher had agency in a curriculum area so heavily dominated by government regulation is a moot point (see later in this chapter in relation to the national curriculum in England, and see Chapter 12).

Key questions for reflection

In what ways might Kieran have made sense of the learning and teaching?
What are the key features of teaching and learning apparent in the two examples?

In this chapter we explore curriculum and pedagogy with a particular focus on teachers' agency and children's agency. The first part of the chapter outlines some of the theories that have influenced our thinking, particularly sociologically oriented ideas of competence and performance. Next, we consider pedagogy and the ways in which it can enhance or diminish children's agency. The final part of the chapter examines national curricula and the extent to which the national curriculum in England, and its development, is likely to enhance agency.

Understanding curriculum and pedagogy

The curriculum is something that is experienced most directly by children and teachers as the activities, subjects, lessons and, in general, the timetables of the school year. In fact, curriculum has been defined as 'the principle by which units of time and their contents are brought into special relationship with each other' (Bernstein, 1971b, p. 48). The succinctness of this definition is useful for its clarity but it may be somewhat limited to fully capture all the essential elements of curriculum. The *Cambridge Primary Review* developed the following definition: 'What is intended to be taught and learned overall (the planned curriculum); what is taught (the curriculum as enacted); what is learned (the curriculum as experienced)' (Alexander, 2010, p. 250). This definition seems to locate agency for the curriculum primarily with the teacher, as 'what is intended' is largely determined by the teacher and the school, not by pupils. It is the teachers, the school *and* the children who bring the contents of the curriculum into special relationship with each other.

Similar arguments can be made about pedagogy, which is very often defined as something largely determined by adults (Rogers, 2013). By contrast, our understanding of pedagogy includes teacher, child and a particular idea of 'culture' (as suggested in the chapter by Baumfield in Wyse et al., 2012). Bernstein wrote that, 'if the culture of the teacher is to become part of the consciousness of the child, then the culture of the child must first be in the consciousness of the teacher' (Bernstein, 1971a, p. 61). Bernstein signalled the gap that very often exists between knowledge that is required to be learned in schools and the everyday knowledge that children bring to the classroom. Similar arguments have been made by Lingard, who writes of a 'pedagogy of indifference' to children's narratives (Lingard, 2007) and the need for adults to create appropriate bridges from informal learning experiences into the codified curriculum knowledge of schools.

Bernstein distinguished two types of pedagogy in infant education: invisible and visible. In later work these types were redefined to account for the changing political terrain that had moved towards greater state intervention in education, and a new culture of managerialism in schools with more explicit forms of regulation and evaluation. Invisible and visible pedagogies were redefined by Bernstein as *competence* and *performance* models (although Bernstein was not thinking specifically about the education of young children). In competence models, which are most closely associated with child-centred pedagogies (Rogers and Lapping, 2012), Bernstein noted that there are few specifically defined pedagogic spaces, and that learners (or acquirers, as he put it) have considerable control (or agency) over the construction of spaces as pedagogic sites. By contrast, in performance models, higher levels of adult-directed learning incorporate specific pedagogic practices that are clearly defined and structured. Seen from the child's perspective the criteria for achieving the right answer (as in the opening example in this chapter) are made relatively explicit by the teacher's pedagogy, and success relies less on producing a personal or original contribution and more on reproducing specialist (disciplinary) knowledge (see also Ivinson and Duveen, 2006).

If we return to the examples at the beginning of this chapter, the first example might be described in Bernstein's terms as a performance mode in which it is *absences*, what is not known by the learner, that are evaluated, and control by the teacher is explicit – for example, the teacher telling Kieran that his suggestion of the word 'tree' was wrong. By contrast, the second example might be described as a competence mode because the *presences* derived from children's interests, and their argument about what they know, were evaluated and extended – for example, when the researcher supported the children's ideas about the letter 'M' and the sound /m/. Adult control in the second example is not altogether absent: the researcher simply had a less directive role, and built their interaction around the children's interests.

The differences in pedagogy that centre on control by adults and/or children that Bernstein theorised have, to some degree, also been the subject of philosophical thinking. The philosopher John Dewey argued that the best teaching ensured an interaction between the child's experiences and ideas, and the school's aim to inculcate learning. The teacher's role, however, was vital: 'Guidance [i.e. by the teacher] is not external imposition. *It is freeing the life-process for its own most adequate fulfilment*' (Dewey, 1902, p. 17. Italics in original). This idea of freeing the child's innate curiosity and desire for learning is a powerful one, so powerful, in fact, that it causes us to rethink previous definitions of curriculum. Our definition of curriculum for this chapter is the provision of education that develops learning through the interaction of children's interests and teachers' aims. At the level of national curriculum children's interests and teachers' aims are framed within a national representation of social aims, meanings and values, and as a representation of nation states' aspirations for their children as future citizens.

The central unifying idea in this chapter is 'agency', which we define as the capacity for people to exercise control over their social situation in ways meaningful to them. For children in educational settings this means having the capacity to make choices and to participate actively in the decision-making processes in the classroom. For teachers, agency includes the extent to which they can exercise power in order to develop curricula and pedagogy in the context of their own classrooms and schools. Agency is central to the pedagogic relationship formed between learners and educators, between children and adults. Children's and teachers' agency is visible through the interactions of teachers and learners, adults and children, and between children themselves. Pedagogy is contingent, reciprocal and is part of shared meanings within particular social and cultural contexts. Pedagogy also has the potential to promote both children's agency and teacher's agency, as we argue throughout the chapter.

Key questions for reflection

To what extent are you able to build on children's needs and interests in your teaching? What are the constraints and challenges of working in this way?

Agency and pedagogy

Our exploration of agency and pedagogy is further illustrated by ethnographic research conducted in three reception classrooms over a full school year (Rogers and Evans, 2008). The project was conceived within a socio-cultural framework in which children were seen as being able to enact their agency. The project recognised the importance of children's active involvement in the positive development of self-regulation and self-efficacy (Carpendale and Lewis, 2006), focusing on children's perspectives on their play. The study was also built on the idea that children are 'both restricted and encapsulated by social structures and as persons acting within or towards the structure' (Prout, 2005, p. 50). Thus there may be both cultural and local differences in how agency is perceived stemming from wide variation in an individual's or society's construction of childhood. For example, the concept that children should be 'seen but not heard' stems from a particular concept of childhood, in complete contrast to the idea that children have the right to be consulted on all matters that affect them (see Chapter 2).

All children in the research attended one of three reception classes, and were either four or five years old at the time of the project. Play in these reception classes was organised around typical provision in the UK as follows: constructive play (manipulative object play such as construction kits, sand and water), symbolic play (role-play, small-world play) and increasingly, as children matured, games with rules. Alongside this provision for play were areas for work, tables at which children would sit to undertake more formal activities in preparation for school. Even in their physical features, these reception classes incorporated two contrasted pedagogies, one that is for play, the other for work. Though attempts to blur the boundaries between work and play have been made in the Early Years Foundation Stage in England, a statutory play-based curriculum framework for children from birth to the end of the reception year, divisions between play and work persist. In order to access the children's perspectives, the study used extended observations of children's play across a school year, gathering data from a range of child-focused sources such as group activities, conversations with the children, children's photos and drawings. The project highlighted the cultural norms, rules and rituals of the classroom, and how these shape children's experiences of the curriculum.

The research found that children actively participated in shaping the pedagogical decisions made by adults. In the context of their play the children had developed a range of strategies such as stalling, resisting teacher's requests and balancing compliance with negotiation over where to play and for how long. Such strategies challenged and, through reflection on practice, subsequently altered the teachers' pedagogical approaches, which was in all three classrooms dominated by the need to meet pre-specified objectives particularly for literacy as set out in the national curriculum. The study concluded that children's agency is often limited by the need to negotiate and cooperate with peers and comply with a teacher's particular pedagogical approach. The power relations between peers and between adults and children will inevitably affect the degree to which children experience a sense of agency.

Key questions for reflection

How have you exercised agency as part of your teaching?
How have you ensured agency for the children you have taught?

Agency and national curricula

The competence and performance models, and their implications for teachers' and children's agency, that we have presented so far in this chapter can also be reflected on in the context of national curricula. Indeed, as you will see, national curricula and assessment have increasingly impacted on pedagogy. National curricula are an important influence on both teachers' agency and children's agency. A national curriculum places requirements on teachers to teach specified curriculum content, and the degree to which children are encouraged to make choices over their learning is also constrained or enabled by national curricula. To further understand the pressure on teachers' agency and children's agency we now look at the development of the national curriculum in England.

Prior to the Education Reform Act 1988 (ERA), which applied mainly to England and Wales, schools and teachers in England had significant levels of autonomy over the school curriculum. Teachers were expected to independently plan the learning for their class of children (see the example that begins the introduction chapter of this book). It is sometimes difficult for teachers in training today to appreciate quite how much control teachers had over the curriculum prior to 1988. A programme of study might have begun with the teacher establishing a topic or theme that would be the focus for a half term or term (usually schools mapped these topics across the whole school curriculum to cover the children's time at the school). This topic or theme might initially be represented as a mind map. The children in the class would be encouraged to suggest the kinds of things that they would like to learn about in relation to the topic. The teacher would then merge the children's interests with what the teacher felt should be covered, in order to establish their more detailed lesson planning – for example, in relation to activities to be undertaken, including the use of things like local trips to places of interest that were appropriate for the topic. Teachers were encouraged to deviate even from this relatively flexible form of curriculum planning if something interesting arose during teaching. For example, to experience, study, discuss and respond in writing and drawing to an unusual weather event if the topic was a broadly scientific one. Most of the classroom tasks would be related to the topic but some subjects of the curriculum were not exclusively linked. For example, mathematics was an area that was frequently covered through the use of separate planning and/or the use of published schemes. Music and PE were other subjects that were less likely to be linked to the topic. Schools had responsibility to ensure that the progression of children's learning was appropriate – for example, ensuring that content was not repeated and that the curriculum enabled children's development.

The ERA resulted in the first national curriculum for more than 100 years (the *Revised Code* of the nineteenth century can be seen as a very much earlier form of national curriculum), and located the power to control this and other aspects of education in the hands of the Secretary of State for Education. The advent of this first national curriculum, and associated national testing and assessment mechanisms, was the start of a trajectory of erosion of schools' and teachers' agency over the curriculum in the period from 1988 to the present day (see Lowe (2007), or Cunningham (2010) for detailed discussion of this period).

A key concept of the debate about whether a national curriculum was desirable was the idea of *entitlement*. Concern had been expressed that the curriculum that pupils experienced prior to 1988 could be repetitive and lacking appropriate progression, particularly if they moved schools (although there was little research evidence to support these assertions). Progression, in the context of this critique, was not envisaged as understanding of child development, a concept and way of thinking about learning that had considerable support at the time, but more about sequences of curriculum content and their organisation as part of the school timetable. It was further argued that pupils were entitled to a *broad and balanced* curriculum. A broad curriculum is one that covers sufficient areas of the curriculum; a balanced curriculum is one where the emphasis on different curriculum areas, such as subjects, is appropriate. In relation to agency, it may be the case that greater entitlement comes from a more differentiated curriculum that is responsive to children's needs and interests, than one which is nationally uniform attempting to ensure that all children experience the same curriculum.

Key question for reflection

To what extent do you think that the distinction between 'core' and 'foundation' subjects in the 2014 curriculum in England is helpful to ensure a 'balanced' curriculum?

In 1988 the Conservative government of the day established the first national curriculum of the twentieth century in the face of strong opposition revealed in the responses to a national consultation (Haviland, 1988; we return to the significance of national consultations later in the chapter). In 1994 Sir Ron Dearing was commissioned by government to review the national curriculum and its assessment, in particular to respond to complaints by teachers that the curriculum was overloaded. The revised document made superficial changes but the problems with overload continued (Wyse *et al.*, 2010).

In 2010, towards the end of the New Labour government which had first come into power in 1997, a new national curriculum was published online for implementation by England's primary schools. This curriculum had been developed by Sir Jim Rose as a result of his review for the New Labour government. Then, in the same year, a Conservative–Liberal Democrat government was elected. One of their first actions was to completely remove the New Labour curriculum, archive it, and announce yet another review of the national curriculum. Although there were some problems with the New Labour curriculum, it did have some noteworthy features. Its attention to active forms of creativity for pupils was greater than the previous national curriculum. Encouraging children to actively create things based on appropriate opportunities to make choices can support their agency. The curriculum did suffer from some lack of coherence, partly as a result of a proliferation of web pages and other documentation. However, the decision by the Conservative–Liberal Democrat government in 2010 not to attempt a more reasoned analysis of the previous curriculum, with a view to building on it in a professional and sustained manner, was regrettable. It appeared that political ideology and politicians' personal beliefs had once again dominated national curriculum development at the expense of a more considered view on the basis of research and scholarship. A fundamental aspect of teacher agency is the opportunity to influence national educational policy. Indeed, the Conservative–Liberal Democrat government of 2010 onwards suggested that teachers should have more agency in relation to the curriculum through greater control over its organisation, and that government should reduce bureaucracy, and prescribe less.

Agency and public consultation

Like the national curriculum of the ERA, the proposed 2014 national curriculum was preceded by a national public consultation on its merits. This consultation attracted more than 17,000 responses that included responses from organisations and from individuals. However, the analysis of the report on the consultation, and the government's response to this report, reveals that, in spite of a majority negative response to the national curriculum proposals, the Secretary of State implemented the proposals largely unchanged (see Table 4.1).

A key issue for this chapter is the extent to which teachers and children might have agency over the 2014 curriculum. It is stated in the preamble to the national curriculum that, '2.1 The school curriculum comprises all learning and other experiences that each school plans for its pupils. The national curriculum forms one part of the school curriculum' (DfE, 2013, p. 2). Then, in the second of the two national curriculum aims:

> The national curriculum is just one element in the education of every child. There is time and space in the school day and in each week, term and year to range beyond the national curriculum specifications. The national curriculum provides an outline of core knowledge around which teachers can develop exciting and stimulating lessons to promote the development of pupils' knowledge, understanding and skills as part of the wider school curriculum. (DfE, 2013, p. 6)

Michael Gove, the Secretary of State for Education (2010–14), had repeatedly claimed that he wanted teachers to have more autonomy over their work, including over the curriculum. It is, of course, the case that free schools and academies are not required to follow the national curriculum, but Gove's claims were made on behalf of all teachers. Yet reading the requirements of the national curriculum one is left with doubts that there will be sufficient time for other areas of the curriculum as the amount of content to be covered is still extensive. The content of the core curriculum subjects is more extensive than the foundation subjects. English is particularly problematic including as it does pages and pages of appendices on spelling, grammar and punctuation. As statutory assessment also influences the extent to which certain aspects of the curriculum are emphasised, the decision to include spelling grammar and punctuation in statutory national testing, and

Table 4.1 Secondary analysis of public consultation and government response to proposals for national curriculum (9 May 2013)[3]

Q	Topic	Responses	Majority view	Overall	Respondents' views	Government's response
1	General comments on NC aims	2,469	901 36%	Negative	Curriculum aims are too focused on knowledge	We were not convinced that the aims should be changed
2	Teachers should shape their own curriculum aims	3,638	1,616 44%	Positive	It should be teachers' role to define curriculum subject aims	The national curriculum provides pupils with an introduction to the essential knowledge that they need to be educated citizens …
3	Content of subjects – English	3,682	Numbers and percentages not given	Unclear due to absence of numbers	English attracted more comment than other subjects Discrete speaking and listening strand called for [People] said there was an overemphasis on phonics, punctuation, spelling and grammar (numbers and percentages not given for responses to this)	A new section on spoken language skills and included further content on the importance of vocabulary development No comment or action on spelling, punctuation and grammar
	Content of subjects – History	3,682	Numbers and percentages not given	Negative	Respondents raised a range of issues which included a concern that teaching history chronologically would not allow teachers to revisit certain periods or consolidate learning effectively	We have slimmed down the new programmes of study

the decision to intensify the use of the phonics screening check (see Chapter 6), will lead to all the well-understood pressures of high-stakes assessment, including narrowing of the curriculum.

Although the foundation subjects only have two pages of requirements per subject, the statutory content of, for example, history still appears to be onerous when you take into account that early years and primary teachers can usually only devote about one or two hours per week at most to history. Most worrying overall has been the move away from the modest freedoms for teachers of the national curriculum of 1999 onwards to even more restrictions on teachers' opportunity to exercise agency over the curriculum, and increasingly restricted opportunity for their agency over pedagogy – for example, in the case of the requirement to adopt a particular model of phonics teacher enforced through the phonics texts of all six-year-old children in England.

Key questions for reflection

If you became the Secretary of State for Education what would be your five priorities for changing the national curriculum?

As a teacher what kinds of direct action can you take in order to influence national developments in curriculum and pedagogy?

As a result of reading this chapter what will you do differently in your teaching?

If teacher and child agency appears to be compromised in England, how does this issue emerge internationally? There is only space in this chapter to offer brief examples but we begin with an overview from the perspective of international testing of pupils, and then briefly consider a positive example from closer to home, Scotland's *Curriculum for Excellence*.

The influence of international testing of pupils' levels of achievement has grown over the last decade. One such testing programme is the Programme for International Student Assessment (PISA), which is a triennial international survey that tests fifteen-year-old pupils' reading, mathematics, or science in each year of assessment. These kinds of testing programmes produce league tables of the countries who have agreed to be included. Politicians have become more and more sensitive to perceived poor performance in these league tables, and consequently this has influenced their thinking about curriculum and pedagogy.

There are many problems with trying to compare the effectiveness of the work of teachers, and of pupils' learning, in the different cultural contexts of nation states through such international tests. However, in addition to achievement data, PISA also includes other data such as surveys of head teachers' views. Of relevance to our consideration of teacher agency in this chapter, one PISA analysis examined head teachers' views about schools' and teachers' control over the curriculum and compared this with the pupil achievement data for learning to read. It was found that:

> At the country level, the greater the number of schools that have the responsibility to define and elaborate their curricula and assessments, the better the performance of the entire school system, even after accounting for national income. *School systems that grant schools greater discretion in deciding student-assessment policies, the courses offered, the content of those courses, and the textbooks used are also those systems that show higher reading scores overall.* This association is observed even though having the responsibility to design curricula is not always related to better performance for an individual school.
> (OECD, 2011, p. 2, emphasis added)

In other words, there is evidence here that when schools, and hence their teachers, have control over their curriculum, or are able to exercise agency, student learning outcomes are better.

As we said earlier in the chapter it is sometimes difficult for new teachers to appreciate the possibilities that a positive enactment of agency can bring. For example, if you have never experienced appropriate levels of control over the curriculum then it is a challenge to appreciate how greater agency might be enacted. It is also difficult to appreciate that a national curriculum might be able to explicitly encourage children's and teachers' agency. To finish the chapter, the example nearer to home we have selected is from Scotland's *Curriculum for Excellence*.

The programmes of study in *Curriculum for Excellence* are represented as *experiences and outcomes*. For the curriculum subject of language the elements are all divided up into the *organisers* of listening and talking; reading; and writing. The requirements are preceded by a list of aspects that pupils are expected to have opportunities to engage with. These include, 'engage with and create a wide range of texts' (Scottish Government, n.d., p. 24). An interesting feature of the language of these aspects and the requirements more generally is the use of the personal pronoun 'I', implying that the curriculum is pupil-centred. For example, 'I develop and extend my literacy skills when I have opportunities to: communicate, collaborate and build relationships' (Scottish Government, n.d., p. 24). Although there is the perhaps predictable over-prioritisation of the learning of phonemes ahead of ideas such as 'I enjoy exploring and choosing stories', the requirements for writing are unusually clear in relation to the agency of pupils. For writing, the requirements in the primary education stages include, 'I enjoy creating texts of *my choice* and *I regularly select* subject, purpose, format and resources to suit the needs of my audience' (Scottish Government, n.d., p. 33, emphasis added). This is, indeed, a powerful statement because children's agency, through making choices, is explicit in a national curriculum text.

Future visions

Teachers' agency and children's agency should be central to the pedagogic relationship. Pedagogies which are contingent, reciprocal and foster shared meaning best promote learning and development. In order to nurture children's sense of agency within the pedagogic relationship adults need to feel confident and empowered to make decisions based on their professional knowledge and understanding of the children whom they teach.

One condition for the fostering of teacher agency is curricula that enable space for teachers to create their own programmes of study at the level of the classroom, leaving room for eliciting and building upon children's interests. Although the rhetoric from government in England has included advocacy of teacher autonomy over the curriculum it is difficult to see how this will be achieved in view of the quite substantial content that statutorily has to be covered from 2014 onwards. Although the freedom over the curriculum given to academies and free schools appears to be genuine, the statutory assessment and accountability system is likely to be in tension with this.

The careful balance between children's interests and teacher's and schools' aims has to be reflected in the way that national curricula express and define the knowledge to be taught and learned. This should not simply be about facts to be learned and content to be covered but based on a transactional theory of knowledge, a transaction where knowledge is best understood as relationships between actions and consequences (Biesta, 2014), and hence a concept of curriculum that is more about possibilities than certainties. So, for example, teaching about the origins of the human species could include views about creationism and about Darwinism (Biesta, 2014), but with rigorous attention to the place of evidence and belief in relation to both, not a laissez faire 'anything goes' approach. The idea of a transactional theory of knowledge highlights the intricate relationship between curriculum and pedagogy as it is enacted in the classroom.

During the ten-year period of reviews of the national curriculum it was suggested by some that a percentage balance between statutory content and teacher-determined content might be a way to protect against the well-documented problems with curriculum content overload (Wyse, 2008). In our view this remains an important possibility for future curricula. Such a model requires very careful thought about the time likely to be taken to deliver statutory content. If this is calculated appropriately then teacher-determined and pupil-determined content would be a more realistic prospect. There would also be a need to moderate pressures from the assessment and accountability systems (for example, the pressure to deliver phonics teaching as part of the English subject curriculum). To our knowledge such a balance has not been implemented and evaluated in any nation state.

It is possible that the presence of a national curriculum *per se* has such a damaging impact on teacher agency over the curriculum that a national curriculum is inappropriate. A more radical alternative would be to offer the freedoms over the curriculum that are currently available to the private sector, to academies and free schools, to all schools. Government could then develop evidence-based curriculum guidance available to schools to select to use if they thought it was of sufficient quality. However, this is at odds with Conservative ideology that argues for the importance of free markets including in the promotion of curriculum and pedagogy resources. Government-designed resources, it is questionably argued in our view, restrict the opportunities for other promoters of resources to prosper.

National curricula are often promoted by governments as a representation of national values, as an entitlement to pupils, and therefore something that the populace, as representative of the state, should have a voice in. Teacher agency, indeed the agency of all in society, is in part represented at a high level by public consultation. Full public consultation is a necessary feature of the development of national curricula if they are, indeed, a representation of national values. The policy decision following public consultation should be built upon rigorous analysis of responses, and such analysis be fairly and decisively acted on. Effective consultation requires governments to have transparent methodologies for the analysis of consultation responses, including equitable ways to balance organisational responses with responses from individual members of the public. Once rigorous analysis has been carried out the majority views should be acted on. Rigorous analysis is more likely if carried out by analysts who are independent of government.

The history of curriculum development in England has shown that the views of secretaries of state about curriculum and pedagogy are frequently at odds with rigorous theory, research and knowledge based on the history of educational practice. As we have shown in this chapter, on occasion these views can be blatantly at odds with majority opinions – for example, expressed in public consultations. It appears then that the power invested in the Secretary of State for Education to develop the national curriculum and assessment system in England is inappropriate because it has resulted in the restriction of the agency of too many schools, teachers and children. The inroads by government into curriculum since 1988 have more recently included inroads into pedagogy – for example, in the teaching of reading. The next UK government should enact legislation to remove the direct power of the Secretary of State to establish the national curriculum and its statutory assessment, and instead put statutory power in the hands of schools, teachers and local regions.

Notes

1 In England, the term 'reception class' refers to the first class in primary school that children attend. Reception starts statutorily in the term of a child's fifth birthday, but in practice most children enter school at four now.
2 The extract was taken from a research project on pedagogy in reception and Year 1 classrooms (all names are pseudonyms).
3 Full tables and commentary can be found here: http://ioelondonblog.wordpress.com/2013/09/20/what-are-consultations-for/

Further reading

Rogers, S. (forthcoming). *Child Centred Education Reconsidered*. London: Routledge.
Drawing on a wide literature and empirical research, this book reconsiders child-centred education for the twenty-first-century classroom.

Priestly, M., and Biesta, G. (eds). (2013). *Reinventing the Curriculum: New Trends in Curriculum Policy and Practice*. London: Bloomsbury.
An interesting edited book that focuses mainly on the pros and cons of *Curriculum for Excellence* in Scotland. Includes a powerful chapter on children's rights. http://www.educationscotland.gov.uk/thecurriculum/whatiscurriculumforexcellence/
Scotland's national curriculum called *Curriculum for Excellence*. Notable for the different way it was established compared to England. It is also a through curriculum from early years to post-sixteen, and includes a programmes of study strand explicitly encouraging children to make choices.

Wyse, D., Hayward, L., Higgins, S. and Livingston, K. (2014). Editorial: Creating curricula: aims, knowledge, and control, a special edition of the Curriculum Journal. *The Curriculum Journal*. 25 (1). 2–6.
Introduces a set of papers about aims, knowledge and control in the curriculum. Also features reviews of two books about the curriculum, one of which is reviewed both by a practitioner and an academic.

References

Alexander, R. (ed.). (2010). *Children, their World, their Education: Final Report and Recommendations of the Cambridge Primary Review*. London: Routledge.
Bernstein, B. (1971a). *Class, Codes and Control, Volume 1: Theoretical Studies Towards a Sociology of Language*. London: Routledge and Kegan Paul.
Bernstein, B. (1971b). On the Classification and Framing of Educational Knowledge. In M. Young (ed.), *Knowledge and Control: New Directions for the Sociology of Education*. London: Collier MacMillan. 47–69.
Bernstein, B. (1975). *Class Pedagogies: Visible and Invisible*. Paris: Organisation for Economic Cooperation and Development.
Bernstein, S. (2000). *Pedagogy, Symbolic Control and Identity: Theory, Research and Critique* (rev. edn). Oxford: Rowman and Littlefield.
Biesta, G. (2014) Pragmatising the Curriculum: Bringing Knowledge Back into the Curriculum Conversation, but Via Pragmatism. *The Curriculum Journal*. 25 (1). 29–49.
Carpendale, J. and Lewis, M. (2006). *How Children Develop Social Understanding*. Oxford: Wiley Blackwell.
Cunningham, P. (2010). *Politics and the Primary Classroom*. London: Routledge.
Department for Education. (2013). *The National Curriculum in England: Framework Document*. London: Department for Education.
Dewey, J. (1902). *The Child and the Curriculum*. Chicago: University of Chicago Press.

Haviland, J. (1988). *Take Care, Mr Baker!* London: Fourth Estate.

Ivinson, G. and Duveen, G. (2006). Children's Recontextualisation of Pedagogy. In R. Moore, M. Arnott, J. Beck and H. Daniels (eds), *Knowledge, Power and Educational Reform: Applying the Sociology of Basil Bernstein*. London: Routledge. 109–25.

Lingard, B. (2007). Pedagogies of Indifference. *International Journal of Inclusive Education*. 11 (3). 245–66.

Lowe, R. (2007). *The Death of Progressivism: How Teachers Lost Control of the Classroom*. London: Routledge.

Organisation for Economic Cooperation and Development (OECD). (2011). School Autonomy and Accountability: Are They Related to Student Performance? *PISA in Focus*, October (9). 1–4.

Prout, A. (2005). *The Future of Childhood*. London: Routledge.

Rogers, S. (2013). The Pedagogization of Play: A Bernsteinian Perspective. In O. Lillemyr, S. Dockett and B. Perry (eds), *Varied Perspectives on Play and Learning: Theory and Research on Early Years Education*. Charlotte, NC: IAP.

Rogers, S. and Evans, J. (2008) *Inside Role Play: Researching Children's Perspectives in Early Childhood*. London: Routledge.

Rogers, S. and Lapping, C. (2012). Recontextualising 'Play' in Early Years Pedagogy: Competence, Performance and Excess in Policy and Practice. *British Journal of Educational Studies*. 60 (3). 243–60.

Scottish Government. (n.d.). *Curriculum for Excellence: Experiences and Outcomes [print version]*. Edinburgh: Scottish Government.

Wyse, D. (2008). Primary Education: Who's in Control? *Education Review*. 21 (1). 76–82.

Wyse, D. (2010). Contextualised Phonics Teaching. In K. Hall, U. Goswami, C. Harrison, S. Ellis and J. Soler (eds), *Interdisciplinary Perspectives on Learning to Read: Culture, Cognition and Pedagogy*. London: Routledge.

Wyse, D., McCreery, E. and Torrance, H. (2010). The Trajectory and Impact of National Reform: Curriculum and Assessment in English Primary Schools. In R. Alexander, C. Doddington, J. Gray, L. Hargreaves and R. Kershner (eds), *The Cambridge Primary Review Research Surveys*. London: Routledge.

Wyse, D., Baumfield, V., Egan, D., Hayward, L., Hulme, M., Menter, I., Gallagher, C., Leitch, R., Livingston, K. and Lingard, B. (2012). *Creating the Curriculum*. London: Routledge.

Chapter 5

High stakes assessment, teachers and children

Guy Roberts-Holmes

Chapter summary

This chapter critically examines the purposes of education within the rapidly changing policy landscape of England. It explores professionals' accounts of day-to-day experiences in order to analyse and understand some of the implications of the forces that drive policy and affect practice. In particular, the chapter looks at the ways in which the phenomena of concepts such as performativity, standards, and school readiness are in tension with child-centred education. This tension is exemplified in the contradictions between the child-centred holistic approach of England's Early Years Foundation Stage (EYFS) and high stakes assessment. The chapter examines the nature and impact of such tensions and seeks out alternative future possibilities and visions, particularly children's *learning stories*.

We've been told by the Head, that the EYFS is no longer a stage in its own right looking holistically at young children … she says it is merely a precursor to Key Stage 1 (KS1). So formal learning is now coming down from Year 1, through Reception and into the Nursery class with the three-year-olds that I teach … We were explicitly asked by our head teacher to make nursery 'more formal' in order to ensure children are not being left behind. 'More formal' means more direct teaching of maths and phonics … The effect of us spending more time on teaching maths and phonics means that we spend less time supporting the children in free-flow child-initiated play … In my school the EYFS is being pressured into becoming a clone of KS1. The philosophy and values of the EYFS are being eroded.

(Nursery teacher, north London primary school)

The ideas above, expressed in the words of the nursery teacher, are linked to many of this chapter's concerns. The opening example illustrates how the lived experience of an individual, such as this nursery teacher, connects to policies that have an impact on her setting, on the way she experiences herself as a professional and upon the children she works with. She shows herself aware of how the purpose of the provision, her role and the ways in which staff and children interact are being changed in ways that she does not agree with. There is a sense of processes which devalue early years provision: 'merely a precursor to Key Stage 1 (KS1)' and 'becoming a clone of KS1'. KS1 refers to 'statutory guidance' on how to 'prepare for and administer' Key Stage 1 national curriculum assessments in England (DfE, 2013a). Her work is being changed in ways that do not seem appropriate to her: to make nursery "more formal"' and 'being pressured'. This demonstrates the ways in which this teacher considers that she is losing control of her child-centred pedagogical principles, reflected in her analysis that the EYFS is 'no longer a stage in its own right looking holistically at young children' and the 'philosophy and values of the EYFS are being eroded'. How far the negative experiences of teachers such as the one quoted here reflect a national picture is not yet established. The research from which the nursery teacher's perceptions were recorded was small scale, so it is possible that other early years teachers have been able to maintain the ethos of the EYFS and provide for balanced and child-led learning experiences in spite of top-down pressures. Rogers' (2010) research on co-constructed learning in role play is a case in point (2010, pp. 152–65). Nevertheless, recent concerns have been raised about a 'deficit' approach to early years provision in relation to primary education and upon an increased emphasis upon short-term fixed 'standards' rather than life-long learning dispositions:

> The government has intervened increasingly through early years policy … aiming to control the diversity of states in which children appear through the (primary) school doors … Tension has been mounting amongst early years educationalists … as they perceive that those leaving the Foundation Stage and arriving at primary school are being measured against a 'deficit model', a set of inappropriate, one-size-fits-all standards of 'readiness' for school.
>
> (Whitebread and Bingham, 2012, p. 1)

Governments often justify such a 'standards' and 'school readiness' agenda by stating that an 'earlier the better' approach is necessary because of the need to 'win' in a 'global race' which begins in the early years. The election of the Coalition government in 2010, for example, heralded an era of increased emphasis on such ideas of educational competition and of the accountability of provision: 'What really matters is how we're doing compared with our international competitors. That is what will define our economic growth and our country's future. The truth is, at the moment we are standing still while others race past' (DfE, 2010, p. 3). This competitive accountability has been reflected within early years reforms. For example, 'a slimmed down' Early Years Foundation Stage curriculum (DfE, 2011) was introduced which focused upon the basics of Maths and English; a revised EYFS Profile in which five-year-old children are ranked and classified according to prescribed 'good levels of development' (GLD) (DfE, 2012b). At the same time, there has been a significant 'toughening up' of national regulations and inspection of the early years. This has been described as the 'schoolification' of the early years. 'Schoolification' means that a narrow view of 'school readiness' is made central to early years, rather than broader understandings of life-long learning dispositions, wellbeing and holistic learning. Such dispositions are central to the EYFS principles. These were as follows:

> Every child is a unique child, who is constantly learning and can be resilient, capable, confident and self assured: children learn to be strong and independent through positive relationships; children learn and develop well in enabling environments, in which their experiences respond to their individual needs … and children develop and learn in different ways and at different rates.
>
> (DfES, 2008, p. 3)

Within these 2008 principles the role of learning dispositions, such as confidence, resilience and self-belief, are pre-eminent and the diversity of children's varied learning approaches is emphasised. The importance of relationships and environments are prioritised in young children's education, rather than cognitive knowledge. Since the introduction of the EYFS Profile (DfE, 2012a), children, teachers and schools have become increasingly preoccupied with assessment testing and phonics screening checks, as children, teachers and institutions are increasingly held to account for their 'performance' in national assessments (Bradbury, 2013; Roberts-Holmes, 2014). A danger with this 'performativity' culture (Ball, 2003) is that many of the youngest children in the school system have been assessed as not making the required 'good level of development' or 'standard' (Bradbury, 2013). So, within such a short-term test-driven regime, children aged five are deemed to have 'failed' and be in 'deficit' to 'norms', with all the implications of reduced expectations that this implies. For example, in 2013, at the end of reception year profile assessments, only 52 per cent of children were deemed to have achieved their 'Good Level of Development' and the figures were worse for summer-born children who were that much younger, with only 30 per cent reaching their Good Level of Development (DFE, 2012a). This is potentially problematic because the learning experiences that young children have in their early years may have a critical impact upon their confidence, self-image and motivations as a learner throughout their school careers (Sylva, 2000; Whitebread and Bingham, 2012).

Holistic approaches and the Early Years Foundation Stage

Evidence from a range of sources and disciplines, including neuroscience (Rushton, 2011), developmental psychology (Whitebread and Bingham, 2012) and educational research (Sylva *et al.*, 2004), suggests that children's long-term wellbeing and future academic success in school is supported by fostering and encouraging young children's learning dispositions and characteristics of effective learning rather than short-term cognitive goals. For example, one of the central findings of the Effective Provision of Pre-School Education (EPPE) project (Sylva *et al.*, 2004) was that early childhood settings that viewed cognitive and social development as complementary, managed to achieve the best outcomes for children. EPPE 2004 has had a significant impact upon the principles, curriculum and pedagogy of the *EYFS* (2008) so that the merged concepts of care and education became central. This holistic approach to learning was reflected in the original Early Years Foundation Stage Profile (EYFSP) (2008), a statutory means and format to assess young children's progress, which placed equal emphasis upon emotional and social learning dispositions as upon cognitive development. With recently raised thresholds in maths and literacy (including the Year 1 Phonics Check), the emphasis for early years assessment has shifted away from an equal focus upon emotional, personal and social learning dispositions combined with numeracy and literacy, learning towards more formalised cognitive testing (Roberts-Holmes, 2014). So, the following example demonstrates the detailed and specific maths knowledge required of young children:

> Children use everyday language to talk about size, weight, capacity, position, distance, time and money to compare quantities and objects and to solve problems. They recognise, create and describe patterns. They explore characteristics of everyday objects and shapes and use mathematical language to describe them.
>
> (DfE, 2012b, p. 1)

This is from the Standards and Testing Document titled *EYFS Profile Exemplification for the Level of Learning and Development Expected at the End of the EYFS* (DfE, 2012a). It shows the ways in which the EYFS has become a knowledge-driven curriculum with its lists of cognitive requirements such as the use of mathematical language. This trend towards more formalised learning, particularly in numeracy and literacy, is set to continue, with a concomitantly reduced focus upon personal and emotional learning dispositions. For example, from September 2016, the government has announced its intention to introduce a Reception Baseline Check which will test four-year-olds' basic numeracy and literacy and track this through to age eleven in Year 6 of primary school (DfE, 2014). Such a policy shift towards more formalised assessment beginning in the first few weeks of a child's arrival at primary school may have the effect of formalising early years teachers' pedagogy.

In contrast, the *EYFS* (2008) was centrally concerned with a child-centred pedagogy and the holistic process of learning rather than being assessment and content driven. For example, the EYFS pedagogical advice encouraged play, participation, meaningful social interaction and co-construction among children and their teachers. Not surprisingly the early years community widely embraced the EYFS when it was first introduced since it was in tune with well-established holistic child-centred approaches to children, care and education. The *EYFS* (2008) principles stated that children were unique, strong and learn in an enabling environment through positive relationships. Theoretically, such a position was underpinned by a Vygotskian socio-cultural and social constructivist developmental model (Vygotsky, 1978) in which the child is constructed as a competent co-constructor of knowledge with other children and adults in child-centred meaningful activities such as play. Play-based experiential learning was a central pedagogical feature: 'play underpins all development and learning for young children ... and it is through play that they develop intellectually, creatively, physically, socially and emotionally' (DfES, 2008, p. 7).

Within the EYFS, co-constructive learning is encouraged through a process of 'sustained shared thinking' (SST) which occurs between children themselves and/or with an adult (Sylva *et al.*, 2004). Sustained shared thinking is defined as an 'interaction where two or more individuals "work together" in an intellectual way to solve a problem, clarify a concept, evaluate activities, or extend a narrative' (Sylva *et al.*, 2004, p. 718). Sylva *et al.* identified that children's freely chosen play activities often provided the best opportunities for teachers to extend children's thinking along with teacher-initiated group work. The key to such shared cooperative learning is the sensitivity and responsiveness of the teacher. Neo-Vygotskians such as Karpov (2005) suggest that a teacher needs to model the learning and needs to include the child in a process of co-construction.

This first section of the chapter has illustrated the ways in which the EYFS principles were built around the importance of co-construction, of free play and child-centredness, and that these principles are in tension with the kinds of assessment policies and pressures towards 'schoolification'.

Children's learning dispositions

The learning experiences that young children have in their early years may have a critical impact upon their confidence, self-image and motivations as a learner throughout their school careers.

Key questions for reflection

Thinking about the example at the beginning of the chapter, summarise some of the key ideas that are explicitly or implicitly referred to by the teacher. Link these to the commentary in the chapter.

Choose one of the key ideas and consider what opposing arguments advocating the different positions might be?

How do you think the daily experiences of children in early years education might be affected by these different positions?

The most important impact of early education appears to be on children's aspirations, motivations and school commitment. These are moulded through experiences in the pre-school classroom which enable children to enter school with a positive outlook and begin a school career of commitment and social responsibility.

(Sylva, 2000, p. 709)

Central to engendering such a 'positive outlook' is the development of positive learning dispositions which enable children to have a healthy self-image of themselves as learners. Dweck and Leggett (1988) identified two basic types of learners – masterful learners and helpless learners – both of which were developed in the early years. Masterful learners, on the one hand, tended to be those children who have a positive self-image of themselves as learners and who believe that they can overcome setbacks and obstacles with further effort: they tended to have high levels of resilience. Helpless learners, on the other hand, tended to have a poor self-image of themselves as learners and believed that their low level of ability was innate and fixed. The reality is, of course, that such learning beliefs are likely to be located on a spectrum and are contextually dependent as well as cognitively and developmentally related. In a similar way, Carr (2011) understands important dispositions as being related to children being ready, willing and able to learn, and dependent upon the child seeing themselves as a competent learner in a sensitive and responsive context where their learning is encouraged and supported.

Given this understanding, the limitations of the current test-driven, performativity context of many early years settings is all too apparent. Such contexts have the unfortunate potential to inadvertently classify some children as successful and 'good' learners while others are classified as 'poor' and 'deficit' learners. In such ranking, classification and ordering based upon so-called 'ability' becomes internalised by young children (and their families), and they will quickly learn to associate themselves with particular learning dispositions, either positively or negatively. So, for example, at the end of their reception year, children are assessed across a range of indexes and their 'levels of development' are graded from one to three, ranked, and reported upon. The following is a sample from the EYFSP guidance:

The Good Level of Development (GLD) across Early Learning Goals (ELG).
To calculate the average points score for **all 17 ELG's** attribute:
Emerging = 1
Expected = 2
Exceeding = 3

From this you will be able measure the total number of points achieved on the EYFSP for each child and use the data to calculate average scores for a cohort, class, individual or vulnerable group. The national average will be calculated based on every child's score.

(Edulink, 2013)

Such a crude and simplistic classification system, with ever-higher thresholds and levels of achievement in numeracy and literacy, means that a high proportion of young children are labelled as 'falling behind' (Bradbury, 2011, p. 656). This approach 'denies the impact of structural inequality and lays all responsibility for performance at the feet of teachers and individual schools' (Lingard *et al.*, 2013, p. 552).

Katz and Raths (1985) noted that, although teaching of knowledge and skills might be effective in the short term for some children, the particular ways these are taught can have adverse consequences upon some children's learning dispositions. The use of didactic teaching and learning, which is engendered by high stakes testing and assessment and the associated pedagogies, does not mean that the acquired skills and knowledge will be applied. For example, a child may be successfully taught letter names and phonemes but that does not necessarily lead to their enjoyment of reading, or to a desire to read on their own for enjoyment. Indeed, without meaningful learning, participation and the generation of positive learning dispositions, any short-term learning may subsequently be lost. So, long-term wellbeing and success at school are supported by young children acquiring positive learning dispositions in the early years. However, as stated earlier, the current trend is away from learning dispositions and towards more formalised cognitive learning.

'School readiness', and the 'standards' agenda

This movement towards more formalised cognitive learning is apparent when the early years is considered as the first stage in a 'delivery chain' (Ball *et al.*, 2012) that connects 'standards' from the early years to primary schools to secondary schools to local authorities (LAs) to the DfE (Department of Education). So, for example, the continuous chain of assessment begins with the EYFSP (Early Years Foundation Stage Profile) at age five (to be replaced in 2016 by the Reception Baseline Check when children are four); the Phonics Screening Test at age six; statutory tests at age six and eleven. Within the 'delivery chain' there is a tendency for initiatives within the school system to hierarchically cascade down into the early years. So, early years testing and the Phonics Screening Check, which are inspected by Ofsted within the context of a primary school's data, are supposed to ensure the delivery of children who are ready for the rapid skills and knowledge acquisition needed in the primary school. In this way, the early years is increasingly subservient to the demands of the Primary National Curriculum (Moss, 2012) as school readiness performance 'policy technologies' (Ball, 2013) have a disciplinary effect upon early years teachers' pedagogy and interpretation of the EYFS. In Foucauldian terms, teachers and children's 'visibility' has increased through the use of such assessment policy technologies, leading to an increase in the 'objectification of those who are subjected' (Foucault, 1979). This means that early years children and teachers are statistically objectified, ranked and judged by the national tests that they are subjected to.

The early years 'school readiness' assessment discourse is the first stage of a process that measures children against predetermined, sequential and normative outcomes throughout their schooling career 'without society having to address its underlying structural flaws of inequality, injustice and exploitation' (Dhalberg *et al.*, 2013, p. vii). In Foucault's terms, the devising and use of a series of normative stages quickly becomes officially sanctioned 'truths' which are used to regulate and govern children and the way practitioners are able to work with them. So, for example, the DfE requires early years teachers to use developmental 'statements', placed in 'bands' to judge children. The following sample is titled 'Mathematics: Numbers' for 22–36 months:

- Selects a small number of objects from a group when asked, for example, 'please give me one', 'please give me two'
- Recites some number names in sequence
- Creates and experiments with symbols and marks
- Representing ideas of number
- Begins to make comparisons between quantities
- Uses some language of quantities, such as 'more' and 'a lot'
- Knows that a group of things changes in quantity when something is added or taken away. (DfE 2012b, p. 32)

Looked at from this perspective, early childhood educators are required to use developmental 'truths' such as the EYFS Development Matters monthly milestones of the young child to frame and control their work and its 'worth' or value. Early years teachers participating in the research cited in this chapter increasingly struggled to make sense of deeply held child-centred values while performing to 'school readiness' agendas and the requirements of the increasingly knowledge-based normative stages and judgements demanded of them.

The following quote from a reception teacher is taken from a qualitative research study that involved twenty early years teachers' understandings of recent assessment changes. The quote was typical of the frustrations felt by the teachers: 'We are trying to keep the "wolf of schoolification" at bay, we stand guard at the threshold but it is very tiring defending your stance all the time' (Reception teacher, Central London). The teachers firmly believed that children learn through play and experiential learning but they felt an increasing pressure to adapt their pedagogy to ensure the children's 'success' in formalised assessment. So, as in the quote above, the teachers, spoke of their weariness, frustration and anger at trying to make sense of the contradictory pedagogical approaches within their early years classrooms. The 'wolf of schoolification' was an apt metaphor for the anxiety, stress and tiredness felt by the sample of early years teachers.

Key questions for reflection

What do you think are the effects of the 'delivery chain' on the relationship between child and early years professional?

The discussion refers to a 'struggle' between 'child-centred values' and 'school readiness agendas'. In what ways do you think a teacher might experience this as a struggle?

A nursery teacher in the research noted that he did phonics teaching with the three-year-olds but then 'tucked this away and got on with the real business of working with the children'. The teacher was aware of the potentially damaging effects of high stakes assessment and strove to ensure that the children were 'not harmed'. This experienced nursery teacher was *policy literate*: a confident articulator of pedagogical knowledge, and able to both accommodate and resist the effect of the assessment regime on his teaching. This is perhaps an example of a teacher who 'cynically complied' (Bradbury, 2013) with the school's performance demands because he was obliged to, while at the same time arguing that inappropriately formal teaching of phonics to three-year-olds wasn't 'particularly useful'.

The plethora of high stakes performance data from Reception class to Year 6 (used by the inspectorate Ofsted to hold early years settings and primary schools to account) brings the early years under the disciplinary and punitive power of simplistic statistical interpretation and analysis. Complex early years principles, curriculum and pedagogy become reduced to crude data: literacy and numeracy figures couched within the misleading notion of 'good levels of development'. Within this assessment regime the subtlety and sensitivity of SST and the co-construction of knowledge espoused in the *EYFS* (2008) and associated guidance is reduced to numbers. Stobart (2008, in Bradbury, 2013) notes that such high stakes tests are no longer simply a judgement of an individual pupil's attainment, but, also, a judgement of a teacher's performance. In this way, early years teachers are increasingly judged by the data as either being 'good' or 'bad'. Focusing upon early years data and crudely associating this with good or bad teaching ensures that early years teachers' pedagogy and their interpretation of curriculum is 'done' according to the assessment regimes' requirements. Bradbury notes 'the power of neo-liberal technologies to "remake" teachers as different types of professionals, to discipline the parameters of their understandings of what being a "good" teacher can be' (2012, p. 178). Early years teachers are caught between the pressures of curriculum prescription as discussed above and the disciplines of performativity potentially leading to a confusing splitting or 'schizophrenia of values and purposes' (Ball, 2003, p. 223). Their own beliefs and values are constantly being challenged and undermined by such pressures, as illustrated in the following testimony:

> The emphasis is now on literacy and maths. The pressure is now to get them all to the expected levels for literacy and maths, when actually the early years framework doesn't lend itself to that at all! It's confusing and unrealistic. It's a nightmare!
> (T. Early Years Foundation Stage Co-Coordinator, north London primary school)

This experienced teacher found such constant policy shifts confusing and difficult to manage. This uncertainty and instability can have emotional consequences for early years teachers:

> All these changes are killing me! … I'm constantly stressed out and feel like I'm fighting against myself sometimes. I want the children to do well but I feel like I don't know what I'm doing now! I know how young children learn at this age but people further up the school are constantly saying 'Oh why haven't you done this?' and its all the pressures and you start questioning yourself.
> (T. Early Years Foundation Stage Coordinator, north London primary school)

Over a decade ago Ball noted the emotional impacts of the performativity regime upon secondary school teachers: 'within all this, the contentments of stability are increasingly elusive, purposes are made contradictory, motivations become blurred and self worth is uncertain. We are unsure what aspects of work are valued and how to prioritize efforts' (2003, p. 220). Such professional tensions can be experienced by early years professionals as they try to make sense of the contradictory tensions between the child-centred EYFS and the current data-driven performativity regime in the early years.

Key questions for reflection

Discuss the meaning and implication of the term 'good levels of development'. In considering your answer, consider some of the following:

- 'good' for whom?
- the strengths and limitations of creating and using data in the way this chapter has discussed
- how children are conceived of within this 'regime' and its production of data.

Education and economic necessity

It appears that the main driving force of early years education policy has become to serve the needs of the economy by providing future workers (Bradbury, 2012, 2013; Moss, 2012). Ball notes that 'within policy, education is now regarded primarily from an economic point of view' (2013, p. 14) and that education policy has become 'subordinate to the necessities of international competition' (2013, p. 61). So getting children 'ready for school' also becomes a non-negotiable economic necessity. For example, in the English government's document *More Great Childcare* (DfE, 2013b) getting early years children ready for school was justified by competition in a 'global race':

> If we want our children to succeed at school, go on to university or into an apprenticeship and thrive in later life, we must get it right in the early years. More great childcare is vital to ensuring we can compete in the global race, by helping parents back to work and readying children for school and, eventually, employment.
>
> (DfE, 2013b, p. 6)

In policies such as *More Great Childcare* the early years is simplistically reduced to the first stage on a conveyor belt that seamlessly moves children through primary and secondary school and into university, apprenticeships and the world of work. This view of education is normalised, as if it is the only approach or truth available, and, therefore, needs no justification. Moss (2012) has termed the ascendency of such simplistic reduction as the 'discourse of no alternative' (DONA) in which all other discourses and alternatives are silenced. Thus education, including the early years, is increasingly captured by a reductionist discourse. Similarly, Ball notes that the social purposes of education are 'increasingly side-lined' to economics (2013, p. 14). Within this discourse early years has become the first necessary condition for survival in the global race (Moss, 2012).

Future visions

In this chapter I have presented two main lines of argument: a) that high stakes testing does not necessarily lead to long-term improved outcomes for children and b) that the current English government's 'earlier the better' approach has some damaging consequences. Indeed, for the many children who are unsuccessful in their attempts to make the required thresholds, the testing regime may have negative short- and long-term consequences as these young children experience 'failure' and the consequent feelings of being 'helpless learners' (Whitebread and Bingham, 2012). In order that early years children's learning experiences are such that they develop positive life-long learning dispositions, it is necessary for the government to listen to and trust early years teachers' professional judgements and considerable knowledge regarding democratic, participatory and child-centred assessment practices. For example, the use of children's *learning stories*, commonly found within the social pedagogy tradition of countries such as Sweden, Denmark and New Zealand (Carr and Lee, 2012), is an alternative form of assessment that eschews the hierarchical, crude and simplistic testing critiqued in this chapter. Learning stories involves young children and teachers in a process of dialogue and narrative, documenting learning processes and dispositions through a variety of means including notes, digital recordings and children's artefacts and is not bound by any fixed notion of expectations and norms (Moss, 2012).

The learning stories approach is similar to New Zealand's *Te Whariki* curriculum in which children learn through responsive and reciprocal relationships (Carr and Lee, 2012). Central to the *Te Whariki* curriculum are co-constructed *learning journeys* or learning stories between the child and teacher. A child's learning story makes explicit to the child and their family aspects of the child's learning and in particular their development of positive learning dispositions. Conversations about the children's learning journeys can encourage young children's self-awareness that their learning is contextually specific, dynamic and variable. The use of learning stories in this way demands educated early years teachers who are capable of developing opportunities and strategies for listening to and reflecting with children about their ideas (Carr, 2011). This process of reflection upon learning was encouraged in the EYFS in England through the process of SST (Sylva *et al.*, 2004), in which children and teachers articulate their ideas together.

Approaches such as learning stories – with their focus on identifying the positive aspects of children's learning, the recognition that self-image is easily damaged and their focus on child development – is in stark contrast to the current English performativity regime of high stakes assessment and inappropriate pressures for early intervention. The hierarchical ranking, grouping and classification of young children by so-called 'ability' determined by numeracy and literacy tests is located in a different paradigm to the learning stories approach. Moss (2012) argues that the learning stories approach is one way in which to 'unmask' the supposedly 'neutral and independent' early years testing and accountability regimes that are akin to 'political violence' (Foucault, 1974, p. 171, in Moss, 2012, p. 152). This can allow early years teachers to be critically self-reflexive and raise their awareness of the ways in which they are 'governed by disciplinary power' and thus potentially to engage in a process of 'care of the self' through locating new spaces, alternative discourses and resistances.

Further reading

Moss, P. (2014). *Transformative Change and Real Utopias in Early Childhood Education: A Story of Democracy, Experimentation and Potentiality*. London: Routledge.
In the first chapter of the book, titled 'The Dictatorship of No Alternative: The Emergent Global Model of Early Childhood Education', Moss offers a powerful critique of neo-liberalism and its effects upon early childhood education.

Brooker, L. (2011). Developing Learning Dispositions for Life. In T. Waller, J. Whitmarsh and K. Clark, *Making Sense of Theory and Practice in Early Childhood: The Power of Ideas*. Maidenhead: Open University Press. Ch. 6. 83–98.
Learning dispositions are central to effective learning and this chapter clearly demonstrates this important relationship.

Carr, M. and Lee, W. (2012). *Learning Stories: Constructing Learner Identities in Early Education*. London: Sage.
A user-friendly and optimistic account of child-centred approaches to recording young children's learning journeys.

Roberts-Holmes, G. (2014). The 'Datafication' of Early Years Pedagogy: 'if the teaching is good, the data should be good and if there's bad teaching, there is bad data'. *Journal of Education Policy*. DOI: 10.1080/02680939.2014.924561
An empirically based critical analysis of the ways in which early childhood education is increasingly determined by the collection and presentation of government-required data.

References

Ball, S. (2003). The Teacher's Soul and the Terrors of Performativity. *Journal of Education Policy*. 18 (2), 215–28.
Ball, S. (2013). *The Education Debate: Politics and Policy in the 21st Century*. Bristol: Policy Press.
Ball, S., Maguire, M., Braun, A., Perryman, J. and Hoskins, K. (2012). Assessment Technologies in Schools: 'Deliverology' and the 'Play of Dominations'. *Research Papers in Education*, 27 (5). 513–33.
Bradbury, A. (2011). Education Policy and the 'Ideal Learner': Producing Recognisable Learner-subjects through Early Years Assessment. *British Journal of Sociology of Education*. 34 (1). 1–19.
Bradbury, A. (2012). 'I feel absolutely incompetent': Professionalism, Policy and Early Childhood Teachers. *Contemporary Issues in Early Childhood*. 13 (3). 175–86.
Bradbury, A. (2013). *Towards an Understanding Early Years Inequality: Policy, Assessment and Young Children's Identities*. London: Routledge.
Carr, M. (2011). Young Children Reflecting on their Learning: Teachers' Conversation Strategies. *Early Years: An International Research Journal*. 31 (3). 257–70.
Carr, M. and Lee, W. (2012). *Learning Stories: Constructing Learner Identities in Early Education*. London: Sage.
Department for Education and Skills (2008). *Early Years Foundation Stage: Setting the Standards for Learning, Development and Care for Children from Birth to Five*. Nottingham: Department for Education and Skills.
Department for Education (DfE) (2010). *The Importance of Teaching: The Schools White Paper*. London: Department for Education.
Department for Education (DfE) (2011). *Statutory Framework for the Early Years Foundation Stage*. London: Department for Education.
Department for Education (DfE) (2012a). *EYFS Profile Exemplification for the Level of Learning and Development Expected at the End of the EYFS*. London: Department for Education.

Department for Education (DfE) (2012b). *Development Matters in the Early Years Foundation Stage (EYFS)*. London: Department for Education.

Department for Education (DfE) (2013a). *Key Stage 1: Assessment and Reporting Arrangements*. London: Department for Education and Standards and Testing Agency.

Department for Education (DfE) (2013b). *More Great Childcare*. London: Department for Education.

Department for Education (2014). *Reforming Assessment and Accountability for Primary Schools*. London: Department for Education.

Dhalberg, G., Moss, P. and Pence, A. (2013). *Beyond Quality in Early Childhood Education and Care*. London: Routledge.

Dweck, C. and Leggett, C. (1988). A Socio-cognitive Approach to Motivation and Achievement. *Psychological Review*. 95. 256–73.

Edulink (2013) *The Revised Early Years Foundation Stage Profile*. Available at: https://www.edulink. networcs.net/sites/teachlearn/early/Resources. Accessed 29 September 2013.

Foucault, M. (1979). *Discipline and Punish: The Birth of the Prison*. London: Penguin.

Gillborn, D. and Youdell, D. (2000). *Rationing Education: Policy Practice Reform and Equity*. Buckingham: Open University Press.

Karpov, Y. V. (2005). *The Neo-Vygotskian Approach to Child Development*. New York: Cambridge University Press.

Katz, L. and Raths, J. D. (1985). Dispositions as Goals for Teacher Education. *Teaching and Teacher Education*. 1 (4). 301–7.

Lingard, B., Martino, W. and Rezai-Rashti, G. (2013). Testing Regimes, Accountabilities and Education Policy: Commensurate Global and National Developments. *Journal of Education Policy*. 28 (5). 539–56.

Moss, P. (ed.) (2012). *Early Childhood and Compulsory Education: Reconceptualising the Relationship*. London: Routledge.

Roberts-Holmes, G. (2014). The 'Datafication' of Early Years Pedagogy: 'if the teaching is good, the data should be good and if there's bad teaching, there is bad data'. *Journal of Education Policy*. DOI: 10.1080/02680939.2014.924561

Rogers, S. (2010). Powerful Pedagogies and Playful Resistance. In L. Brooker and S. Edward (eds), *Engaging Play*. Maidenhead: McGraw Hill, Open University Press. Ch. 11. 152–65.

Rushton, S. (2011). Neuroscience, Early Childhood Education and Play: We are Doing it Right! *Early Childhood Education Journal*. 39 (1). 89–94. DOI 10.1007/s10643-011-0447

Stobart, G. (2008). *Testing Times: The Uses and Abuses of Assessment*. London: Routledge.

Sylva, K. (2000). Early Childhood Education to Ensure a 'Fair Start' for All. In T. Cox (ed.), *The National Curriculum and the Early Years*. London: Falmer Press.

Sylva, K., Melhuish, T., Sammons, P., Siraj-Blatchford, I. and Taggart, B. (2004). *The Effective Provision of Pre-School Education Project: Findings from Pre-School to End of Key Stage 1*. Available at: http://www.education.gov.uk/publications/eOrderingDownload/SSU-SF-2004-01.pdf. Accessed 22 August 2014.

Vygotsky, L. S. (1978). *Mind and Society: The Development of Higher Mental Process*. Cambridge, MA: Harvard University Press.

Whitebread, D. and Bingham, S. (2012). *School Readiness: A Critical Review of Perspectives and Evidence*. TACTYC Occasional Paper No. 2.

Chapter 6

Technology and education

Lynn Roberts

Chapter summary

This chapter considers how changes in technology relate to primary education and early years provision. Recent years have seen, for example, the reduction in cost and increase in the availability of mobile computing devices that can access the web, the increase of opportunities for synchronous and asynchronous communication and for social networking. The chapter explores two areas: first, relationships between new media, meaning-making and life within and outside the classroom and, second, new technology and literacy practices. This chapter shows that interaction between educational settings and new technology is possible, desirable and could be a more powerful element of future practices.

What relevance might a child's photograph of a big blue diamond, shown in Figure 6.1, have to technology and education? It was taken by a seven-year-old girl, Sarah, during a 'digital shoebox' project which explored how technology could support links between home and school, with children taking mobile phones home and collecting images, uploading them to the online photosharing site Flickr (www.flickr.com) and then using the photographs in school-based literacy work. Sarah was a quiet member of her class, working at a higher level than average in terms of expectations for her age in literacy, numeracy and science, but sometimes lacking the confidence to participate in all aspects of lessons. The second session of the project involved Sarah visiting the local library to access Flickr, viewing the photos, sorting them into sets and adding descriptions, tags and titles. Sarah's 'album' consisted of four photographs of her pets, five of her toys and two of her parents. In the plenary of the session Sarah showed her set to the other children in her class, who were clearly interested. The photograph that consistently attracted the most attention was Sarah's image of her 'blue diamond'. The class wanted to know, where had the diamond come from? Were there any others? When did Sarah get it? What did she do with it?

The diamond was later chosen by all children in the group as an image that featured in their literacy work and it attained something akin to cult status. In a task that involved the creation of small booklets, in a literacy lesson where text and images were merged, the photograph was used multiple times, featuring three or four times in some booklets that only had space for a total of eight images. When asked in a group interview which was their favourite photo, all children identified the diamond. The power

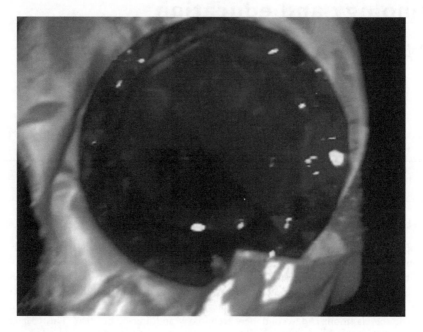

Figure 6.1 Sarah's diamond: 'the blue dimand is a big dimand and a realy preayy dimond' (caption by Sarah in *Flickr*).

of the image in the way it was appropriated by the class was at first positive but then caused Sarah some more complicated emotions as the following informal conversation, which was recorded while Sarah selected two photographs for a final, collaborative story-writing activity, shows:

SARAH: I don't like girly things.
TEACHER: OK, not girly things.
SARAH: And not the diamond.
TEACHER: Why not the diamond?
SARAH: Because whenever ... Maybe if I don't choose the diamond, maybe people won't choose it.
TEACHER: Don't you want them to choose it?
SARAH: Not *all* the time ... If they do all the time then I get a bit annoyed.
TEACHER: Why do you get annoyed?
SARAH: 'Cos they choose it all the time and if they choose it all the time, I get a bit ... I don't think I want them to do it every time.
TEACHER: You don't think it's nice that they're choosing your picture?
SARAH: Well, it is. But it's just everybody's choosing it and everybody wants one now.
TEACHER: I know, it's a pain isn't it? OK, you choose the two photos you want ...
SARAH: Everybody's telling me that they want one and I'm like 'maybe' ...
TEACHER: Well, you just have to say no, they can't have one – yours is the only one!

Lessons were being learned not just about the possibilities of technology, but also issues of ownership and collaboration. In a similar way to the other children, Sarah made use of photographs not taken by her. In the three booklets authored by Sarah in school, a total of 23 images were used. Sixteen of these were her own photographs, eight were other children's and, of those eight images, four had been taken by Mark, her closest friend in the project.

Sarah's experience was part of a project carried out in London that used mobile phone technology to engage with children's interests and experience outside school.[1] I was able to revisit a school that I had previously worked in as a class teacher to support and research the project, working as a teacher with groups of eight children at a time from a Year 2 class (children aged seven to eight years). The children were provided with mobile phones to capture images from home, then share them in an online environment and use the photographs as a learning resource in school. The project built on the Home–School Knowledge Exchange (HSKE) project carried out as part of the Teaching and Learning Research Programme (TLRP) which had aimed 'to develop, understand, measure, evaluate and disseminate ways in which pupil attainment and learning disposition can be enhanced by a process of knowledge exchange and transition between parents and teachers' (Hughes and Pollard, 2006, p. 385). As part of the HSKE project, physical shoeboxes filled with a variety of artefacts had been taken home by children in Key Stage 1 (aged five to seven years), and then brought back into school in order to support a range of literacy-related activities. A 'digital shoebox' project explored how technology could support the process further, enabling different elements of life outside school to be captured, shared and reused. Key questions included: how do children use digital artefacts? In what ways does the use of digital artefacts support/facilitate the teaching of literacy in the primary curriculum?

The collection and curation of the images in an online area for the digital shoebox project set the tone for the subsequent sessions and had a lasting effect on how the images were viewed and revisited. Being able to tag, title and share images allowed the children to explore a different kind of communication, a different type of literacy, a way of conveying and reading information that would have been very difficult, or even impossible, using text alone: '[t]he concept of creating cataloguing systems by the use of tags, some self-generated, some suggested by existing content, is a potential key skill for (new) media and digital literacies' (Potter, 2008, p. 23). The 'digital shoebox' project only touched the surface of how such skills could be incorporated in the curriculum, but potential areas to explore did emerge. The appearance of the 'blue diamond' as an in-joke with the group, for example, links well with adult uses of Flickr. Online photosharing spaces often develop 'memes' – the term 'meme' referring to 'the process whereby a cultural unit, maybe a word or sign, passes around a group, embedding itself within the culture' (Davies, 2006, p. 226). In the sessions of this project, the meme was contained within the group in class, but it would have been interesting to use 'our' blue diamond as a way of venturing into the wider photosharing world, learning more about the role of tags and how to search, making links, commenting on and collecting images from others.

Key questions for reflection

What are the opportunities and challenges of using mobile phones as part of classroom work?
What other possibilities can you think of that combine technology, school and home?

Technology at home and school

We live in a world infused by technology and, while it can be misleading to assume all children have the same exposure to information and communications technologies (ICT) at home, many are growing up 'at ease with digital devices that are rapidly becoming the tools of the culture at home, at school, at work and in the community' (NAEYC, 2012, as cited in Holloway *et al.*, 2013, p. 10). Schools in Victorian England were built in ways that screened out the world beyond the classroom with large windows being positioned to let in plenty of light, but often too high to provide a view of life outside. In the same buildings today, interactive whiteboards (IWBs) are a standard feature – providing a window not just on the local environment but enabling and encouraging a global outlook too. For the children and teachers within classrooms, technology has blurred school boundaries and their 'walls' have vanished, or maybe at least become semi-permeable (Potter, 2011). Sarah's experiences, for example, show how technology can offer opportunities to innovate with different relations between the school and home, based on the opportunities of new technology contextualised within carefully constructed pedagogy. It can be seen as responding to needs to maximise the potential of home–school relations. The example illustrates how Sarah's use of technology captured elements of her home experience and brought it into relationship with her learning experiences in class. She developed her skills in accessing information, making meaning of her material and in reflecting upon, editing and communicating her work and ideas to others.

If education is to be relevant and meaningful for children in early years and primary settings, technology needs to be a key component of life within the classroom. Many schools ensure impenetrable firewalls 'protect' children from the outside world, in this example Flickr was only accessible from the local library, as the local authority had blocked all access from schools. However, this protective approach could be seen as a focus on the wrong dangers. In a world where the formation of self-identity is dominated by practices of consumption (Giddens, 1991; Miller, 1987) there is maybe more of a need to inform and empower: to equip children with ways to be active agents and creators with technology. There is a danger otherwise that highly visible equipment such as a new ICT suite or set of laptops merely has a 'totemic' value, demonstrating to key stakeholders that schools are part of the new Information Age but not developing learning significantly (Selwyn, 2007, p. 38).

In many ways technology such as IWBs could even be seen to encourage a more didactic style of teaching, not so different to the Victorian classroom. The decisions made by a teacher about how software and games are used and supported in a primary classroom are key in influencing the learning experience created. It is not technology alone that drives positive innovation in education, but a combination of understanding the new potentials of the technology in relation to effective pedagogy.

The tensions, between concerns about technology and the potentials for technology, were revealed during a Massive Open Online Course (MOOC) about ICT in Primary Education (Coursera, 2014). Participants from 170 different countries were able to share experiences of how ICT has transformed learning in their experience as teachers, policymakers and researchers. The most frequently mentioned theme within a discussion thread considering changes in teaching and learning was 'access to information', with examples being given focusing not only how to access online information, but also questioning on how to do so safely, critically and responsibly. A smaller, but nevertheless prominent theme in the MOOC discussion on the nature of change in education, focused on how children are not only able access information, but can use ICT to create and share their own ideas with the wider world. In the example at the beginning of this chapter, Sarah and her fellow pupils were able to share their stories and photo albums with friends and family in simple ways that generated a real, responsive audience to class-based work. Technology was not only positioned to provide this channel of communication through the classroom walls, it is also a medium more closely related to children's lived experiences.

The introduction of technology into learning contexts alone cannot transform relations between schools and the wider community, particularly in view of the problems with the links between home and school that have been recognised for many years. The mismatch between home and school is not a unique situation for the UK. For example, the power of linking 'funds of knowledge' from life outside school within a classroom environment has been identified in many different learning contexts. The term 'funds of knowledge' was developed by Luis Moll and his colleagues working with Hispanic communities in Arizona through considering the 'historically accumulated and culturally developed bodies of knowledge and skills essential for household or individual functioning and well-being' (Moll et al., 1992, p. 133). Moll argued that there is a need for connections to be made between the educational resources of home and school, and that the students' community, and its funds of knowledge, should be seen 'as the most important resource for reorganising instruction in ways that far exceed the limits of current schooling' (Moll and Greenberg, 1990, p. 345). In creating links between home, school and community, Moll suggested that,

> the 'teacher' in these home based contexts of learning will come to know the child as a 'whole' person, not merely as a 'student', taking into account or having knowledge about the multiple spheres of activity within which the child is enmeshed. In comparison, the typical teacher–student relationship seems 'thin' and 'single-stranded', as the teacher 'knows' the students only from their performance within rather limited classroom contexts.
>
> (Moll et al., 1992, pp. 133–4)

While the strength of the argument that teachers should be able to see the multifaceted 'whole' of the children they work with is clear, how to gain that knowledge and experience within existing school systems is not straightforward. The digital shoebox project described at the beginning of this chapter only provided a small step to incorporating children's knowledge and experience outside school within the classroom; nevertheless, some of Moll's experiences in Arizona resonate with my experience as a researcher in the UK.

Sarah had been particularly enthusiastic about working with the images collected from home and consistently wanted to stay and work on her booklets through break times and during Friday afternoon's 'golden time' in class when the children were usually free to play games and choose their own activities. Sarah's mother noticed the way her daughter had enjoyed having the chance to bring elements of her home identity into school; in the 'any additional comments' box of the questionnaire, she noted that, 'I think this project gives children a chance to express what things and people in their life are important. It also gives children a look into others' lives and what things they enjoy.' From my perspective, as the teacher-researcher in these sessions, I would echo the comments from Sarah's mother; furthermore, I found the images a remarkably easy way to build a relationship with a group of previously unknown children, facilitating my awareness of their interests and needs in a classroom environment. Using Moll's (1992) terminology, the activities enabled me to develop a 'thicker' more 'multistranded' awareness not only of the needs of the children, but also of their existing skills and literacy practices. The group of children enjoyed being able to develop new media skills in 'curating' the images and publishing short stories and poems using the photographs. Interestingly, the group did not see these sessions as 'literacy' or even 'work', even though the lessons had been carefully planned to meet the learning objectives for the school's existing literacy curriculum. This leads to questions around what literacy is in the world today, how literacy practices are connected to technological developments and what this means in educational contexts.

Literacy and schooling

Sarah's work with the process of creating and accessing imagery, of curating it and developing links with her learning reveal the opportunities for new ways of engaging with literacy in school. One of the key themes within the changing relationship between school as a learning space and new technology concerns the nature of literacy. From the perspectives of theory, research and policy, tensions have been identified between more traditional perspectives on how schools position literacy within their teaching and perspectives that respond to newer, emergent notions and experiences of 'multiple literacies'. Snyder, for example, asserts the multimodal nature of literacy: 'being literate is to do with understanding how the different modalities are combined in complex ways to create meaning' (2002, p. 3). A recurrent theme in the literature has been that social and technological developments challenge existing definitions of literacy and that the rate of change needs to be better reflected in the ways literacy is understood within education. Educationists such as Bearne (2003), argue that the concept of what it is to be literate is being questioned, which, in turn, is connected to the ways in which primary education gives attention to literacy in curricula and in assessment. The privilege of the written word is no longer adequate, with literacy being increasingly qualified using terms such as 'digital', 'visual' and 'multimodal' alongside a noticeable shift towards the dominance of the image and the screen (Kress, 2003).

The tension between the institutional pace of change in schools and new media developments in the wider world is not a neutral or insignificant one for learners and teachers. The correlation between children's socio-economic background and eventual success in formal education is a source of continued concern. There is an ongoing, global pattern of success for children whose 'way of being' (or 'habitus') is closely matched to the school habitus and this is, in turn, related to social and economic status (Bourdieu, 1997). A large part of what forms these habita, especially for children in early years and primary education, is connected to literacy and ways of understanding and being understood. If school-based literacy is out of step with communication in the wider world, when children negotiate the move from their 'primary discourse' of home to a 'secondary discourse' of school (Gee, 1991), those whose home literacies are not so aligned with school literacies are disadvantaged. There is a danger, with the emergence of 'new literacies', that school and home literacies will drift more widely apart and the potential for the mismatch between home and school could increase, with some children not having the additional experience at home that enables the bridge between everyday literacies and the more narrowly formulated school literacies to be created.

Schools have a key role in mediating the process by which an individual becomes literate, reflecting and reforming societal values of what constitutes literacy and culture (Roth, 1984). Roth's comments propose a relationship between schools and a dominant, unitary culture, arguing, for example, that, 'schools, acting as agents for the culture, control the extent to which personal knowledge may enter into the public knowledge of school curriculum; they thus have a direct influence upon cultural continuity and critical change' (Roth, 1984, p. 103). Although such an outlook of schools can be critiqued as not being as relevant in a multilingual, multicultural society (that includes other educational influences in children's lives), it is, nevertheless, significant the extent to which the wealth of literacy practices and experiences that children bring into school are acknowledged, developed and formalised through the curriculum. One of the common ways of approaching the inclusion of new media in curricula is from the perspective of children in primary education as meaning-makers, reflected in Burnett *et al.*'s (2006, p. 11) call for research that examines the impact of 'digital innovations' on classroom literacy as: 'they challenge the very definitions and contexts of literacy practice ... and involve children and young people in new ways of taking and making meaning'. Such thinking has an effect on the curriculum and pedagogy concerning the ways in which literacy itself is framed and taught.

Burnett *et al.* researched some of the ways in which new technology might transform literacy practices in the classroom and concluded that new media are transforming the way children write as well as the kinds of texts they produce. The findings from the research were that children:

- showed 'a keen interest to the challenge of working onscreen'
- had 'a high level of motivation in exploring the potential of the medium and developing their skills and language use'
- evidenced 'a fairly sophisticated awareness of the ways in which meaning can be created with interactive multimodal texts'
- were 'able to make sense of and use a wide range of texts and quickly became confident in their ability to create meaning in different ways'. (2006, pp. 25–6)

Burnett *et al.* conclude that these areas are 'largely overlooked by current policy and practice in the teaching of literacy, which tends to confine the role of ICT to that of a typewriter or tool for consolidating traditional literacy skills' (Burnett *et al.*, 2006, p. 26). Such literature calls for the concept of literacy to be stretched and developed: for the expansion of 'traditional' focus on reading and writing to be replaced by 'literacies' better reflecting contemporary lived experience, for a more 'open pedagogy where learning is not pre-determined but generated based on a functional need to continue to learn to play the game better – children thrive as literate beings, continuously seeking out more knowledge' (Vasquez, 2004 p. 215). Lankshear and Knobel (2007, p. 9) refer to different 'mindsets' in literacy practices, labelling the more traditional mindset – 1 – as 'centred', hierarchical and individualistic while seeing mindset 2 as more distributed, collective and open. School literacy is often focused on individual work, more 'mindset 1', yet many projects involving technology are more group oriented, matching the ethos behind 'mindset 2'. Lankshear and Knobel (2007, p. 9) suggest there is both 'new technical stuff' and new 'ethos stuff' involved in these new literacies, the new technical stuff allowing easy creation, editing, sampling, publishing and remixing of images, music, texts, films; the new ethos stuff being 'more participatory', 'collaborative' and 'distributed' in nature than conventional literacies. That is, they are less 'published', 'individuated' and 'author-centric' than conventional literacies. They are also less expert-dominated than conventional literacies. The rules and norms that govern them are more fluid and less abiding than those we typically associate with established literacies (Lankshear and Knobel, 2007, p. 9).

Key questions for reflection

What do you understand the term 'literacy' to mean?

List the changes in your own lifetime concerning 'different kinds of communication between people' in relation to new technology.

Consider how you see your own experience of 'literacy' – have any of these experiences of new technology changed how you see literacy and what it means to be literate?

Consider young children's experiences of new technology and how they might see 'literacy': do you think their experiences and views are parallel or different to your own?

Participatory digital literacy

Work involving the creation of animations and films reflecting these ideas of participatory, collaborative digital literacies is becoming increasingly common in early years settings. The following case study provides one example of participatory digital literacy. A Primary PGCE student at the Institute of Education, London, carried out a short piece of action research in class.[2] Unlike many moving image projects, which can take weeks to develop with a class, often involving external experts, this case study focused on developing a more 'everyday' use of animation in class, the study was framed around three key questions:

- How can schools make best use of children's prior knowledge?
- What opportunities does technology offer for new forms of interaction?
- Do multimodal approaches offer an alternative vision of literacy in early years education?

The project initially involved structured teaching with small groups of children to create animations of the life cycle of a butterfly. The children were shown how to animate a plasticine caterpillar to move down a slide at the beginning of the session (see Figure 6.2). The conversations taking place around this activity highlighted some of the ways children's understanding of media creation is often reliant on a teacher being less present, in order to facilitate the children's work. In the following extract, the animation process mystifies one child even though it was taking place with the group of children as active participants.

> CHILD L: I can't do that, how did you do that?
> TEACHER: Do what?
> L: Make it go down the slide!

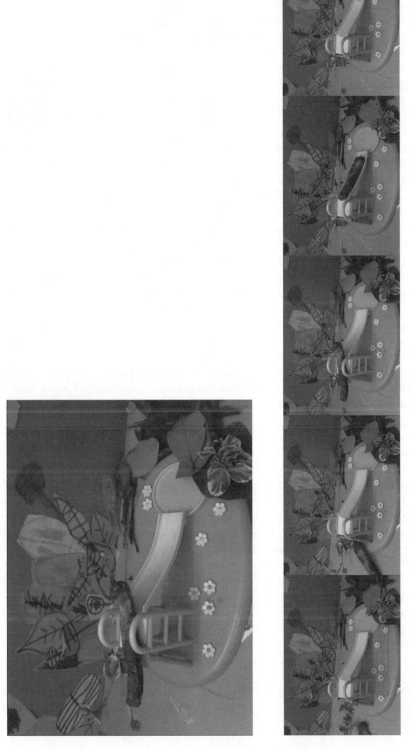

Figure 6.2 and 6.3 Caterpillar and slide in introductory activity to animation.

TEACHER: I didn't do anything, do you remember how we made it go down the slide together?

L: No, how did you … Move? [gesticulates at iPad]

TEACHER: Nothing, remember we did it together … move it a bit, take a photo. These are all just the photos together to make it look like it's moving.

This conversation, and others that took place, suggested to the teacher who had created the activity that, although the children had experienced work with the iPads before, there was a tendency for adults to control the process from their starting points, with a view of a finished product. Reflection on the limitations of too much teacher control led to the creation of a more open animation space, with an iPad set up on a table with animation software running, enabling the class to create their own animations during free-flow activity times. The children initially used the models and story of the life cycle of a butterfly animation, but then developed more fluid narrative episodes, with assorted leaves, a plastic cheetah and a large paper spider being among some of the objects brought to life. The children were able to develop their experience and understanding of 'digital mark-making', making decisions collaboratively over objects to use and where to move them, considering the interplay between the objects.

If children are to become digitally literate and able to understand and create multimodal texts, they need to have experience of creating the different combinations of images, words, colours, sounds and layout. Such processes raise fundamental questions about what 'becoming literate' means in a multimedia world (Flewitt, 2012, p. 295). In the PGCE student's project, children were able to work together to create a joint end project. One of the main questions the project raises is how to align this socialised nature of creativity with school-based work and assessment. For example, one child asked 'are we going to do one each?' While this could show a high level of engagement and interest in creating the animations, it could also suggest that group outputs are not always acknowledged or valued in our education system, raising some key issues around creativity, collaboration and the role of the teacher in working with technology in this way.

A key consideration in relation to new media and education is the importance of rigorous understanding of the nature of difference. Difference can relate to styles of learning, differences in culture or how the home economic environment affects access and attitude. The caterpillar task, and its way of viewing new media and literacy, required rethinking about literacy and new media as a social practice. It also raised questions about policy and curriculum through thinking about literacy as a social practice and location as part of social justice – for example, the ways that schools can address inequity of access and exclusions concerning gender or race. Vasquez framed two interconnected questions for enquiry: 'What does it mean for learning to be social? What happens to literacy development in these social spaces?' (2004, p. 204), and called for an 'open pedagogy where print text is not privileged over all texts', becoming 'one of many symbol systems used as a generative multimodal tool for cultivating different forms of literate behaviours beyond those traditionally associated with literacy, such as reading and writing' (2004, p. 215).

Future visions

In the current debates on the place of technology in the curriculum, a strong emphasis on the importance of computer science has dominated discussion (for example, in

England's national curriculum), with global media portraying the shift to 'computing' as a new direction led by a strong economic rationale. Eric Schmidt, CEO of Google, has suggested that a 'great computing heritage' in education has been thrown away in the UK and that creative industries need not only people who can use the software, but also those who can understand how it is made, something the current education system is not providing (Schmidt, 2011). However, just as with other claims and ideas surrounding technology in education, the divide between past and present is not so clear cut. There is a long history of supporting computational thinking in learning and teaching, and this tradition of learning with technology is important to consider within the present context. Children in primary and early years settings have been exploring key computing concepts through the use of programmable toys, as well as text-based programming languages, for over 40 years. In developing the programming language Logo in the 1960s and 70s and considering its implications for education, Papert used the teaching of maths as an example to suggest that a central problem is the difficulty of finding ways to draw on 'the child's vast experience of oral mathematics' (Papert, 1993, p. 16) and that computers could offer something new. Papert advocated that, by enabling children to interact with computers and to create their own 'microworlds' using Logo, allowing them to draw on their 'own special mathematical knowledge about quantities, about space, about the reliability of various reasoning processes', they would 'pursue mathematical activity because the world in which they are drawn requires that they develop particular mathematical skills' (Papert, 1993, pp.16–17). Although Logo did have an impact in primary schools, Mitch Resnick, who worked with Papert and continues to develop his ideas further, said,

> thousands of schools taught millions of students to write programs in Papert's Logo programming language. But the initial enthusiasm didn't last. Many teachers and students had difficulty learning to program in Logo, since the language was full of non-intuitive syntax and punctuation. To make matters worse, Logo was often introduced through activities that did not sustain the interest of either teachers or students. Many classrooms taught Logo as an end unto itself, rather than as a new means for students to express themselves and explore what Papert called 'powerful ideas'.
>
> (Resnick, 2012, p. 42)

It is this emphasis on programming as a language to express ideas *and* a vehicle to explore powerful ideas that is key in considering the new emphasis on teaching of computer science in school.

In an interesting parallel with the arguments made by Lankshear and Knobel (2007) about the different 'mindsets' involved in developing new media literacy, Resnick (2012) and others in MIT have moved Logo in line with this 'new media ethos', developing Logo into the visual programming language Scratch to become a more social, shared and collaborative experience. Scratch has been designed to be 'more tinkerable, more meaningful, and more social' (Resnick, 2012, p. 42) with a key element to its rapid success on a global scale being the ability to share your program and remix other's in an online community. The programming skills and concepts being learned by children with Scratch are undoubtedly useful, but these are often only being developed because the language allows children to express themselves creatively in making games, animations and telling stories which can then be shared with a wider audience. The emphasis on the 'social' nature of Scratch, the importance of collaboration and the need to use technology for a purpose resonates with the existing research on the interaction between technology and pedagogy and is a key element to consider in planning learning and teaching in an early years setting.

In the two examples presented in this chapter, collaboration between learners both in and beyond the classroom emerged as an important theme. Collecting and curating photographs in the digital shoebox project created new social networks between the children, teacher and parents. Images and captions were uploaded both at home and school and, as the project progressed, parental comments began to feature in the online albums with anecdotes and contexts about the photographs appearing. In class, simply being able to share and explore images and remix them in learning activities allowed the children to make use of each other's photographs in ways that both supported the development of individual social relationships and created a sense of group identity.

In the animation project, although children were engaged with the teacher-led, structured activity of animating the life cycle of a butterfly, the more significant learning took place within the self-selecting groups formed when the animation resources were left available for children and this learning had a strong collaborative element. Making an animation required: someone to take the photographs; someone to move the objects; a stage to be created; and a possible narrative to be developed. These activities involved a level of discussion and shared thinking the children readily engaged with in ways that surprised the teaching staff present.

Collaboration is often seen as a supportive element of early years pedagogy. Piaget suggested that in order to understand the world there is a need 'to cease to look upon one's own point of view as the only possible one, and to co-ordinate it with that of others' (Piaget, 1959, p. 277). It is not always clear in an early years setting what is real collaboration and what is simply sharing the same physical space. Charles Crook has noted that while there is enthusiasm for pupils to learn collaboratively in education, 'observations of young children's spontaneous interactions during routine small group work imply that the quality of collaboration is typically rather poor' (Crook, 1998, p. 237), which leads to the question of whether true collaborative learning is a realistic ambition with very young children. In writing about the role of technology in supporting social exchange, Crook suggests that technology does offer a special potential for supporting the development of collaborative learning in early education by providing an authentic context for social interaction. This was clearly visible in the animation project, where the children needed to take turns, problem-solve and interact *at* computers in order to create a shared outcome in a process of communal purpose. In planning activities with technology, the relationship between computers and collaboration should be carefully considered and made use of.

It seems unlikely that iPads will replace teachers, but practices around technology are developing and changing. Barnatt (2009) recommends teachers to adopt the role of a facilitator more than that of a 'broadcaster', and to change attitudes to a 'mashup mentality' where the educator thinks about and changes the ways of creating contact between themselves, pupils and learning. Learning has always taken place beyond the classroom walls, but technology allows links to be made between locations more easily. In the digital shoebox example, funds of knowledge from home could be used productively in school-based work, with technology not only providing a way of capturing those home-based experiences but also a way of sharing and working with images in ways more aligned with children's experience of literacy outside school. Opportunities are provided for a wider community to be involved in formal education – not just in relation to the way parents, teachers and children are able to share ideas and experiences online as in the digital shoebox project, but also in more ambitious projects, such as Sugatra Mitra's 'granny cloud' where adults volunteer to scaffold children's learning globally via Skype (https://www.theschoolinthecloud.org/). Technology can support children to explore different views of the world from beyond the classroom, but, equally, it enables educators to see more clearly and understand children's experience of the world. In early years settings in particular, a multimodal approach to literacy and communication allows ideas to be shared and recorded more easily than in situations where the only technology is pencil, crayons and paper.

Notes

1 Consent was given to use this material in line with BERA ethics guidelines and names have been changed to respect confidentiality.
2 I would like to acknowledge Alasdair Mussell Webber's New Media Specialism Project on 'Making Things Come Alive: Animation in the Early Years Classroom', April 2014.

Further reading

Lankshear, C. and Knobel, M. (2007). *A New Literacies Sampler*. New York: Peter Lang.
This book is a useful support in considering what 'new literacies' are, how people are using them in their everyday lives and how these new literacy practices relate to learning and education.

http://scratch.mit.edu/info/research/
It is worth exploring some of the research papers written about using Scratch collated by MIT. The research listed on their website is focused on Scratch as a visual programming language, but the concepts considered in the papers apply to other programming languages and activities too. If you are designing learning activities for children using Scratch or something similar, it is useful to engage with these wider discussions and debates and to think about coding creatively and how to meet the needs of the learners in your class.

Selwyn, N., Potter, J. and Cranmer, S. (2010) *Primary Schools and ICT: Learning from Learner Perspectives*. London: Continuum.
This book is an engaging exploration of children's ideas and interests in using technology; by considering learner voice, some clear, practical recommendations are made for developing practice in primary schools.

Papert, S. (1993). *The Children's Machine: Rethinking School in the Age of the Computer*. New York: HarperCollins.
This chapter has considered some of the optimism around technology and Seymour Papert is one of the key exponents of creating change through using computers in education. He has written a series of books that are useful in exploring these ideas more, including *Mindstorms* in 1980 and *The Children's Machine*, over a decade later examining the progress that had (and hadn't) taken place. These are not recent books, but are interesting to read and helpful in framing the current debates surrounding technology and education.

References

Barnatt, C. (2009). Higher Education 2.0. *International Journal of Management Education*. 7 (3). 47–56.

Bearne, E. (2003). Rethinking Literacy: Communication, Representation and Text. *Reading Literacy and Language*. 37 (3). 98–103.

Benjamin, L. (1988). A History of Teaching Machines. *American Psychologist*. 43 (9). 703–12.

Bourdieu, P. (1997). The Forms of Capita. In A. H. Halsey, H. Lauder, H. P. Brown and A. Stuart-Wells (eds), *Education, Culture, Economy and Society*. Oxford: Oxford University Press. 46–58.

Burnett, C., Dickinson, P., Myers, J. and Merchant, G. (2006) Digital Connections: Transforming Literacy in the Primary School. *Cambridge Journal of Education*. 36 (1). 11–29.

Coursera (2014). MOOC. ICT in Primary Education: Transforming Children's Learning Across the Curriculum. https://www.coursera.org/course/ictinprimary

Crook, C. (1998). Children as Computer Users: The Case of Collaborative Learning. *Computers and Education*. 30 (3). 237–47.

Daniels, H. (2001). *Vygotsky and Pedagogy*. London: RoutledgeFalmer.

Davies, J. (2006). Affinities and Beyond! Developing Ways of Seeing in Online Spaces, *E–Learning*. 3 (2). 217–34.

De Castell, S. and Luke, A. (1983). Defining 'literacy' in North America Schools: Social and Historical Conditions and Consequences. *Journal of Curriculum Studies*. 15 (4). 373–89.

Docking, J. (1990). *Primary Schools and Parents, Rights, Responsibilities and Relationships*. London: Hodder and Stoughton.

Flewitt, R. (2012). Multimodal Perspectives on Early Childhood Literacies. In J. Larson and J. Marsh (eds), *The Sage Handbook of Early Childhood Literacy*. London: Sage. 295–309.

Gee, J. P. (1991). What is Literacy? In C. Mitchell and K. Weiler (eds), *Rewriting Literacy: Culture and the Discourse of the Other*. New York: Bergin and Garvey. 159–212.

Giddens, A. (1991). Modernity and Self-identity: Self and Society in the Late Modern Age. Cambridge: Polity Press.

Holloway, D., Green, L. and Livingstone, S. (2013). *Zero to Eight. Young Children and their Internet Use*. LSE, London: EU Kids Online.

Hughes, M. and Pollard, A. (2006). Home–School Knowledge Exchange in Context. *Educational Review*. 58 (4). 385–95.

Kress, G. (2003). *Literacy in the New Media Age*. London: Routledge.

Lankshear, C. and Snyder, I. with Green, B. (2000). *Teachers and Techno-literacy: Managing Literacy, Technology and Learning in Schools*. St Leonards: Allen and Unwin.

Lankshear, C. and Knobel, M. (2007). *A New Literacies Sampler*. New York: Peter Lang.

Miller, D. (1987). *Material and Mass Consumption*. Oxford: Blackwell.

Moll, L. and Greenberg, J. (1990). Creating Zones of Possibilities: Combining Social Contexts for Instruction. In L. Moll (ed.), *Vygotsky and Education*. Cambridge: Cambridge University Press. 319–48.

Moll, L. C., Amanti, C., Neff, D. and Gonzalez, N. (1992). Funds of Knowledge for Teaching: Using a Qualitative Approach to Connect Homes and Classrooms. *Theory Into Practice*. 31 (2). 132–41.

Papert, S. (1984). Trying to Predict the Future. *Popular Computing*. 3 (13). 30–44.

Papert, S. (1993). *The Children's Machine: Rethinking School in the Age of the Computer*. New York: HarperCollins.

Piaget, J. (1959). *The Language and Thought of the Child*. Hove: Psychology Press.

Potter, J. (2008). Photoshopping/Photosharing: New Media, Digital Literacies and Curatorship. In M. Knobel and C. Lankshear (eds), *DIY Media*. New York: Peter Lang.

Potter, J. (2011) New Literacies, New Practices and Learner Research: Across the Semi-permeable Membrane between Home and School. *Lifelong Learning in Europe*. 16 (3). 174–81.

Resnick, M. (2012) Reviving Papert's Dream. *Educational Techology*. 52 (4). Available at: http://web.media.mit.edu/~mres/papers/educational-technology-2012.pdf

Roth, R. (1984). Schooling, Literacy Acquisition and Cultural Transmission. *Journal of Education*. 166 (1). 291–308.

Schmidt, E. (2011). *Television and the Internet Shared Opportunity*. Available at: http://www. theguardian.com/media/interactive/2011/aug/26/eric-schmidt-mactaggart-lecture-full-text. Accessed 9 October 2014.

Selwyn, N. (2007). Plus ca change, plus c'est la meme chose: Considering the Probable Futures of Education Technology. In D. Kritt and L. Winegar (eds), *Education and Technology: Critical Perspectives and Possible Futures*. Lanham: Rowman and Littlefield. 31–46.

Snyder, I. A. (2002). Silicon Literacies. In D. Barton (ed.), *Silicon Literacies: Communication, Innovation and Education in the Electronic Age*. London: Routledge. 3–12.

Vasquez, V. (2004) *Negotiating Critical Literacies with Young Children*. Mahwah, NJ: Routledge.

Part III

Teacher development

Chapter 7

Expertise, knowledge and pedagogy

Tony Eaude

Chapter summary

This chapter considers how primary classteachers with a high level of expertise work, the teacher knowledge involved and the implications for pedagogy, drawing on research on expertise and teacher expertise. Among the key features of teacher expertise are a combination of propositional, procedural and personal/interpersonal knowledge and 'case knowledge' to enable rapid, intuitive responses. Since primary classteachers' aims are multiple, broad and long term, their expertise involves pedagogical content knowledge across several subject areas, and helping children make links across these. Their craft knowledge involves many relatively small but important actions and interactions to match learning opportunities to young children's level of understanding and take account of their responses. An extensive repertoire of pedagogies and a reciprocal approach sensitive to different children's needs and responses are important in the busy, unpredictable world of the primary classroom. Since teacher agency, autonomy and confidence are essential for manifesting expertise, a culture of compliance and performativity militates against teachers acting in these ways.

1. The class is busy working at maths problems. The teacher is marking and discussing a child's work. Eight-year-old Martin, behind her, picks up a wooden block and prepares to throw it at another child. At that moment, the teacher calls out, without turning her head, to ask Martin to distribute new materials – and straightaway he agrees to do so. The crisis is averted.
2. A visitor watches a history lesson with a class of eleven-year-olds about the aftermath of World War II in Germany as a part of a topic on the impact of war on societies. The children are encouraged to talk and write in relatively short bursts, to keep some with a low attention span involved. At one point, the class is divided by a rope representing the Berlin Wall to help them understand what it might feel like to be separated from friends. The children debate, role-play, write, draw and think, so that the session proves to be more than just a history lesson. The visitor is impressed and asks the teacher how she planned and decided when to change activities. She is unsure, saying that this is largely based on hunch and her knowledge of the class.
3. The teacher wants a class of seven-year-olds to work more scientifically, hypothesising, experimenting, observing, recording and interpreting in small groups and

discussing the results as a class. The first week, there is much enthusiasm, but little focus. In later weeks, children are encouraged to concentrate on one new aspect, but without ignoring others. Gradually, but unevenly, over several weeks, the teacher helps to articulate what he expects and so to shape the children's understanding of what scientific method involves.

These three examples illustrate how classteachers with a high level of expertise working with young children act and think. The first may seem unremarkable, the sort of thing an observer might see several times a day. In the second, the teacher keeps the class engaged and involved, improvising during the lesson, within a framework of broad objectives. In the third, the teacher controls the task to make it manageable, gradually building on previous weeks' learning.

This chapter is based on the belief that primary classteachers' expertise is subtle but hard to articulate; and tries to identify its key features, as discussed in Eaude (2012, 2014). It starts by considering the theory on expertise, in general, and teacher expertise, before discussing different types of teacher knowledge. This is followed by an exploration of the primary classteacher's role and the implications for pedagogy, taking account of the constraints which may make manifesting expertise difficult. It is suggested that primary classteachers' expertise involves many, varied interactions such as those described above; and that a high level of autonomy and trust is necessary.

Alexander (2000) indicates that different cultures have strong traditions of pedagogy, with teachers in France and Russia, for instance, using class discussion extensively and those in Michigan, USA, tending to adopt more informal approaches. This chapter does not argue for or against particular styles of teaching, but highlights features common to teachers with a high level of expertise with young children, recognising that those used will vary depending on the context and task. However, since primary classteachers require a broad range of pedagogies, those with a high level of expertise show most of these at some time.

This discussion takes place in the context, in England and in many other countries, of an increased emphasis in recent years on measurable outcomes and results, especially in literacy and numeracy. This is accompanied by what the *Cambridge Primary Review* (Alexander, 2010) called a 'culture of compliance', backed by high-stakes assessment and accountability mechanisms. This has resulted in a narrow curriculum and a loss of autonomy for teachers, especially in primary schools. While recent government rhetoric in England has called for greater teacher autonomy, how the curriculum is taught seems likely still to be strongly influenced by assessment and accountability mechanisms.

Features of expertise

Research suggests (e.g. Sternberg and Horvath, 1995; Glaser, 1999) that expertise in any field – taxi driving or tree surgery, singing or surfing – is:

- prototypical, within broad, fluid boundaries, so that how experts in any field operate varies;
- situated, and context-dependent, so that an expert in one respect may be less expert in another, even in a similar field;
- mostly tacit (Polanyi, 1967), so that expertise is easily recognised, but its constituent aspects hard to identify or to articulate.

Tacit knowledge is:

- acquired without a high degree of direct input, not primarily from instruction but from experience of operating within a given context;
- essentially procedural, knowing how best to undertake specific tasks in particular situations, involving more than a set of abstract rules; and
- used in ways intricately bound up with one's own goals, so that one's own circumstances, dispositions and personalities may lead to different approaches to meet these. (See Elliott *et al.*, 2011, p. 85)

This might suggest that one cannot identify the constituent elements of expertise. However, drawing on Berliner's (2001, pp. 463–4) summary of Glaser's work, the following propositions can be made:

- expertise is specific to a domain, developed over hundreds and thousands of hours, and continues to develop;
- development of expertise is not linear, with plateaux occurring, indicating shifts of understanding;
- expert knowledge is structured better for use in performance;
- experts represent problems in qualitatively different – deeper and richer – ways;
- experts recognise meaningful patterns more quickly;
- experts are more flexible and more opportunistic planners;
- experts impose meaning on, and are less easily misled by, ambiguous stimuli;
- experts may start to solve a problem more slowly but overall they are faster problem-solvers;
- experts are usually more constrained by task requirements and the social constraints of the situation (though I suggest that experts recognise rather than are constrained by these);
- experts develop automaticity to allow conscious processing of more complex information;
- experts have developed self-regulatory processes as they engage in their activities.

Expertise is not just a characteristic of the person, but of the interaction of the person and the working environment (Berliner, 2001, p. 466), especially where the aims of the role and the actions required to meet these are complex. Expertise is manifested differently in static and in fluid situations. In the former, such as a chess match or designing a building, one can deliberate about what to do next. In the latter, such as playing rugby or teaching a class, one relies more on intuition, because there is little time to deliberate. This does not imply a lack of planning, but an ability to adapt rapidly in response to events.

Experts working in complex social situations have acquired intuitive specialist knowledge to meet the everyday demands of these (see Ruthven *et al.*, 2004, p. 1). Such 'knowledge in action' takes account of the social, physical and cultural context, structuring the resources available and incorporating a degree of flexibility, to respond to the uncertainty and contingency usual in real life. This highlights ways of working, taking account of, interpreting and responding to, the changing situation, with expertise dependent on how knowledge can be used quickly and efficiently to meet often-multiple goals.

While it is tempting to imagine that some people are 'naturals', expertise has to be worked at constantly. Experience is necessary but not enough. Expertise is learned, but only with difficulty, over a long period of time, often unevenly. Since different aspects may develop at different rates, an outstanding tailor, or trampolinist, or teacher is likely to be more expert in some respects than in others.

Thinking about expertise

Consider an activity in which you have a high level of expertise: anything from driving to drumming, manicure to mechanics. Do not be modest!
Think about the following:

- how do you plan when approaching a difficult problem?
- how do you respond to unexpected difficulties?
- how conscious are you of your actions/thought processes when engaged in the activity?

Now compare notes with other people who have chosen a different activity.
To what extent does this fit with the general points above?

Teacher expertise

Judgements about teachers' competence are often based on observation of single lessons, results in tests or a combination of both. However, as Shulman (2004, p. 396) observes:

> Most of the embarrassments of pedagogy that I encounter are not the inability of teachers to teach well, for an hour or even a day. Rather they flow from an inability to sustain episodes of teaching and learning over time that unfold, accumulate, into meaningful understanding in students.

Teaching has multiple aims, for instance related to academic attainment and to values and attitudes, and to cater for a whole group's varying aptitudes and needs. Success involves much more than test results. Teaching a class of children is complicated, unpredictable and multifaceted. Think back to the three examples at the start of the chapter. In the first, the teacher – somehow – intervened at the right moment to avoid a problem. In the second, she kept adapting the lesson to maintain the children's involvement. In the third, the expertise lay in enabling ways of working over time. So, these three no more capture the whole range of a teacher's expertise than discussing only an artist's brushstroke or use of colour, or how a doctor greets or examines a patient. Teacher expertise resides in the interplay of many different aspects, creating a process more subtle than the sum of its component parts. The broader the aims, the more complex the teacher's expertise; and many teachers, however experienced, may never develop a high level of expertise.

The *Cambridge Primary Review* (Alexander, 2010, pp. 417–18) draws on research from the USA to identify thirteen areas of teacher expertise, here reordered and grouped under five headings:

- Structuring and using teacher knowledge
  better use of knowledge;
  extensive pedagogical content knowledge, including deep representations of subject matter;

- Setting objectives and providing feedback
  more challenging objectives;
  better monitoring of learning and providing feedback to students;
  better adaptation and modifications of goals for diverse learners, including better skills for improvisation;
- Understanding and responding to events
  better perception of classroom events including a better ability to read cues from students;
  better problem-solving strategies;
  more frequent testing of hypotheses;
  better decision-making;
- Creating and sustaining a climate and context for learning
  better classroom climate;
  greater sensitivity to context;
- Manifesting attitudes and beliefs
  greater respect for students;
  display of more passion for teaching.

Alexander (2010, p. 418) reports Berliner's conclusion that these were 'correlated with measures such as students' higher levels of achievement, deep rather than surface understanding of subject matter, higher motivation to learn and feelings of self-efficacy … especially … with younger and low-income pupils'.

We shall return to the implications for pedagogy in the primary classroom of the list above, which indicates that teaching requires much more than good subject knowledge. However, since this is emphasised in selecting and training teachers, the types of knowledge required for teaching merits detailed examination.

Thinking about teachers' subject knowledge

How important is teachers' own subject knowledge in teaching six-year-olds? Or ten-year-olds?
Why?
Does this vary between subjects?
Can teachers have too much subject knowledge? If so, what may be the problem(s)?

Types of teacher knowledge

Knowledge is often equated with information. However, one must distinguish between propositional and procedural knowledge. The former is factual information, the latter ways of working. Most tasks require some propositional knowledge, but teaching, as a practical activity – like riding a bicycle, cooking a meal or designing a building – involves procedural as well as propositional knowledge. Moreover, skilled interpersonal relations are crucial for effective teaching (see Elliott *et al.*, 2011), with Eaude (2012) highlighting the importance for teachers of young children of personal and interpersonal knowledge – that of oneself, of others and how these interact.

Teachers with a high level of expertise have built up, over time, a bank of 'case knowledge', of similar situations on which they draw in responding to a particular event. This may refer to aspects such as understanding an individual or group's behaviours, interpreting mistakes and recognising when to alter initial assumptions and hypotheses. As Shulman (2004, p. 404) writes, 'one of the most important things that young teachers learn from experience is what students *don't* understand, what enduring misconceptions they have'. This highlights a distinction between theoretical and experiential knowledge, that learned from books or lectures and that gained by experience. Neither, on its own, is enough. The former must be drawn from the more general, sometimes counter-intuitive, insights of research. The latter must be internalised by action and reflection on one's own context and experience and is often characterised as domain and craft knowledge (see Alexander, 2010, pp. 413–14).

The term 'domain' is defined only loosely, as a category broader than a timetabled subject, but 'domain knowledge' is that associated with a discipline, such as science or geography, drama or photography. The ability to demonstrate how to work in particular ways is one crucial element of teacher knowledge. While not the same as subject knowledge, domain knowledge can easily be misunderstood to mean the same. Expertise depends on how knowledge is structured and used. While teachers require a certain level of subject knowledge, what matters more is pedagogical content knowledge – often shortened to PCK – which Shulman (2004, p. 203) defines as:

> a particular form of content knowledge that embodies the aspect of content most germane to its teachability ... the most useful forms of representation ... the most powerful analogies, illustrations, examples, explanations and demonstrations ... the ways of formulating the subject that make it comprehensible to others.

Therefore, the teacher's subject knowledge matters mainly in so far as it enables her to present subject matter in ways which help particular learners or groups; and detailed subject knowledge may be a hindrance working with young children, unless well used. Teachers' craft knowledge is procedural, manifested in how they actually work, making generalisations difficult. Expertise, especially in teaching, consists of the ability to act rapidly and appropriately, with intuitive processes usually preceding, but backed up, when necessary, by deliberative ones (see Eraut, 2000, p. 258). The more reciprocal the teaching, the more aspects such as understanding children's responses and how one's own actions affect these matter. We shall return to what craft knowledge 'looks like' in the primary classroom.

Using teacher knowledge

Berlak and Berlak (1981) argue that teaching inherently involves a series of dilemmas, to which the teacher must find what they call 'patterns of resolution'. Examples of dilemmas are those between:

- catering for the individual and for the whole class;
- offering care and challenge; and
- encouraging autonomy and interdependence.

In Alexander's words (1995, p. 67), 'teaching is essentially a series of compromises'. This involves making judgements between often-conflicting demands, depending on the situation. As Shulman (2004, p. 550) observes, 'what intervenes between knowledge and application is the process of *judgement* … Human judgement bridges the universal terms of theory and the gritty particularities of situated practice.' Experienced teachers and novices differ less in their capacity to identify good solutions, than avoiding bad decisions. As Elliott *et al.* (2011, pp. 99–100) state:

> What most characterises the expert teacher is the ability to undertake a selected course of action with a high level of interpersonal competence, and to adjust one's own behaviour in accordance with the unfolding nature of the situation. Both strategy selection and its execution may be compounded by the presence of anxiety or stress. Thus, a further component of teacher expertise is likely to involve the capacity for self-regulation, particularly with regard to strongly emotional issues.

The adult–child relationship is not a one-way process. In Kimes Myers' (1997, p. 8) words, 'when we engage in relationships with young children … the child within us also has a developing edge'. Since young children often provoke responses which bring out the adult's hidden vulnerabilities, those who teach them with a high level of expertise have a deep understanding of themselves, their strengths and vulnerabilities, and of other people's.

Teaching with a high level of expertise involves matching pedagogy to the needs of a particular child or group, rather than following the manual or collecting 'tips for teachers'. As Hargreaves (2003, p. 161) writes, 'teachers are not deliverers but developers of learning. Those who focus only on teaching techniques and curriculum standards … promote a diminished view of teaching and teacher professionalism that has no place in a sophisticated knowledge society.'

Such a society increasingly emphasises deep learning, based on concepts rather than content. So, teachers should see themselves as catalysts for learning, not curriculum-deliverers (see Twiselton, 2006), and agents, rather than victims, of change (Whitty, 2008, p. 45). This is a different way of understanding what teaching involves from one which emphasises instruction, delivery and compliance and is especially relevant to working with young children.

Thinking about the primary classteacher's role

Discuss, preferably in a small group, for a class in a particular primary age group you have observed or taught:

1. How can the teacher's subject knowledge be used in maths, history and art, and how might these be linked?
2. Which aspects of craft knowledge do you think most important?
3. Consider relationships between the teacher and the class.

Remember that answers to these questions will vary according to context. There is no one right answer.

What is special about the primary classteacher's role?

Most of the points made so far could apply to those teaching children of any age. However, to gain further insight into primary classteachers' expertise, let us consider:

- what is distinctive about young children's learning;
- the primary classteacher's role and the context in which she carries this out; and
- the relational and emotional aspects of the role.

Piaget (e.g. 1954) characterised the seven to eleven age group as the concrete-operational stage, when children begin thinking logically about concrete events, but have difficulty understanding and using abstract or hypothetical concepts to decide what will happen on a particular occasion. However, a strongly age-related view of stages is challenged by those such as Donaldson (1992) who demonstrated that children's understanding and response depends heavily on the nature of the task and the child's relationship with adults setting it. She argued that, with age, children become able to use different 'modes' and that more experienced learners select the mode appropriate to the type and difficulty of the task.

Bruner (2006, p. 69) identifies enactive, iconic and symbolic modes of representation, broadly involving actions, drawing and symbols, of which language is the most prominent. Young children tend to benefit from working from first-hand experience rather than abstract principle. They learn concepts slowly, over time, through a range of experiences through which the relationships between concepts are understood and internalised. While language becomes increasingly significant in the primary years, spoken language is, for most children, easier to use than written language, as either reader or writer. Even an experienced learner may benefit from using enactive and iconic modes when trying to grasp unfamiliar ideas. This implies that any learner, for tasks at the limit of their understanding, benefits from using an 'earlier' (or more than one) mode of representation.

This accords with the findings of neuroeducational research (e.g. Goswami and Bryant, 2010; Cowan, 2012) that:

- emotion and cognition are closely linked, with emotional responses tending to dominate except where these are consciously regulated;
- learning involves several interlinked mechanisms, some unconscious, others increasingly involving conscious control; and
- learning, especially deep, conceptual understanding, is enhanced by using different means of representing experience and material being presented in a variety of ways.

This body of research indicates that how the brain develops means that children only gradually become able to carry out some functions effectively, including processing emotional responses and exercising conscious control. The primary years are important for improving executive function, the conscious use of inhibitory mechanisms and meta-cognition to regulate immediate responses, relying less on external reward or sanction. Conscious reasoning makes considerable demands on working memory (the processes used to store, organise and manipulate information temporarily) which is vital to enable abstract and generalised thinking. The ability to use working memory efficiently develops only gradually and is impaired by anxiety. So children need opportunities and encouragement to improve executive function, through discussion, reflection and practice in an unthreatening environment.

Primary classteachers spend a considerable amount of time with a class, during any week and throughout the year, and usually have to teach most subject areas. This provides the opportunity to build close relationships and a deep understanding of the class and individuals within it. Classteachers cannot have as much subject knowledge in every subject as a specialist in only one, but they are well placed to make links across the whole curriculum and to encourage, over time, the attitudes, values and dispositions for lifelong and lifewide learning (see Claxton and Carr, 2004; Claxton, 2007, for more academic; and Claxton, 2002, for practical discussion). Their expertise resides more in ensuring breadth and balance and enabling links across different subject areas, and with children's experience outside school, which is especially significant for those least experienced in, or engaged with, school learning.

Out of school, children can usually speak and move when they want. In a class of up to 30, they are expected to wait. This can easily lead to children becoming passive and disengaged, or disruptive. It is easy to become anonymous in the crowd; or to gain attention by standing out from it. Their teachers must try to meet individual needs while catering for those of the whole group. This requires skill in interacting with the group, without wasting time and energy, if children are to be actively engaged, as in the history lesson described above. So classteachers must be attuned to children's emotional and cognitive cues and responses – and their own. The need to respond appropriately to children with a wide variety of backgrounds and abilities means that personal/interpersonal knowledge based on relationships of mutual trust matters particularly when learners are inexperienced or unsure.

Which aspects of pedagogy are most important in the primary classroom?

Think about and write down which pedagogical approaches are most likely to help a class of primary-age children:

- become 'readers' (as opposed to just decode written words)
- think, and act, like a scientist or a historian or an artist
- adopt good learning behaviours (think beforehand of three or four)
- develop intrinsic motivation.

Be aware that these will not just involve one approach, so there is no one right answer.
Again, discuss and compare your answers with others in a group.
Does this suggest areas for you, or others, to research further?

Implications for pedagogy

This section considers the areas of teacher expertise highlighted above more specifically in relation to the primary classteacher's role.

Structuring and using teacher knowledge

The *Cambridge Primary Review* (Alexander, 2010, p. 55) argues that 'teachers should work towards a pedagogy of repertoire rather than recipe, and of principle rather than prescription'. Given the range of subjects to be taught, the types of knowledge to be learned and how young children learn best, those teaching a class of young children must be able to adopt different versions of teaching such as facilitation and negotiation, rather than rely on transmission (see Alexander, 2008, pp. 78–81).

Structuring and using teacher knowledge appropriately is essential to try to ensure that tasks are within what Vygotsky (1978) called the Zone of Proximal Development – that is, just beyond the child's current level of understanding. In some ways, this match may be easier with young children than with older students because the subject knowledge required is less. In others, it may be harder because of the greater distance between the teacher's understanding and the children's, re-emphasising that teachers must interpret a range of cues, both cognitive and behavioural, about children's current level of under-standing. This reinforces the importance of pedagogical content knowledge rather than subject knowledge as such.

However, two difficult issues arise:

- the different levels of subject knowledge required to teach different age groups in the primary years; and
- the level of knowledge required in some subjects.

Teaching eleven-year-olds usually requires more subject knowledge than teaching six-year-olds and some subjects seem to require more procedural knowledge, especially, than others. For instance, teaching music or a modern foreign language at anything other than the most basic level needs an understanding of pitch and rhythm, and of vocabulary and grammar. While the same might be said of any subject, textbooks and written resources may provide more help – for instance, in science or history. This is not to say that teachers should just follow the manual but does explain why there may be a case for specialists in some subjects, especially with ten- or eleven-year-olds. While a subject specialist will usually understand more of the content, and procedural knowledge, associated with a discipline, he is unlikely to be able to draw parallels and analogies with other subject areas – or to have as close a relationship or knowledge of children's strengths and weaknesses, aptitudes and difficulties as the classteacher.

Setting objectives and providing feedback

Setting objectives and providing feedback is central to how teachers work. Part of the rhetoric of successive governments, with which it is hard to disagree, is that teachers should have high expectations. However, primary classteachers also require broad expec-tations, across and beyond the formal curriculum, and realistic ones if children are not to be bored or demotivated, by experiences being too undemanding or too difficult.

Young children benefit from praise and reinforcement, rather than a diet of criticism. But constant praise, especially for low-level tasks, does little to provide constructive feed-back about how to improve. As Alexander (1995, p. 206) writes,

> praise may not be what it seems. For one thing, it becomes devalued if it is used too often and without discrimination; for another the use of overt praise may be at vari-ance with other messages about children's work which a teacher is conveying and which children readily pick up.

Moreover, as Dweck (2000) indicates, children benefit from praise for behaviours rather than intelligence if they are to develop a growth mindset necessary to avoid a sense of learned helplessness when faced with difficulties.

Feedback works both from adult to child and from child to adult. The latter enables the teacher to understand the child (or children's) current level of understanding and alter the pitch of the task accordingly, as is necessary if teaching is to be reciprocal. This reaffirms that teaching entails understanding and responding to events, with young children's unpredictability emphasising the interpretation of cues, especially to discover areas of misunderstanding (see Hattie, 2012, for a detailed discussion of feedback).

Understanding and responding to events

Elliott *et al.* (2011, p. 99) suggest that skills such as:

- 'withitness' (being aware of events taking place);
- the capacity to manage multiple events concurrently;
- the skilful use and regulation of voice;
- the subtle deployment of non-verbal behaviour; and
- sensitivity in the control of spoken communication patterns

are among those which teachers use to demonstrate expertise and authority. The classroom is such a busy place (unless one restricts children's active participation) that teachers have to know, and respond to, what is happening in several places at once. Responses may be verbal or with a smile, a frown or a gesture – even doing nothing – depending on the situation and the class. The need to judge rapidly how best to respond is one reason why expertise as a classteacher is so hard to describe and even harder to acquire.

Five important aspects of student teachers' craft knowledge identified by John (2000, pp. 98–101) are:

- problem avoidance;
- interpretation of pupil cues;
- opportunity creation;
- mood assessment; and
- improvisation.

Teachers with a high level of expertise anticipate and avoid problems, as with Martin in the first example at the beginning of this chapter. Teaching a class requires peripheral vision, the ability, like a good driver, to see what is going on around while focused on the task in hand; and to be attuned to a range of cues, emotional, behavioural and cognitive, to adapt one's pedagogy. The ability to recognise patterns of what is happening, or likely to happen, helps such teachers avoid difficulties or identify and cope with them swiftly. They create opportunities and enable and encourage children to do so and follow them through, maybe following a perceptive remark or one indicating a misunderstanding. Since the mood of a classroom can change rapidly, especially with young children – for instance, after lunch, on a windy day or for particular activities – one difficult but important skill is knowing when, and how, to influence this, perhaps with humour or a warning, with a change of activity or how children are expected to work.

Schön (1987) distinguishes between reflection on action and reflection in action – the former deliberative and analytical, the latter more intuitive and enabling appropriate decisions to be made in-the-moment. While most teachers reflect on their teaching, reflection in action is one mark of really expert teachers. Sometimes, this may involve very rapid reflection, sometimes immediate, intuitive responses. Sawyer (2004) describes this as 'disciplined improvisation', in contrast to 'scripted instruction'. This does not imply an unplanned approach, but being able to improvise fluidly and confidently within broad structures and frameworks. It does not mean that teachers should not have learning objectives, but that they should be wary of sticking too closely to these.

Creating and sustaining a climate and context for learning

Creating and sustaining an inclusive climate for learning, over time, is a vital aspect of primary classteachers' expertise. This is harder than it may appear. While inclusion is often used to mean ensuring that children of all abilities can participate and that bullying does not occur, or is rapidly addressed when it does, there are subtler forms of exclusion. For instance, if ability and intelligence is seen mostly in terms of attainment in reading and writing and mathematics, other types of intelligence, such as musical or interpersonal, as suggested by Gardner (1993), will be devalued. Young children can achieve far more than adults expect when tasks are meaningful to them. To be inclusive, the primary curriculum must be broad and balanced (see Alexander, 2010), with opportunities for varied types of activity and ways of representing experience. If tasks are to be active and engaging, especially for those children whose culture and background are less congruent with the school's expectations, teachers must draw, and build, on children's 'funds of knowledge', from outside school (see Hogg, 2011).

Experts usually keep the task simple so that they focus on what matters most; and know the limits of their expertise. However, they do not oversimplify – for instance, a pianist leaving out difficult parts of a concerto or a doctor ignoring unfamiliar symptoms. For primary classteachers, expertise involves opening up, and keeping open, possibilities for different children in a diverse group, rather than oversimplifying or restricting learning opportunities.

Exercising expertise in changing situations requires confidence. Primary classteachers may gain confidence from many sources, such as deep knowledge of the subject, or class, or their own sense of expertise. However, one should be cautious. Confidence may be misplaced; and too great a level of confidence on the teacher's part may create a sense of dependency, especially working with young children. Therefore, teachers may, at times, have to show uncertainty so that, despite being confident in their own knowledge, they encourage and enable children to question, challenge and be critical. If children are to develop creativity and independence the teacher must be in control, but not too controlling.

Manifesting attitudes and beliefs

Showing respect for all children is harder than it seems. In subtle (and sometimes not-so-subtle) ways, teachers indicate a greater interest in some children, and their responses, than others. For instance, high-attaining or articulate children are often listened to more than others; and those in the early stages of learning English or who find reading difficult may be regarded as of lower ability. As Shulman (2004, p. 413) suggests, 'you must respect the intelligence and understanding of your students *especially* when they misunderstand'. When children are prepared to articulate their thought processes and so risk being ridiculed or thought stupid, they offer the teacher valuable clues. So teachers with a high level of expertise are not patronising and value errors as well as right answers, using children's naïve conceptions to understand how they are thinking and their learning can be enhanced.

While 'passion for teaching' may evoke a wry smile from the exhausted student or teacher, a commitment to, and an enthusiasm for, children and their learning is essential especially with young children, since they are unlikely to engage with learning if their teacher does not show enthusiasm and enjoyment. Given the power of example, especially in learning procedural knowledge, young children benefit from what Rogoff (1990) calls an apprenticeship approach, where children learn more from watching and asking than from direct instruction – for instance, in becoming a reader or thinking critically. So teachers provide valuable role models and their role is not just that of technician. However, Jackson *et al.* (1993, pp. 286–7) comment that the teachers they studied did not use 'role model' much, perhaps because it seems too 'heroic', but spoke rather of 'humbler virtues' such as:

- showing respect for others;
- demonstrating what it means to be intellectually absorbed;
- paying close attention to what is being said;
- being a 'good sport'; and
- showing that it is OK to make mistakes and to be confused.

New visions

How teachers select and carry out appropriate strategies is affected by anxiety, emphasising that they must be able to regulate their own responses, particularly when strongly emotionally affected. Primary classteachers' confidence is easily undermined by inherent and external factors. Among the former is the unpredictability of the primary classroom. Young children's responses tend to be more volatile and less predictable than those of older children, since they find self-regulation more difficult, especially in a group. Children's conduct is strongly influenced by the reactions of others. For example, a silly noise or pulling a face may prompt others to follow suit, usually to the amusement of everyone except the teacher; their teachers tend to be worried about losing control and so become controlling, reducing children's agency.

A second inherent factor is isolation. This may be surprising, given the thousands of interactions involved, but the imbalance of age, and of power, in the classroom and the expectation that teachers will take the lead means that they may feel very alone, resulting in a tendency not to trust their own judgement, especially under pressure.

External expectations exercise a strong influence on how teachers use their expertise. As Berliner (2001, pp. 465–6) indicates,

> policies from the principals, superintendents and school board ... along with expectations of the community ... subtly but powerfully, affect teachers' attitudes, beliefs, enthusiasms, sense of efficacy, conception of their responsibilities, and teaching practices.

A sense of being trusted contributes to a secure sense of identity as a teacher. Nias (1989) indicated that the close link between primary teachers' personal and professional identities affects them particularly strongly when expected to comply against their own better judgement.

Among the external constraints which affect primary classteachers' identity and ability to exercise expertise are a prescriptive curriculum and high-stakes assessment and accountability. The former reduces teachers' scope for making adaptations for a specific group and tends to encourage content coverage rather than deep learning or reciprocal teaching. High-stakes assessment and accountability makes all but the most confident teachers concentrate on the subjects assessed, performativity, content, pace and compliance. OECD (2009) argues for teacher autonomy as long as suitable accountability mechanisms are in place. So a balance is needed between encouraging teacher autonomy and checking how well teachers teach. But the pressure to cover a great deal of content or to be judged outstanding in every lesson limits the chance of teachers manifesting a high level of expertise. Detailed prescription of what is to be taught, allied with high-stakes accountability, risks undermining teachers' sense of agency and constraining their expertise (see Chapter 4 for an in-depth exploration of agency and the curriculum).

This chapter started with three examples of primary classteachers at work: an incident, a lesson and a series of lessons. Their expertise resides not in any one of these but a complex interaction of immediate and long-term interactions to meet multiple aims; and is broader and more holistic than subject specialists' narrower but deeper expertise. Since teaching a class of young children is very demanding, this depends on judgement, requiring propositional, procedural and personal/interpersonal knowledge, with a combination of theoretical and experiential knowledge helping to create case knowledge about similar situations. Pedagogical content knowledge is more important than subject knowledge, as such, especially with less experienced learners. Craft knowledge is multifaceted, but often intuitive, to cope with the fluid world of the classroom, and is linked closely to personal and interpersonal knowledge of how one affects, and is affected by, a class of young children, and by external expectations.

There is considerable scope for empirical research into primary classteachers' expertise and how it is best developed. However, this must take account of the breadth of opportunities and challenges of the primary classteacher's role rather than assume that their expertise is easily compared with that of the subject specialist. In policy terms, the complexity of the primary classteacher's role and what this involves needs greater recognition rather than limiting this by narrowing the range of learning opportunities available to children. If primary classteachers' expertise is to be valued and developed, there must be less emphasis on performativity backed by high-stakes accountability and more on teacher autonomy. This will be a key element in a new vision of classteachers able to equip young children with the skills, attitudes and dispositions to cope confidently with a world of rapid change.

Further reading

Eaude, T. (2012). *How do Expert Primary Classteachers Really Work? A Critical Guide for Teachers, Headteachers and Teacher Educators*. St Albans: Critical. www.criticalpublishing.com
A short book summarising key aspects of research on expertise and teacher expertise to identify what is specific to primary classteachers.

Elliott, J. G., Stemler, S. E., Sternberg, R. J., Grigorenko, E. L. and Hoffman, N. (2011). The Socially Skilled Teacher and the Development of Tacit Knowledge. *British Educational Research Journal.* 37 (1). 83–103.
A thoughtful article on the interactive nature of teaching and how the subtle processes involved can be developed.

Glaser, R. (1999). Expert Knowledge and Processes of Thinking. In R. McCormick and C. Paechter (eds), *Learning and Knowledge.* London: Paul Chapman. 88–102.
A chapter which discusses the features of expertise in general, providing a useful overview, without being specific to teaching.

Sternberg, R. J. and Horvath, J. A. (1995). A Prototype View of Expert Teaching. *Educational Researcher.* 24 (6). 9–17.
A short, classic article exploring expertise in relation to teaching.

References

Alexander, R. (1995). *Versions of Primary Education.* London: Routledge.
Alexander, R. (2000). *Culture and Pedagogy: International Comparisons in Primary Education.* Oxford: Blackwell.
Alexander, R. (2008). *Essays on Pedagogy.* Abingdon: Routledge.
Alexander, R. (ed.). (2010). *Children, their World, their Education: Final Report and Recommendations of the Cambridge Primary Review.* Abingdon: Routledge.
Berlak, A. and Berlak, H. (1981). *Dilemmas of Schooling: Teaching and Social Change.* London: Methuen.
Berliner, D. C. (2001). Learning About and Learning From Expert Teachers. *International Journal of Educational Research.* 35. 463–82.
Bruner, J. S. (2006). *In Search of Pedagogy: The Selected Work of Jerome S. Bruner (Volume 1).* London: Routledge.
Claxton, G. (2002). *Building Learning Power: Helping Young People become Better Learners.* Bristol: TLO.
Claxton, G. (2007). Expanding Young People's Capacity to Learn. *British Journal of Educational Studies.* 55 (2). 115–34.
Claxton, G. and Carr, M. (2004). A Framework for Teaching Learning: The Dynamics of Disposition. *Early Years.* 24 (1). 87–97.
Cowan, N. (2012). Working Memory: The Seat of Learning and Comprehension. In S. Della Sala and M. Anderson. *Neuroscience in Education: The Good, the Bad and the Ugly.* Oxford: Oxford University Press. 111–27.
Donaldson, M. (1992). *Human Minds: An Exploration.* London: Allen Lane.
Dweck, C. S. (2000). *Self Theories: Their Role in Motivation, Personality and Development.* Philadelphia: Psychology Press.
Eaude, T. (2012). *How do Expert Primary Classteachers Really Work? A Critical Guide for Teachers, Headteachers and Teacher Educators.* St Albans: Critical. www.criticalpublishing.com
Eaude, T. (2014). What Makes Primary Classteachers Special? Exploring the Features of Expertise in the Primary Classroom. *Teachers and Teaching: Theory and Practice.* 20 (1). 4–18.
Elliott, J. G., Stemler, S. E., Sternberg, R. J., Grigorenko, E. L. and Hoffman, N. (2011). The Socially Skilled Teacher and the Development of Tacit Knowledge. *British Educational Research Journal.* 37 (1). 83–103.
Eraut, M. (2000). The Intuitive Practitioner: A Critical Overview. In T. Atkinson and G. Claxton (eds), *The Intuitive Practitioner: On the Value of Not Always Knowing What One is Doing.* Buckingham: Open University Press. 255–68.
Gardner, H. (1993). *Frames of Mind: The Theory of Multiple Intelligences.* London: Fontana.

Glaser, R. (1999). Expert Knowledge and Processes of Thinking. In R. McCormick and C. Paechter (eds), *Learning and Knowledge*. London: Paul Chapman. 88–102.

Goswami, U. and Bryant, P. (2010). Children's Cognitive Development and Learning. In *The Cambridge Primary Review Research Surveys*. Abingdon: Routledge. 141–69.

Hargreaves, A. (2003) *Teaching in the Knowledge Society: Education in the Age of Insecurity*. Maidenhead: Open University Press.

Hattie, J. (2012). *Visible Learning for Teachers: Maximising Impact on Learning*. London: Routledge.

Hogg, L. (2011). Funds of Knowledge: An Investigation of Coherence within the Literature. *Teaching and Teacher Education*. 27. 666–77.

Jackson, P. W., Boostrom, R. E. and Hansen, D. J. (1993) *The Moral Life of Schools*. San Francisco: Jossey Bass.

John, P. (2000). Awareness and Intuition: How Student Teachers Read their own Lessons. In T. Atkinson and G. Claxton (eds), *The Intuitive Practitioner: On the Value of Not Always Knowing What One is Doing*. Buckingham: Open University Press. 84–106.

Kimes Myers, B. (1997). *Young Children and Spirituality*. London: Routledge.

Nias, J. (1989). *Primary Teachers Talking: A Study of Teaching as Work*. London: Routledge.

OECD (2009). *School Autonomy and Accountability: Are They Related to Student Performance?* PISA in Focus 9. Available at: http://www.oecd.org/pisa/pisaproducts/pisainfocus/48910490.pdf

Piaget, J. (1954). *The Construction of Reality in the Child*. London: Routledge & Kegan Paul.

Polanyi, M. (1967). *The Tacit Dimension*. London: Routledge & Kegan Paul.

Rogoff, B. (1990). *Apprenticeship in Thinking: Cognitive Development in Social Context*. Oxford: Oxford University Press.

Ruthven, K., Hennessey, S. and Deaney, R. (2004). *Eliciting Situated Expertise in ICT-integrated Mathematics and Science Teaching*. University of Cambridge/ESRC. Available at: http://www.leeds.ac.uk/educol/documents/189417.pdf

Sawyer, R. K. (2004). Creative Teaching: Collaborative Discussion as Disciplined Improvisation. *Educational Researcher*. 33 (2). 12–20.

Schön, D. (1987). *Educating the Reflective Practitioner*. San Francisco: Jossey Bass.

Shulman, L. S. (2004). *The Wisdom of Practice: Essays on Teaching, Learning and Learning to Teach*. San Francisco: Jossey Bass.

Sternberg, R. J. and Horvath, J. A. (1995). A Prototype View of Expert Teaching. *Educational Researcher*. 24 (6). 9–17.

Twiselton, S. (2006). The Problem with English: The Exploration and Development of Student Teachers' English Subject Knowledge in Primary Classrooms. *Literacy*. 40 (2). 88–96.

Vygotsky, L. S. (1978). *Mind in Society: The Development of Higher Psychological Processes*. Cambridge, MA: Harvard University Press.

Whitty, G. (2008). Changing Modes of Teacher Professionalism: Traditional, Managerial, Collaborative and Democratic. In B. Cunningham (ed.), *Exploring Professionalism*. London: Institute of Education, University of London. 28–49.

Chapter 8

Language and culture in foreign language teaching

Paula Ambrossi

Chapter summary

Languages, in their grammar and vocabulary, reflect the historical evolution of their culture, including legacies of conquest and invasion. This chapter is grounded in a social constructivist approach to teaching and learning, examining how we shape and are shaped by language and culture. It also addresses why teaching should explain some historical origins of the vocabulary of the language being learned.

Foreign languages in primary schools are discussed from the point of view of past and present curriculum initiatives, and the impact of these on current practice. A case is made for cross-curricular teaching involving discussions around culture. Spanish is used as an exemplar, drawing mainly on Spanish history from Moorish Spain to the 'discovery' of the Americas. Encouraging teachers to engage with these issues (as opposed to engaging only with new language) is seen not only as inclusive practice, but also essential in order to motivate children and to help them learn.

STUDENT (S): Well, I don't think we should celebrate acts of violence and exploitation. The Conquistadores did nothing positive for the land and people they discovered and conquered. They just exploited and stripped the native peoples of their own language and identity.

TUTOR (T): I'm not sure myself how I feel about this either, because if it weren't for them I would not be standing here talking Spanish to you right now. I am, in a way, the product of a violent historical act. To wish the Spanish Conquest away is to wish myself away. If I were a native my voice would never have reached you.

S: But how can you know that?

T: I can't. But I do know that my identity is not one thing or the other, and that I'd be nowhere without either culture having met.

S: Still, making a film about the Conquistadores seems to me like we're glorifying or celebrating invasion.

T: But that will not be our starting point. We will be looking at when the invaders themselves were conquered. Imagine the many children of Muslim background in inner London schools, what their reaction might be when they find out that a significant part of the Spanish language is of Arabic origin. What might their responses be when you get them to think about the reasons behind that?

The example above, paraphrased from a primary education teacher training session for students specialising in Spanish, demonstrates the strong views held by some trainees in relation to the historic links covered during the course. The exchange is a very good prompt for this chapter's main message: that language teaching and learning is more than acquisition of vocabulary and grammar in order to speak, read or write. We learn a new language in order to access new visions and understandings, whatever our age or foreign language proficiency. This is, in effect, the purpose of study of a foreign language in England's national curriculum, implemented from September 2014 onwards.

The interaction between tutor and trainee teachers above arose from a focus on the historical origins of Spanish language and culture. The historical sequence is that, after 700 years of Roman invasion and 300 years of Visigoth kingdoms, around the eighth century AD the Berber Moors arrived from the Islamic Golden Age into the Dark Ages of Europe, changing Spain forever. When they arrived they found a southern Spain unrecognisable to us now. In the 400 years that followed, the Moors gave the Iberian peninsula irrigation, architecture, scientific curiosity, mathematics, music, art, a love of learning and education, as well as developing an organised city with a form of religious tolerance. Islam had breathed in the wealth of knowledge from the Greek and Hindu cultures, perfected it and added to it, and gave it to the people they conquered.

On 2 January 1492, the Spanish Christian crusaders 'rid Spain' of the last Moor strong-hold in Granada (expelling also all the Jews). This is exactly the same year when Spain sent Christopher Columbus to look for a better route to the West Indies. Columbus died believing he had arrived in the West Indies, unaware of the extensive land he had 'discovered'. The continent was subsequently named, in all probability, after the Italian explorer Americo Vespucci.

The historical basis of modern Spain, its language and culture, differs from the evolution of other languages and cultures. So Spain, the Spanish culture and language are used as an exemplar in this chapter but with the intention to apply the implications more widely.

The chapter begins with a brief overview of social constructivist views relevant to the discussion of culture, language and identity. It then continues by applying social constructivism to the development of intercultural understanding. In the following section, which considers foreign languages in Primary Schools in England, the focus is on how intercultural understanding may be fostered while, at the same time, fulfilling the requirements of the national curriculum, which was revised with effect from September 2014. Cross-curricular approaches are discussed in the section which follows, together with practical pedagogical strategies for the models suggested. The advantages and disadvantages of each are identified for enabling effective teaching and learning. Implementing curriculum requirements while at the same time motivating teachers, not only to provide foreign language teaching and learning, but also to foster intercultural understanding, is the focus of the section on 'Motivation to teach language'. In this, the co-construction of intercultural understanding by teachers and children is an underlying concept. The chapter then concludes by foregrounding the challenges posed by over-focus on linguistic features of a language. In setting out the vision of developing intercultural understanding, there is emphasis on the role of a school's leadership team to enable implementation of the foreign language curriculum through one of the three models.

A social constructivist view of culture, language and identity

The connection between culture and language is well established (Valdes, 1986; Sercu, 2005; Nunan and Choi, 2010). Language, as well as facilitating communication, permeates and structures our way of thinking about the world. The interaction between language and culture has become better understood since its first conceptualisation, and we now understand how complex any concept of culture and identity is. In addition to the importance of wider aspects such as language, culture is defined in the chapter as those shared 'external' elements and events which work as a kind of signpost for our 'internal' identities:

> Culture, as we have said, has to do with the artefacts, ways of doing, etc. shared by a group of people. Identity is the acceptance and internalization of the artefacts and ways of doing by a member of that group.
>
> (Nunan and Choi, 2010, p. 5)

There is a constant interplay and readjustment between the external world and the internal self, made more complex by the idea that what we perceive as external comes from ourselves too. The dividing line between our minds and the external world is not clearcut or stable; we are involved in an 'ongoing dialectic of our creating things which in turn create us' (Malafouris, 2013, p. 43). Consistent with the close interaction between thoughts and artefacts, but from a different perspective, Vygotsky (1978) emphasised that children's cognitive development takes place within a social context.

The evidence suggests that children co-construct their knowledge and their worlds (Burman, 2008,). They model their understandings on those of parents, carers, teachers and significant others (Rogers, 2008) and this has significance for the attitudes children will acquire and take into adulthood. Much of what of what we believe about our culture and language (and identities) is made powerful by our need to belong and fit in not only with our immediate social group but with groups that, themselves, crave for an historical and geographical bond. This gives identification with the body, the name, the language that we possess. The group bonding is important in feeling oneself protected by a community with shared memories and roots. Integration in a culture provides children with two aspects, crucial in the formation of personality: identity and self-esteem. And many adults continue anchoring themselves to these collective references, more than to their individual desires (Alvarez-Junco, 2001, p. 18, trans. P. Ambrossi).

With reference to teachers who play a fundamental role in what children come to believe, it is argued that they should be enabled to examine their own attitudes to languages and culture and to widen their own understanding. The example at the beginning of this chapter illustrates the point, and the need to recognise what, historically, Europe owes to the Muslim world and Arabic to Spanish.

An example from music is further evidence. If the reader types into YouTube search. 'Radio Tarifa en vivo, la Pastora' a Spanish band called Radio Tarifa can be heard performing their song 'The Shepherdess' ('La Pastora'). In music form, the listener can hear a similar view of what this chapter is trying to convey of the historical influences which contribute to a culture. The Spanish song has Arabic undertones; Tarifa in southern Spain is known as the 'Mediterranean balcony', the closest point to Africa. The common origins of the two cultures may be appreciated by focusing on the affinity between traditional Iberian music and the popular and cultured music of the Mediterranean world.

Developing intercultural understanding

The concept of co-construction of knowledge applies to adults as well as children. It is, therefore, argued that by deconstructing our own understandings and attitudes, recognising that these are often limited by the socio-cultural and physical context which we inhabit, we may become aware of those of others. 'Culture' is an all-encompassing term, but genuine *intercultural understanding* implies recognition of the rich mixture of influences within as well as between communities. The music played by Radio Tarifa is a case in point.

Like music, stories, ideas and actions carry cultural information about a sense of self, about the people that we are, that we could be, or that we would not want to be. Recognition of how we have learned to make sense of our worlds may contribute to acquiring a more critical understanding of our own culture and of developing some intercultural competence.

Viewing identity through the lens of social interactions can give teachers some agency in helping children view and form their sense of identity and understand how people constantly engage in the construction of their own. This ought to be of particular interest to any foreign language teacher who wants children to engage effectively in language learning, and achieve some measure of intercultural competence. One way to broaden the spectrum of possible identities that children could inhabit in their imagination is through poetry, prose, film or role play. The following quotation illustrates the point: 'artistic and discursive genres from different linguistic/cultural traditions can be explored as means to help students to work together to imagine and create more empowering identities' (Lin, 2008, p. 216). Language viewed in this way can also be seen as a performative act:

> As we perform identity with words (rather than reflecting identity in language), we also perform languages with words. What we therefore have to understand is not how this 'thing' called 'language x' or 'language y' does or does not do things to and for people, but rather the multiple investments people bring to their acts, desires, and performances around these language effects.
>
> (Pennycook, 2006, p. 71)

Valuing children's emerging sense of identities involves engaging with their own feelings and thoughts (their voice) as they enact their identities through their use of language. Valuing their voices makes it possible for them to learn to value the voices of others. Discussions about their own and other cultures need to be inclusive, led by any teacher whatever their foreign language skills. Discussions can motivate the learner beyond the classroom and give meaning and significance to the language learned: 'effective communication requires much more than mastering the phonological, lexical, and grammatical subsystems of the language' (Nunan and Choi, 2010, p. 43). Spoken words – as in greetings, animals, colours – are not voice, and it is argued that every lesson should have room for children's voices. Spoken words may, nevertheless, be viewed as a beginning in today's multicultural society and among the many children in schools whose first language is not English.

Foreign languages in primary schools in England

Recent initiatives around language learning in general tend to display a greater awareness of the diversity and respect towards different cultures (Department for Education, 2002, 2005, 2013). Initial drives to encourage and support foreign language learning in England from 2002 onwards produced some insightful and exciting ideas and guidance for the primary schools. However, the ongoing and renewed emphasis in England to improve English and Mathematics performance in Primary schools has presented headteachers with a dilemma regarding how to introduce languages into an already 'crowded' curriculum (Hunt et al., 2005). As Alexander and Flutter (2009, p. 3) have suggested, the primary 'curriculum is not just a political and professional battleground; it is also a conceptual minefield'. In the light of this we recognise that trying to encourage schools to give their time and energy to a reconceptualisation of what foreign languages can look like is a challenging task.

The most recent framework for foreign language teaching in primary schools, implemented in September 2014, specified that a foreign language, ancient or modern, should form part of the national curriculum for seven- to eleven-year-olds (Key Stage 2, Years 3–6). As with its predecessors, for example, in the national curriculum revision of 2002 (Department for Education, 2002), the framework provides a rationale of 'liberation from insularity and an opening to other cultures' (Department for Education, 2013, p. 1). One difference is that the 2013 Framework replaces the teaching of a modern foreign language specified in the 2005 revision of the national curriculum (Department for Education and Skills, 2005), with a foreign language, ancient or modern. The rationale is consistent with the policy document published by Eurydice, the information network on education in Europe for the Directorate General for Information and Culture (2001):

> In addition to covering communication skills, Foreign Language teaching – as nearly all curricula review it – must also allow pupils to broaden their knowledge and deepen their understanding of the people who speak the Foreign Language taught and of their customs and lifestyles. These objectives, formulated in terms of openness to other cultures, often go hand in hand with the aim of promoting personal reflection on their own cultures.
>
> (Eurydice, 2001, p. 196)

The Eurydice statement underlines the focus of this chapter which argues throughout that full understanding needs an awareness of the historical origins of a language and the culture in which it is embedded. Such an appreciation is considered to be fundamental to the value of teaching the mechanics of a language.

Beginning with the formal introduction of foreign language teaching in the primary school from 2002 onwards, and without the constraints of textbooks, to date there has been a significant amount of freedom of innovation and an opportunity to apply the best research-based pedagogies available. In the 2014 national curriculum programme of study at Key Stage 2, the same opportunities apply, with an emphasis on practical communication but greater specification of listening, speaking, reading, writing and appreciation (Department for Education, 2013, p. 2). However, we also live in an age of performance targets, league tables and an atmosphere of suspicion of different cultures which can inhibit both innovation and a genuine intercultural engagement through the learning of a foreign language. How the required skills may be acquired in conjunction with a degree of understanding of a culture is a major issue.

Studying foreign languages in early years and primary offers the opportunity for a cross-curricular approach that can be constructivist in nature. Children can learn through the interconnectedness of subjects, learning not only how to greet someone in their language but why it might be important or valid for us to do so in the first place. If, however, over-emphasis is placed on the oracy and literacy (listening/speaking, reading/writing) of the target language, children cannot give age-appropriate opinions about culture, identity, or anything else that may hold their interest. An emphasis on memorisation rather than exploration will not encourage independent learners (Cable *et al.*, 2012). Rather, it will produce children who learn to be passive, encouraged towards, as Airey (2004) argues, 'surface approaches to learning, instead of the deep/holistic approach … a risk that students no longer focus on understanding, but rather learn what Sawyer (1943: 9) terms *imitation subjects*', thus making the application of learned structures irrelevant for the learner (Airey, 2004, p. 101). For instance, children may learn how to say 'soy moreno' (I have dark skin), but they won't understand that 'moreno' comes from the word 'Moro' (Moor), and that the Moors ruled southern Spain for 400 years, and the impact of this event on Europe, etc. Children and adults can only fully participate in these conversations when using languages they own.

In considering approaches to developing ownership of the target language, three main models have emerged of foreign language delivery in schools (Wade *et al.*, 2009; Cable *et al.*, 2012). These are:

1. Outside language 'expert' coming to the school;
2. Class teacher (or school staff member) delivering the language;
3. A combination of the above.

Each of these would satisfy the requirement to teach a foreign language at Key Stage 2. The first model is 'outsourcing' the language teacher: employing an 'expert' from outside who comes to the school to deliver the lesson. This often happens during the class teacher's non-contact time (used for planning). The implications of this model can be the following:

*   Hopefully, the 'expert' will have a good level of content and pedagogical knowledge about language learning in primary, modelling and teaching – among other aspects, correct pronunciation and written skills. However, there is no clarity as to what constitutes an 'expert', so a school may hire someone who reports to be, for example, a fluent Mandarin speaker, but the school has no immediate way of asserting the actual level of expertise in both speaking and writing of the applicant, nor their relevant pedagogical knowledge.
*   The expert may provide a new and different teaching style to which the children may respond well.
*   There will be a dedicated slot in the timetable for the foreign language lesson which will be adhered to.
*   The outsider does not know the children well enough to differentiate learning as effectively as a class teacher might.
*   There is less opportunity to teach foreign languages cross-curricularly, or of consolidating knowledge throughout the week. The class teacher may not know what the children have been learning.
*   If the teacher is not in the classroom and shows no interest in the foreign language lessons, children might learn from his or her modelling that it is fine to demonstrate (and have) no interest in foreign languages.

The second model some schools have adopted is to have the class teacher or another member of staff from the school delivering the language. In this case the implications can be the following:

- The teacher will be familiar and competent with primary and early years pedagogy.
- If taught by another staff member in the school, it may provide a different delivery style for children.
- Timetabling is more flexible but lessons are likely to be changed or cancelled if something more 'pressing' comes up.
- There may be great variability in the teachers' language skills, which may impact on children's learning. Support around resources and language development will be necessary in many cases.
- The teacher knows the class and can differentiate effectively, getting the most out of each child.
- There are many potentially good opportunities for consolidation of knowledge throughout the week and cross-curricular learning, which is a great asset in language learning.
- The teacher can model an attitude that reinforces the positive aspects of learning a new language, particularly if the teacher is learning with the children as modelling language learning skills can help the children become independent learners.
- Teachers will have to invest time and energy into the lessons, just like they would for science, music or any other foundation subject.

The third model, which can involve team-teaching, has the 'expert' and the class teacher working in collaboration. This approach can provide the most fruitful opportunities as children can have access to the best of both models (Cable *et al.*, 2012). This also allows teachers to develop their language skills and confidence while modelling a positive attitude to the children.

Even though the new foreign languages curriculum for England focuses only on oracy and literacy in terms of attainment, it is worth remembering the purpose of study for foreign languages (and modern foreign languages) for both primary and secondary teaching, as stated by the government in the national curriculum in England *Programmes of Study*, published on 11 September 2013:

> Learning a foreign language is a liberation from insularity and provides an opening to other cultures. A high-quality languages education should foster pupils' curiosity and deepen their understanding of the world. The teaching should enable pupils to express their ideas and thoughts in another language and to understand and respond to its speakers, both in speech and in writing. It should also provide opportunities for them to communicate for practical purposes, learn new ways of thinking and read great literature in the original language. Language teaching should provide the foundation for learning further languages, equipping pupils to study and work in other countries.
> (Department for Education, 2013, p. 1)

There is an expectation of some intercultural understanding in the statement above. The aim of 'fostering curiosity' and 'new ways of thinking' cannot be merely based on the memorisation of words and structures.

The new curriculum also offers the exciting possibility of allowing the study of ancient languages (Latin and Greek) in primary schools. Foreign languages cannot escape the mantle of (and attitudes towards) the classics. Latin and ancient Greek give us access to classic civilisations, and modern foreign languages should be no different for they give us access to exploring our present cultural identity. As humans we learn to listen, to speak, to read and to write because we need to understand and express ourselves.

The purpose of study is ambitious and certainly sets high expectations. It provides us with the idea that focusing solely at the word and structure level (however attractively this may be done) may not engage children's curiosity for the world in the long term. Engaging with a culture's 'content' rather than just its 'words' may motivate children by providing them with plenty of food for thought which stays with them beyond the lesson, encouraging independent learners who *can* and have acquired 'a deeper under-standing of the world' and who *want* to 'express their ideas and thoughts in another language' (Department for Education, 2013, p. 1). Literature in translated form can also offer a rich background for language learning. Many teachers appreciate classical or contemporary literature from abroad. Engaging with the literature of a nation can be a way of encouraging intrinsic motivation in children (or anyone) by inviting their emotional responses to a text. The diverse themes that can be accessed through this art form provide a context for the language that may well last beyond any words learned: 'every reader must be grateful for what translators open up; and will be affected, altered, shifted, and will respond and reciprocate in some fashion and in some degree' (Constantine, 2004, p. 13).

Key questions for reflection

In relation to a modern foreign language taught in your schools think about how much you know about some of the important literature, art and music that the people who speak the language engage with. Then consider how knowledge of these art forms might enhance children's language learning.

Cross-curricular opportunities

Approaching foreign languages in a cross-curricular style can offer teachers more choice as to what aspects of language and culture motivates them the most. Many teachers are drawn to history and, if the school is opting for Latin or Spanish, open discussions may take children towards aspects that can be perceived as 'difficult' events in history, like the ones outlined at the beginning of the chapter. At this point, teachers will be faced with the decision concerning an approach to controversial topics, and the choice they make will send an important message to the children. Teachers might need to think about how they themselves approach these questions. Why, for instance, we will not find any toy Conquistador helmets for sale anywhere, and yet we can feel quite comfortable buying pretend Viking, Roman or Crusader attire. Avoiding a careless or surface-level engagement or overemphasis on certain historical aspects will help steer children away from distorted views about ancient people (Hoodless, 2008) as these distorted views might in turn legitimise the choice of aggression as a mode of 'conquest', disguised almost as 'play'. As teachers we do not need to speak French or Spanish to engage with these issues, but through our attitudes we can, out of ignorance, 'impose' identities on peoples from the past or from other cultures, or perpetuate stereotypes of, for instance, black people (Traille, 2007; Harnett, 2008).

Making links explicit across subjects shows the interconnectedness of things, helping us make sense of the particular in the whole. This is exemplified in the activity in Figure 8.1, where the image can be analysed as a starting point for a unit of work.

The example given in Figure 8.1 highlights the links that can be explored with student teachers using a Spanish event, and which student teachers may then in turn use with the children they teach. These links are particularly relevant to exploring how our language, culture, attitudes, borders and identities are shaped. Unfortunately, many refugee children in our classrooms have had first-hand experience with the conflict of invasion and can find no obvious platform on which to express or understand some of the aspects of what they or others close to them have lived.

Working with languages across the curriculum can be a powerful and unique opportunity towards developing citizens with global awareness, and children who are encouraged to see the whole through exploration and discussion of its parts and context, rather than just having an emphasis on the facts as in words and language structures (Haynes, 2008), important as these are. Teaching foreign languages cross-curricularly also fits with a constructivist approach

Activity rationale:
Recreating the encounter between Europeans and Native Americans can be a powerful experience which can make children reflect, ask questions and challenge previous conceptions. Although the 'outcome' of the activity with children can be a short film or animation (which might eventually be shared with the whole school or parents), the real learning takes place during the process of learning, including discussing the issues.

Figure 8.1 Linking an historical event in Spain with language teaching.

Graphics by P. Ambrossi 2013

to learning. Foreign languages in this instance become 'project-based, process-oriented, product-centred learning within a rich and facilitative multimodal learning environment' (Rüschoff and Ritter, 2001, p. 231). Making links explicit across subjects shows the interconnectedness of things, helping us make sense of the particular in the whole.

Motivation to teach language

Government initiatives can be a good starting point, but inspiring teachers to engage with language and culture is an essential step towards inspiring children. During the first years of teacher training, informed ideas and ideals (not just information) have the greatest hope. Even though some schools might not provide the most fertile soil, new teachers can enter their profession planting seeds and initiatives in a bottom-up approach, carrying energy from within which is informed by research from above.

Most countries in the western world, Asia and the Americas have been teaching foreign languages to their young citizens for decades, which has meant that structures to do so are well established. The curriculum is delivered through textbooks, and in many instances the textbook market has dominated the field, its pedagogy and the imagination of its teachers, but too often without due understanding of the motivation of children.

It is a great credit to any institution that its teachers are encouraged and trained to use their knowledge and creativity when designing and delivering lessons. Not relying on textbooks may allow for the possibility of theory and practice to come face to face most emphatically. It can power the need in foreign language teachers to find approaches to teaching and learning in their actual practice, as applicable to their particular pupils. Being encouraged to think creatively and in explorative ways around teaching and learning has allowed many of our teacher trainees in England to become critical and outstanding practitioners. One example of this is illustrated in the following account, which took place during a school practice in an inner London school.

A ten-year-old Muslim boy had asked a trainee teacher (foreign languages specialist) whether she was a Christian or a Muslim. She was taken aback at first, but then interpreted the boy's confusion in that although she was of Muslim faith, because she was his Spanish teacher the boy had apparently assumed that she must be a 'Catholic' (because she spoke Spanish). This trainee teacher was able to design a sequence of lessons based on children's own understandings and misconceptions. Together, they started by comparing language features between Spanish and Arabic (all the children spoke Arabic at home and were beginning to learn Spanish in school), followed by discussions around whether we can be Muslim and European at the same time.

This type of engagement with languages into aspects of intercultural understanding can go well beyond the cultural 'tourism' one often finds in schools. Baldock (2010) gives a comprehensive account of how interculturalism has worked (or not) in the early years setting; his analysis is also applicable in many ways to older children (and I would argue many university students). He explores how schools often celebrate festivals of other cultures as a mode of 'understanding' that culture, but he cautions against the fact that, although these activities demonstrate a willingness to engage with another culture, they lend themselves too easily to become a form of 'tourism', where the true origins and essence of traditions are ignored or forgotten, instead of being the subject of meaningful discussions.

Discussing other cultures with children, however, can potentially erect the walls around their own culture, creating a '*them*' and '*us*' mindset. The richness of including history in these discussions is that we come to realise that we are not as distant from each other as the modern nation-states notion would have us think.

New visions

The focus of this chapter has been on developing intercultural understanding and, in particular, the relationships between culture and a specific language. Spanish has been used as the exemplar but the points made apply to whichever language is adopted by a school as its foreign language. Without understanding of the inter-relatedness of languages, their origins and the multiplicity of influences which have come to bear on them, it has been argued that the learning is likely to remain at a surface level and unlikely to contribute to awareness of a globalised world. Through cross-curricular study, which draws upon the history, geography, science, mathematics, music, art and literature of a country or countries, there is opportunity for children and their teachers to co-construct meaningful knowledge of the language and its culture.

One challenge to this is to ensure that the requirements of the foreign language programme of study for Key Stage 2 are met. As has been pointed out, it is easier to measure whether the precise targets of listening, speaking, reading and writing, including the specifics of grammar, have been met than to gauge how well a child has been 'liberated' from insularity. It is, too, very difficult to measure the potential impact a teacher's or child's level of interest today might have on future learning. Current practices tend to focus on memory, with some attention to application.

Too much attention to linguistic details at the expense of holistic understanding of language in its cultural context is one of the 'current certainties' in primary foreign languages, a constraint that has to be challenged. One element of addressing the challenge is through the three models of pedagogical practice that have been explored. Of these, one, where class teachers work collaboratively alongside outside language experts, is considered to offer the best opportunity. A new vision is required not only from teachers, but also from schools' leadership teams to enable this to become reality. In this way, class teachers may become engaged with different aspects of the target language and its culture so that they may find what 'speaks to them' in a meaningful way.

Learning a foreign language requires great personal investment and teachers have many pressures on their time. Motivating them through their personal interests can give them reason to begin the journey. They will, after all, be the role models who in turn need to motivate the children, to understand that languages work within human triumphs, defeats and inventiveness. It is this which has made the society in which we live so diverse, a product of conflict and greed as much as of kindness and enlightenment.

Further reading

Department for Education (2013). *National Curriculum in England: Programmes of Study 2013*. Available at: https://www.gov.uk/government/publications/national-curriculum-in-england-languages-progammes-of-study/national-curriculum-in-england-languages-progammes-of-study
This is an outstanding guide to anyone involved in the delivery of languages in its broadest sense.

Deutscher, G. (2010). *Through the Language Glass: Why the World Looks Different in Other Languages*. London: Random House.

This book allows one to think about the nature of languages and what elements the teacher might be able to discuss with children in order to spark their curiosity.

Laird, E. (2007). *CRUSADE*. London: Macmillan.
This history/fiction book is suitable for a ten+ audience. It deals with issues of faith, intolerance and determination, as a boy from the Dark Ages of Europe meets a boy from the Islamic Golden Age. Based around events during the siege of Acre.

Sercu, L. (2005). Teaching Foreign Languages in an Intercultural World. In L. Sercu, E. Bandura, P. Castro, L. Davcheva, C. Laskaridou, M. Del and C. Mendez Garcia (eds), *Foreign Language Teachers and Intercultural Competence: An International Investigation*. Clevedon: Multilingual Matters. 1–18.
This book offers a comprehensive guide as to what engaging with intercultural competence can look like in the classroom, in different contexts.

Hughes, B. (2005). When the Moors Ruled in Europe. Channel 4 Documentary. Available at: http://www.channel4.com/programmes/the-ancient-world-with-bettany-hughes/on-demand/39867-001
The story of the mysterious and misunderstood Moors, the Islamic society that ruled in Spain for 700 years, but whose legacy was virtually erased from western history. Particularly relevant for schools delivering Spanish.

References

Alexander, R. J. and Flutter, J. (2009). *Towards a New Primary Curriculum: A Report from the Cambridge Primary Review. Part 1: Past and Present*. Cambridge: University of Cambridge Faculty of Education.

Alvarez-Junco, J. (2001). *Mater Dolorosa: La Idea De Espana En El Siglo XI (Sorrowful Mother: The Idea of Spain in the Nineteenth Century)*. Translated by P. Ambrossi. Madrid: Taurus. 18.

Airey, J. (2004). Can you Teach it in English? Aspects of the Language Choice Debate in Swedish Higher Education. In R. Wilkinson (ed.), *Integrating Content and Language: Meeting the Challenge of a Multilingual Higher Education*. Maastricht: Maastricht University Press. 97–108.

Baldock, P. (2010). *Understanding Cultural Diversity in the Early Years*. London: Sage.

Burman, E. (2008). *Deconstructing Developmental Psychology 2nd edn*. London: Routledge. 9.

Cable *et al.* (2012). Language Learning at Key Stage 2: Findings from a Longitudinal Study. Education 3–13. *International Journal of Primary, Elementary and Early Years Education*. 40 (4). 363–78.

Constantine, D. (2004). *A Living Language: Newcastle/Bloodaxe Poetry Lectures*. Newcastle: Bloodaxe Books.

Department for Education and Skills (2002). Available at: http://webarchive.nationalarchives.gov.uk/20130401151715/http://www.education.gov.uk/publications/eOrderingDownload/DfESLanguagesStrategy.pdf

Department for Education and Skills, Departmental Report 2005, available at, https://www.gov.uk/government/uploads/system/uploads/attachment_data/file/272106/6522.pdf

Department for Education (2013). *National Curriculum in England: Programmes of Study 2013*. Available at: https://www.gov.uk/government/publications/national-curriculum-in-england-languages-progammes-of-study/national-curriculum-in-england-languages-progammes-of-study

Eurydice (2001). *Foreign Language Teaching in Schools in Europe*. Directorate General for Education and Culture. 196. Available at: http://www.eurydice.org

Harnett, P. (2008). Who Are We? Who Are You? Challenges in Constructing Identities Through Studying the Past: Some Findings from the TEACH Report. In A. Ross and P. Cunningham (eds), *Reflecting on Identities: Research, Practice and Innovation*. London: CiCe. 653–62.

Haynes, J. (2008). *Children as Philosophers: Learning through Enquiry and Dialogue in the Primary Classroom*. London: Taylor & Francis e-Library.

Hoodless, P. (2008). *Teaching History in Primary Schools*. Exeter: Learning Matters.

Hunt, M., Barnes, A., Powell, B., Lindsay, G. and Muijs, D. (2005). Primary Modern Foreign Languages: An Overview of Recent Research, Key Issues and Challenges for Educational Policy and Practice. *Research Papers in Education*. 20 (4). 371–90.

Lin, A. M. Y. (2008). *Problematizing Identity: Everyday Struggles in Language, Culture and Education*. New York: Routledge. 216.

Malafouris, L. (2013). *How Things Shape the Mind: A Theory of Material Engagement*. Massachusetts: Massachusetts Institute of Technology.

Nunan, D. and Choi, J. (2010). Language and Culture: Reflective Narratives and the Emergence of Identity. *London and New York: Routledge*.

Pennycook, A. (2006). Postmodernism in Language Policy. In T. Ricento (ed.), *An Introduction to Language Policy: Theory and Method*. Oxford: Blackwell. 7.

Rogers, S. (2008). Researching Young Children's Perspectives: A Multi-modal Approach. In S. Rogers and J. Evans (eds), *Inside Role-Play in Early Childhood Education: Researching Young Children's Perspectives*. London and New York: Routledge. 39–51.

Rüschoff, B. and Ritter, M. (2001). Technology-Enhanced Language Learning: Construction of Knowledge and Template-Based Learning in the Foreign Language Classroom. *Computer Assisted Language Learning*. 14 (3–4). 219–32.

Sawyer, W. W. (1943). *Mathematician's Delight*. Harmondsworth: Penguin.

Sercu, L. (2005). Teaching Foreign Languages in an Intercultural World. In L. Sercu, E. Bandura, P. Castro, L. Davcheva, C. Laskaridou, M. Del and C. Mendez Garcia (eds), *Foreign Language Teachers and Intercultural Competence: An International Investigation*. Clevedon: Multilingual Matters. 1–18.

Traille, K. (2007). Teaching History Hurts. The Historical Association. *Teaching History*. 127. Available from: http://www.history.org/uk//resources/secondary_resource_704_8.html

Valdes, J. M. (1986). Culture Bound: Bridging the Cultural Gap in Language Teaching. *Cambridge*. Cambridge University Press.

Vygotsky, L. S. (1978). *Mind in Society: The Development of Higher Psychological Processes*. Cambridge, MA: Harvard University Press.

Wade, P., Marshall, H. and O'Donnell, S. (2009). Primary Modern Foreign Languages Longitudinal Survey of Implementation of National Entitlement to Language Learning at Key Stage 2. *Research Report No. RR127*. London: DCSF.

Chapter 9

Inclusion or special educational needs?

Uncertainty in the twenty-first century

Joseph Mintz

Chapter summary

This chapter explores the ongoing uncertainty that pervades how we think about special educational needs, and how different perspectives on inclusion interpenetrate with views on different models of pre- and post-service teacher education in relation to special educational needs. This is illustrated by a case study of working with a child with a diagnosis of dyspraxia in the classroom.

The chapter then goes on to review the recent history of teacher education in relation to special educational needs in the UK and USA. In this context, there follows a discussion on whether there is a special pedagogy for special educational needs, and what implications this has for the work of student teachers and teachers in general. A detailed critique of the work of Lewis and Norwich (2005), currently influential in pre-service teacher education in the UK, concludes that the delineation between special knowledge and special pedagogy is a false and even dangerous dichotomy.

Dougie had problems with writing and physical coordination, sometimes known as dyspraxia, and he had had this diagnosis formally for some time. He presented from the beginning of the year as an able, articulate child, but one who found it very difficult to express his ideas and thoughts in written form. Dougie showed considerable difficulty with spelling, handwriting and the general process of writing, often getting 'stuck' when asked to write. On meeting with Dougie's parents shortly after he started at the school, Dougie's mum, when asked about his social relationships, commented 'Oh, Dougie doesn't do friends.' Dougie, over the course of the year, found it hard to fit in with the other children in class and tended to be quite intellectual, being interested in a whole range of subjects and having a wide-ranging general knowledge compared to the rest of the class. He found it hard to interact with the other children, and had a tendency to irritate them in an almost deliberate way, pinching them or poking them or taking their pencil or book. At the time it seemed to me that Dougie did this as a way of starting a relationship with them, his actions having a playful quality to them, but the other children tended, unsurprisingly, to get annoyed by him and found him a 'pain' to be around.

In the following vignette, I detail Dougie's involvement in a fight with another child and his interactions with me.

Dougie had had a fight with another boy, Jordan, in the after-school football club the day before. Jordan's mother had informed me about this at the start of the new day and I had spoken to the two boys about it. It seems to have started over nothing serious, Jordan had pushed Dougie after he kicked the ball at him, and Dougie had lost his temper. I hadn't seen any evidence of this 'losing temper' by Dougie in class before this. In the afternoon we had a PE lesson and some of the children played a game of football. Perhaps not surprisingly, Dougie and Jordan ended up having another altercation. It happened rather quickly, and I wasn't quite sure what had caused it. Anyhow, Dougie was shouting at Jordan. He sounded very angry, and was almost screaming, he seemed quite different from his normal persona, his usually playful, laconic, lazy self in class. This was scary – I was wondering what was going to happen next – I aimed to stay calm, to try and contain his obvious anger and frustration, but as usual in such situations of displayed anger, worrying whether I would be able to.

'Try and calm down, Dougie.'

Dougie did not respond to this (or did he?) and ran off to hide, curled up in the corner of the small entrance porch that led in to the main building. I went over to him and crouched down next to him.

'Dougie, what's wrong?'

'There's no use in getting yourself all upset like this.'

Dougie's response was, 'Go away. Go away, leave me alone,' said in a hysterical, very pained way. I felt it was important to show him that I was going to try and stay and help him, and said, 'I'm not going to go away. I want to try and help you.'

Dougie kept on repeating, 'Go away, go away …' oblivious to anything I was saying.

I felt somewhat at a loss as to what to do, wishing someone else would come along and help who Dougie was not going to tell to go away.

I decided to leave him for a while and went back to the rest of my class to see how they were getting on. Five minutes later Dougie came back over to the main group, looking a bit calmer and a bit sheepish. He sat on the side. I let him sit there until the end of the lesson. When the lesson had ended I asked him if he was feeling better. He said that he was. We discussed what the problem had been this afternoon and he explained how Jordan had tackled him for the ball (it seems fairly), but how he had got angry and pushed him. I said that I could see that he had felt angry but that he could not just run off when he felt upset. He nodded. We went back to class and Dougie sat in his seat quietly, although he seemed less than present. I was busy with the rest of the class until home time. The next time that I had ten minutes (the morning of the next day at break) I took Dougie aside and discussed with him how he was feeling about the other children in class. Did he want to be friends with any of them? He mentioned a few names. I asked him if he had tried inviting them over to his house? He said that he had with Michael, but that it had not worked out and that they had just ended up fighting. I suggested to him that perhaps sometimes he tries to be friends with the other children by 'winding them up' and perhaps this didn't really work. He just looked blankly at me – not in a way that he hadn't heard me, but rather that he was blocking out this line of thought – his face looked quite hard set. He had done this a few times in the past – I felt exasperated. I could not get through to him, even though in normal class interactions I have a good relationship with him. He seemed unwilling to hear, unable or unwilling to escape from the pattern of rejection and isolation that he found himself in, even though he clearly wanted to be engaged with his classmates on some level. I gave up and sent him back out to play.

Here I present reflections from my time as a class teacher working with one child, Dougie, in a Year 4 class (eight to nine years old) in a mainstream school. Dougie was thought to have a diagnosis of dyspraxia, and in my perception had difficulties with the task of learning that was presented in the context of our classroom, when compared to many of his classmates; I was confronted with the daily challenge of trying to work out how to help him with that learning. Accordingly, I searched for ways to deal with his problems, including seeking advice from other professionals, particularly the school's special educational needs co-ordinator (SENCO). However, much of the time, I just felt uncertain as to what was the best thing to do for him.

As in a number of other interactions over the year with Dougie, the vignette above shows how uncertain and sometimes exasperated I was at times when working with him. There was something incongruous about him. On the one had he would engage you in this almost adult way about topics that interested him, yet would dissolve at times into inexplicable non-communication. As well, as can be seen in the first part of the vignette, when he curled himself up into a ball, it was evident that he was very upset and was suffering. I thought that this was linked in some way to his dyspraxia, but this did not in itself help me to get a purchase on Dougie – there were no concrete cues to hold on to.

The teacher in a primary school is faced with the challenge of achieving this task with 30 children, each of them a *complex individual* – although often the teacher's experience of them is as part of a group. The children also have the difficult challenge of finding their place in a group of their peers, working out how to relate to the adult leader of the group and engaging in the task of learning. In most such class groups in schools, this task of learning seems to be more difficult for some children than for others. There seem to be barriers, whether internally or externally created, to their achieving the smoother progress that some children appear to achieve.

The task of learning

Dougie had very good maths skills and was verbally very able, but found the mechanics and process of writing difficult and had very poor spelling. He enjoyed using computers and was slowly developing the ability to type. With writing, he sometimes put lots of effort in to it, sadly with usually poor results, but sometimes would not be bothered to try at all. As I noted, Dougie's general knowledge was very good; he would often talk about things precociously, discussing technology using quite advanced terms. When he spoke to his peers about things like this, he would often do so in something of an adult way, sometimes going over their heads. He didn't seem to be on the same wavelength as his peers. Discussions with the SENCO during the year led us to devise a typical school programme for him. We were rather unsure of how to help him; however, based on what we knew, we devised an individual education plan (IEP) for Dougie. I reproduce one of the targets from the IEP here, which had as its focus increasing attention to writing tasks:

Target to be achieved	Achievement criteria	Possible techniques	Possible strategies	Ideas to support strategies
To complete tasks within time set	Task observed to be completed within time set on at least five occasions	Achievable tasks set Use of a timer record chart praise/reward for achievement	Praise/reward Write amount of work expected at start of task	Encourage Dougie to fully focus on task

We also worked on strategies to improve his self-esteem and, later in the year, other ideas to help him with writing, such as using the computer for typing. We also implemented a positive behaviour strategy, where Dougie was given reward points at the end of the week, designed to encourage him to see when he had achieved things and to hopefully make him reflect on his tendency to lose his temper and have outbursts. This blend of a cognitive model of attributions (i.e. self-esteem) and behavioural extrinsic motivators was typical of many of the programmes that we would devise in school for children with learning difficulties and, indeed, they did have some effect on Dougie. One notable example occurred when the class had been working for about a month on individual research projects. I had been encouraging him to increase his use of computers in various aspects of his work, as he seemed to show a real interest in them and it made the process of producing work much easier for him when compared to writing by hand. Dougie decided to present his research project using a PowerPoint presentation. This was something that, at the time, was outside of the capability level of most of the other children and they were very impressed by his use of the technology when he made this presentation. I remember being struck by a subtle change that came over him and as well his relation to the group after he made this presentation. He seemed somehow more confident, and the other children also seemed to treat him differently. No longer was he just someone who annoyed them or said things they did not understand, but he was now, even if only on occasion, someone who had powerful things to do and say to them, something, in fact, to contribute to the group's primary task.

Reflecting on Dougie

When you are in the midst of the activity of teaching, of course, you don't often have the luxury or ability to stop and reflect on what influences are extant in your work, yet, reflecting now, it is clear that there were a number of theoretical approaches that were at play in my mind and in the minds of other adults working in the school, when thinking about children such as Dougie. They came to be present in our minds from a range of sources – our training, our perception of government policies, influences from our own time as children in school and from the media. From these sources we had also absorbed ideas about specific conditions – dyspraxia, Asperger's, dyslexia etc. – and had in our minds a set of thoughts, developed to a greater or lesser extent, about what learning was like for children who came under those categories. At the same time, the knowledge I gained about Dougie through my intersubjective relationship, even if imperfect, about Dougie's needs, wants, desires – about him as a person – was also of significance when I made decisions, often in the moment, about how to work with him. The same, of course, was true for the other children in the class.

This tension about what we might term theoretical versus tacit knowledge is one that looms large in debates about education and pedagogy in general. However, it is has particular significance when we consider the context of special educational needs. This is for two reasons. First, as I alluded to when discussing Dougie, the psychological and the medical have a heavy influence in the discourse of the classroom. When we use phrases like 'Dougie has a diagnosis of dyspraxia' we inescapably admit a scientific lens on the human subject, with all the inherent dangers of applying labels to individuals. Many, of course (including, as you will see, myself), argue, in contrast to Barton (1988) that the potential benefits of the scientific lens outweigh the dangers (not that we should ignore these), and that we, in fact, do children a disservice by ignoring its potent role. In other words, the place of theoretical knowledge in special education is highly contested.

The second reason, which is in some ways conceptually aligned to the first, is that there is an ongoing debate, representing, if you like, the two polarities of special education and inclusive education, as to whether there is, in fact, any special pedagogy for special education. Those at the inclusive education pole argue that there is not and what matters is the attitudes and dispositions of teachers, such as a commitment to equality, high expectations for all children and an ability to consider the individual needs of each child. Of course, this is something of a false dichotomy and those at my putative special education pole would not (at least in public) disagree with any of these aims. What is at stake, though, is the balance, and it is here that the two reasons I put forward interpenetrate, because in the end they both turn on the weight we place on sociological versus psychological conceptualisations of special educational needs. How you balance them on the scale of both national policy and local practice (including the practice of the individual teacher in the individual classroom) determines answers to questions such as: what should the balance be between special and mainstream school provision and how best should we prepare teachers for working with children with special educational needs? This second question will now be considered.

Key questions for reflection

How can we conceptualise the terms 'inclusion' and 'special educational needs'?

How should we balance theoretical knowledge about particular categories with experiential knowledge of the child?

Is uncertainty when working with children with special educational needs a good or bad thing?

Debates in preparing teachers for working with children with special educational needs

There are significant theoretical tensions, between sociological and psychological positions, and on the balance between a focus on theoretical as opposed to tacit knowledge. Such tensions have been amply reflected in trends in policy development in relation to both service provision for and teacher training in relation to children with special educational needs. In England, the ideological move towards inclusion heralded by the influential *Warnock Report* (Warnock, 1978) and, to a significant extent, supported by New Labour, has to some extent been reversed by the Conservative–Liberal coalition government since 2010. Their reversal of New Labour's programme of special school closures is a case in point. The Children and Families Act (Department for Education, 2014) has also heralded greater emphasis on the role of specialist skills and knowledge for teachers and other care professionals working with children with SEN. In the USA, although there is a much more clearly embedded tradition of specialist training for special educators, since the passing of the Individuals with Difficulties Education Act (IDEA) in 1997 (Department of Education, 1997), there has also been growing debate about mainstreaming (Kavale, 2002) and the extent to which specialist knowledge, restricted to special education teachers, is the best way to achieve good outcomes across different groups of children (Brownell *et al.*, 2005; Jones and West, 2009). This policy question is linked to an ongoing debate as to whether developing specific understanding about particular diagnostic categories and associated specific teaching strategies does makes teachers more effective practitioners. As noted, there is often an implicit view, from authors writing from a sociological perspective, that professional development which promotes an overall positive disposition and attitude towards inclusion is far more important than specific knowledge about specific conditions (see, for example, Avramidis and Kalyva, 2007; Leatherman and Niemeyer, 2005). Lewis and Norwich (2005), writing from such a perspective, reviewed teacher effectiveness studies to consider whether or not there is a specific SEN pedagogy. In their influential writing, they conclude in quite strong terms that in most cases there is not. Children may need more repetition, over learning or attention to detail, but they characterise this as a change in emphasis, not a qualitatively different pedagogy. Thus they argue that there is no special pedagogy for special education.

Lewis and Norwich's work, following on from Barton (1988) – as well as, importantly, Oliver (1990) in disability studies – has led to the dominance of a concept of inclusive teaching in which there is much less emphasis on knowledge of differing diagnostic categories, and much greater emphasis on an inclusive pedagogy (see, for example, Florian and Black-Hawkins, 2011). This reduces barriers and encourages a diversity of learning strategies tailored to individual needs (i.e. the two poles of inclusive versus special education). Others have disagreed with this balance between the two poles. Osler and Osler (2002) presented data to indicate that, particularly for some impairments, the level of understanding about those conditions and what implications they can have for teaching strategies makes a significant difference to the effectiveness of the teacher in meeting the needs of those children. Drawing on government statistics on academic outcomes for children with SEN, Wedell (2008) argues that student teachers in England and Wales are generally unprepared for meeting the needs of those with SEN and concludes that emphasis in teacher education on subject knowledge rather than on child development and the psychology of learning meant that teachers were not well equipped for supporting children with SEN. In other words, understanding specifically how children with SEN differ from typical development and an understanding of particular approaches to learning when development does vary is important. This builds on earlier concerns identified by Garner (1996a), who reported on the levels of dissatisfaction with training provider teaching in this area and (Garner 1996b) the lack of relative emphasis to special educational needs given by training providers in the UK. In fact, Hodkinson (2009) identifies this tendency towards dissatisfaction as a historical trend going back to the 1960s.

The debate about the balance between theoretical and tacit knowledge in the work of teachers working with children with special educational needs, and in their training, is very much a live and contentious one.

Teacher education and special educational needs

It is important to highlight the historical differences between the training approach taken in the UK as compared to other countries. The USA, as well as many European countries, have a tradition of specialist initial teacher training for SEN teachers, who would, in the past, go on to teach in specialist provisions for children with SEN, although there is an increasing trend for such teachers to start and continue their careers in mainstream settings as well (Hegarty, 1998; Hodkinson, 2009). In contrast, there has never been any established tradition of specialist education for teachers of SEN, at least in initial teacher training, in the UK (Hodkinson, 2009), although the reasons for this are not very clear. It could be that, since 1980, UK education policy has been very heavily influenced by Barton's sociological discourse on special education, although it is also possible that the relatively low levels of funding for initial teacher training in the UK may be equally implicated.

Whatever the historical forces at play, the debate between the inclusive education and special education poles (or the sociological versus psychological positions on special needs) is alive and well in relation to policy on teacher education. In particular, there currently is concern among UK policy-makers that in initial teacher training in the UK there is not enough emphasis on SEN, which, although it is a gross generalisation, mirrors, as I have described, something of an opposite trend in the USA. Particularly influential in this regard has been the report by the UK House of Commons Education and Skills Select Committee (2006) which undertook an in-depth review of SEN provision in schools, and received representations from a range of stakeholders, including teachers, parents, other professionals and special interest groups. The Committee concluded that there was a lack of emphasis on training in SEN in both initial teacher education and continuing professional development (CPD) frameworks and recommended that 'SEN training should become a core, compulsory part of initial teacher training for all teachers' (House of Commons Education and Skills Select Committee, 2006, p. 70). No doubt partly in response to this report, and other policy reports with similar conclusions such as the *Lamb Inquiry* (Lamb, 2009), government policy in the UK since 2008 has placed more emphasis on special educational needs training for teachers, with a range of albeit patchily implemented initiatives. These include a national training programme for special educational needs coordinators (Training and Development Agency for Schools, 2010) and a proposed greater emphasis on SEN in initial teacher training in the Children and Families Act (Department for Education, 2014). The debate about theoretical versus attitude/tacit knowledge is also active, specifically with regards to how teachers should be prepared for working with children with in specific diagnostic categories, such as autism. Simpson (2004) identifies a trend in the USA towards non-categorical and cross-categorical special education initial teacher education programmes, that is to say that many training providers are moving towards programmes which focus on SEN in general, without a specific focus on any one diagnostic category, although when compared to the UK, US programmes still have much more specific content on particular diagnostic categories (Barnhill et al., 2010).

Special pedagogy?

Lewis and Norwich (2005) strongly argued that there was no such thing. If they are right, then the answer to the debates between the inclusive education pole and the special education pole in relation to teacher education seems quite clear. Teachers need to know about broad principles of inclusive pedagogy, but knowing clear, hard facts about autism or attention deficit (hyperactivity) disorder (AD[H]D) or dyspraxia is not a priority. It would not, according this argument, have helped me when working with Dougie to know more about dyspraxia.

Well, in thinking about this argument, I would like to explore Lewis and Norwich's work (2005), which has been influential certainly in the UK, in a bit more depth.

In *Special Teaching for Special Children?*, Lewis and Norwich (2005) differentiate between what they term the 'general differences' and 'unique differences' positions on special educational needs *pedagogy* (my italics). They write that,

> general differences position pedagogy is informed by needs that are specific or distinctive to a group that shares common characteristics. In this position the specific needs of a sub-group of those with disabilities and difficulties are in the foreground; needs that are common to all and unique to individuals, though important, are more in the background.
>
> (Lewis and Norwich, 2005, p. 3)

In contrast, the unique differences position is set out as:

> pedagogic decisions and strategies [that] are informed only by common and individual needs. Unique differences are in the foreground, with common pedagogic needs more in the background. General specific needs are not recognized. This is a position which assumes that while all learners are in one general sense the same, they are also all different. This means that particular pedagogic strategies are relevant or effective for all pupils, irrespective of social background, ethnicity, gender and disability. Differences between individuals are accommodated within this position, not in distinct groups or sub-groups, but in terms of the uniqueness of individual needs and their dependence on the social context. Yet, for this to be so, common pedagogic needs have to be considered in terms of principles that are general and flexible enough to enable wide individual variations to be possible within a common framework.
>
> (Lewis and Norwich, 2005, p. 4)

This could be regarded a useful encapsulation of the special education versus inclusive education polarity. The book is then structured as an investigation as to whether, for any specific group, there is, in fact, any evidence that there is a general differences pedagogy which is effective. A number of individual chapters are contributed, perhaps somewhat paradoxically, by experts in various diagnostic categories, including autism, dyslexia, moderate learning difficulties and so on. Finally, the authors conclude, based on this survey, that – with the exception of specialist services for hearing and visual impairment – there is no good evidence for the existence or effectiveness of a 'general differences' pedagogy and services for children with special educational needs would be more effective if we consigned it to history; they conclude that 'the traditional special needs categories used in the UK, and internationally, have limited usefulness, in the context of planning or monitoring, teaching and learning in most areas' (Lewis and Norwich, 2005, p. 220). The authors also make a very clear distinction between knowledge and pedagogy. There is, they argue, clearly particular knowledge about specific categories of need, but no special pedagogy. It is on this distinction that I want to focus.

'Pedagogy' is a term that is often used within academic and educational debates, and in many courses of initial teacher education, but it is quite hard to pin down what it means. One position is that it is something akin to a science of teaching. Shulman (1987) argues that we need to be able to develop schema of how effective teachers work with children. This could be considered a cognitive account. In contrast, another position, which could be termed 'romantic' or 'constructionist', sometimes associated with a Piagetian perspective, is that pedagogy is the process of child-rearing and development that leads to the formation of an active, choosing individual (see Hamilton, 1999) where the teacher's role is that of a guide. There are also feminist and sociological critiques of these positions, leading to alternative ideas of what pedagogy is. For example, Walkerdine (1984) rejects a scientific view of pedagogy, calling rather for its deconstruction so that we can lay bare the way in which societal inequalities are reproduced via practices in the classroom. Finally, and perhaps more dominantly in recent decades, there is the socio-cultural position on what pedagogy means. In this perspective, the separation between what is learned and how it is learned is challenged. Activity, concept and tools (including, importantly, language) are interdependent. Thus pedagogy is viewed as praxis where there is a dialectic relationship between theory and practice.

I wonder, then – with such a contested term, which wraps around itself differential conceptualisations of learning, teaching and curriculum – what Lewis and Norwich (2005) mean when they aim to separate out pedagogy and knowledge in relation to special needs. In fact, I would argue that, unless one takes a markedly cognitive view of what pedagogy is, it is quite hard to sustain such a split, and that raises the question of why the authors try so hard to maintain it.

This question is given further saliency when we look at the individual chapter contributions on the different diagnostic categories. In fact, in contrast to the overall conclusion that there is no evidence for a 'general differences' position, for a specialist pedagogy, it is actually the case that the individual contributions, in terms of the evidence presented, give a different picture. For example, Porter's (2005) chapter on 'Severe Learning Difficulties' gives a review of a number of studies on working memory, and concludes that:

> In considering the implications of this research one needs to take into account familiarity of material and individual differences but we can hypothesize that individuals will respond better to visual material and small chunks of information especially when this is presented in auditory form and that they need to be helped to use strategies such as rehearsal.
>
> (Porter, 2005, pp. 56–7)

Read's (2005) chapter on 'Dyslexia' (chapter 11) discusses a number of multisensory intervention programmes, focusing particularly on Walker's (2000) review, which concludes, according to Read, that:

> the student with dyslexia may need more input and a different structure of teaching from other children. It also presupposes that the teacher should be aware of (a) the factors associated with the acquisition of literacy, (b) the particular difficulties in literacy that can be noted in dyslexic children, (c) the principles of multisensory teaching, (d) the importance of selecting clear and coherent teaching aims and (e) an awareness of the important role played by both pre-reading strategies and proofreading, as a post-writing strategy, in the teaching of students with dyslexia.
>
> (Read, 2005, p. 141)

Now Read (2005) notes the contested and sometimes uncertain nature of experimental studies in this area – a theme which runs through many of the chapter contributions. However, in both this case and with Porter (2005), it seems quite clear that they are suggesting particular teaching strategies that relate to these particular groups of children, and which it is at least conceivable are different to strategies which might be considered for other children. In other words, they are proposing a special pedagogy.

I would argue that this dismissal of the possibility of a role for special approaches in special education, common among many theorists adopting an inclusive pedagogy stance, is heavily influenced by a Foucaldian critique of psychology, and we can trace the path of this influence through disability studies to inclusive education. Barton (1988) makes this history clear in his seminal 1988 paper. In this critique, when we turn the lens of science on the human subject, we forget that power and knowledge are mutually constitutive, and that what appears as the knowledge of science, actually has a history linked to inequities in power relations. In this critique, science's position of dominance is upended and it makes no sense to think of pedagogy as having a scientific component to it. This is, I would argue, one reason why in the literature on inclusive education, knowledge (i.e. science) and practice become split and seen as separate entities.

However, such a split has dangers. First, science and psychology really can tell us things that we want to know. As we progress in to the twenty-first century the possibilities for developmental psychology and neuroscience to tell us really important things about human activity, and specifically about how different children might learn, is becoming increasingly difficult to ignore. Yes, we need to be careful in interpreting this science – and in some ways it is probably a healthy strategy to always engage in contesting its implications – but to suggest that it does not have implications for how we think about the human mind and its development is really unsupportable. Second, I very much agree with the socio-culturalists that knowledge and practice need to be in constant conversation with one another. A view of pedagogy, as suggested by Lewis and Norwich, where they are split off into different camps, fails to properly encapsulate the activity of teachers and children in the classroom.

It is also important to note another danger inherent in the splitting of knowledge from pedagogy in relation to special needs. Lewis and Norwich (2005) argue that we do not need to know about special pedagogy, but that there is 'split-off' knowledge about particular diagnostic categories which we might want to know about. However, this is a very fine-grained argument, that is easily open to misinterpretation. In particular, the message that teachers might receive is that they don't need to know anything about what science can tell us about diagnostic categories. This is not the message that Lewis and Norwich intend directly, but it might easily be the one that is communicated, particularly in an education system where a sociological discourse facilitates, at least for some, suspicion of the role of psychology in education.

Key question for reflection

What does the term 'pedagogy' mean?

New visions

In Chapter 12 of *Special Teaching for Special Children?*, Portwood (2005) considers 'Dyspraxia'. She lists a number of recommendations, including teaching specific hand-writing strategies such as encouraging children to print or write letters consistently, using paper with widely spaced lines and using a sloping surface for reading (2005, p. 156). Portwood (2005) also notes that significant emotional difficulties can be associated with dyspraxia, and that the evidence for specific intervention programmes – for example, those designed to develop handwriting skills – is quite poor, and that some strategies relevant for children with dyspraxia may overlap with those of other children with par-ticular learning styles.

Looking back on my earlier life as a classroom teacher, and specifically to my work with Dougie, I think that knowing more about dyspraxia would have helped me enormously in working with him. However, in saying this, I think it is important to be clear about where I disagree with Norwich and Lewis. I do agree with them that the sociological critique of special needs highlights real dangers associated with the process of categorisa-tion in special needs and we need to guard against these. However, if in doing so we deny the place of psychology in education, then we rob our children of the chance to benefit from its very real fruits, which, as is argued here, is a serious abrogation of our responsibili-ties as adults and as teachers.

We need teachers who can make use of theoretical knowledge about diagnostic cate-gories sensitively and carefully, wielding it in close 'conversation' with what they know about the individual child.

As I have indicated, teacher training in the UK currently provides very poor provi-sion in relation to special educational needs. We need, I think, to address this deficit; we need to prepare teachers to understand how they can construct a pedagogy for the individual children with special educational needs that they work with, based on their personal knowledge of the child and a clear understanding of what we usefully know about particular diagnostic categories. I am not saying that a diagnostic category tells us everything we need to know about a child, or even that it tells us most of what we need to know. I agree that individual differences – the individual personality, likes, dislikes, strengths and difficulties of a child (the agentic human subject that we meet in inter-subjective encounter) – are always likely to be what is most important. However, the risk with Lewis and Norwich's splitting of knowledge from pedagogy in special educa-tion is that we end up losing the knowledge altogether, and theoretical knowledge organised around diagnostic categories does have really important and useful things to tell us. It is this lesson that teachers, particularly those at the beginning of their careers, need to heed. Specialist knowledge about diagnostic categories in special education, including what we know about best practice approaches to teaching and learning, is important in making sure that teachers can do the best for the children in their classes affected by these conditions. It is not the only or most important thing that they need to know, but it is far from irrelevant and teachers need to engage with what science in its broad sense can tell us about how to work effectively with particular groups of chil-dren. Teacher educators, therefore, have a responsibility to make sure that teachers are prepared for the process of engaging with best practice evidence related to specific diagnostic categories. This is a process that should start in initial teacher education but continue as teachers progress through their careers.

Key questions for reflection

Should teachers be engaging with best practice evidence and research on diagnostic categories in special education?

How can teachers filter what they need to know from the mass of information available in the academy and on the web?

Further reading

Schon, D. A. (1983). *The Reflective Practitioner: How Professionals Think in Action*. New York: Basic Books.

In this seminal text, Schon explores the relationship between theoretical and tacit knowledge in the work of professionals, and tries to give an answer to what goes on 'in the moment' when decisions are made about how to act.

Jordan, R. (2008). Autistic Spectrum Disorders: A Challenge and a Model for Inclusion in Education. *British Journal of Special Education*. 35 (1). 11–15.

In this article, Rita Jordan draws on her extensive experience of autism education and explores the ways in which inclusion does and does not work for this particular group. Her analysis gives another perspective on whether there is or is not a special pedagogy for autism education.

European Agency for Development in Special Needs Education (2012). *Teacher Education for Inclusion*. Brussels: EADSNE. Available at: https://www.european-agency.org/publications/ereports/te4i-profile/te4i-profile-of-inclusive-teachers

This policy report explores different approaches to teacher education for special educational needs across Europe and illustrates how different policy stances reflect some of the tensions between inclusion and special education considered in this chapter.

References

Avramidis, E., and Kalyva, E. (2007). The Influence of Teaching Experience and Professional Development on Greek Teachers' Attitudes Towards Inclusion. *European Journal of Special Needs Education*. 22 (4). 367–89.

Barnhill, G. P., Polloway, E. A. and Sumutka, B. M. (2010). A Survey of Personnel Preparation Practices in Autism Spectrum Disorders. *Focus on Autism and Other Developmental Disabilities*. 26 (2). 75–86.

Barton, L. (1988). *The Politics of Special Educational Needs*. London: Routledge. 219.

Brownell, M. T., Ross, D. D., Colón, E. P. and McCallum, C. L. (2005). Critical Features of Special Education Teacher Preparation: A Comparison with General Teacher Education. *The Journal of Special Education*. 38 (4). 242–52.

Department for Education. Children and Families Act 2014 (2014). England and Wales. Available at: http://www.education.gov.uk/a00221161/

Department of Education (1997) *Individuals with Disabilities Education Act Amendments 1997*. Washington. Available at: http://www2.ed.gov/offices/OSERS/Policy/IDEA/regs.html

Florian, L., and Black-Hawkins, K. (2011). Exploring Inclusive Pedagogy. *British Educational Research Journal*. 37 (5). 813–28.

Garner, P. (1996a). A Special Education? The Experiences of Newly Qualifying Teachers during Initial Training. *British Educational Research Journal*. 22 (2). 155–64.

Garner, P. (1996b). Students' Views on Special Educational Needs Courses in Initial Teacher Education. *British Journal of Special Education*. 23 (4). 176–9.

Hamilton, D. (1999). The Pedagogic Paradox (or Why No Didactics in England?). *Pedagogy, Culture and Society*. 7 (1). 135–52.

Hegarty, S. (1998). Challenges to Inclusive Education: A European Perspective. In S. J. Vitello and D. E. Mithaug (eds), *Inclusive Schooling: National and International Perspectives*. London: Routledge. 151–65.

Hodkinson, A. (2009). Pre-service Teacher Training and Special Educational Needs in England 1970–2008: Is Government Learning the Lessons of the Past or is it Experiencing a Groundhog Day? *European Journal of Special Needs Education*. 24 (3). 277–89.

House of Commons Education and Skills Select Committee. (2006). *Special Educational Needs: Third Report of Session 2005–06*. London: Stationery Office.

Jones, P. and West, E. (2009). Teacher Education: Reflections upon Teacher Education in Severe Difficulties in the USA: Shared Concerns about Quantity and Quality. *British Journal of Special Education*. 36 (2). 69–75.

Kavale, K. A. (2002). Mainstreaming to Full Inclusion: From Orthogenesis to Pathogenesis of an Idea. *International Journal of Disability, Development and Education*. 49 (2). 201–14.

Lamb, B. (2009). *Lamb Inquiry: Special Educational Needs and Parental Confidence*. London: Department for Children, Schools and Families.

Leatherman, J. M. and Niemeyer, J. (2005). Teachers' Attitudes Toward Inclusion: Factors Influencing Classroom Practice. *Journal of Early Childhood Teacher Educators*. 26 (1). 23–36.

Lewis, A. and Norwich, B. (2005) Overview and Discussion: Overall Conclusions. In A. Lewis and B. Norwich (eds), *Special Teaching for Special Children?* Milton Keynes: Open University Press. 206–21.

Oliver, M. (1990). *The Politics of Disablement*. London: Macmillan.

Osler, A. and Osler, C. (2002). Inclusion, Exclusion and Children's Rights: A Case Study of a Student with Asperger Syndrome. *Emotional and Behavioural Difficulties*. 7 (1). 35–54.

Porter, J. (2005). Severe Learning Difficulties. In A. Lewis and B. Norwich (eds), *Special Teaching for Special Children?* Milton Keynes: Open University Press. 53–66.

Portwood, M. (2005). Dyspraxia. In A. Lewis and B. Norwich (eds), *Special Teaching for Special Children?* Milton Keynes: Open University Press. 150–65.

Read, G. (2005). Dyslexia. In A. Lewis and B. Norwich (eds), *Special Teaching for Special Children?* Milton Keynes: Open University Press. 138–49.

Shulman, L. S. (1987). Knowledge and Teaching: Foundations of a New Reform. *Harvard Educational Review*. 57 (1). 1–22.

Simpson, R. L., Lacava, P. G. and Graner, P. S. (2004). The No Child Left Behind Act Challenges and Implications for Educators. *Intervention in School and Clinic*. 40 (2). 67–75.

Training and Development Agency for Schools. (2010). *The National SENCO Award*. London. Available at: http://www.education.gov.uk/schools/careers/traininganddevelopment/b00201451/sen-skills/advanced-skills

Vygotsky, L. S. (1978). *Mind in Society: The Development of Higher Psychological Processes*. Cambridge, MA: Harvard University Press.

Walker, J. (2000). Teaching Basic Reading and Spelling. In J. Townend and M. Turner (eds), *Dyslexia Practice*. New York: Springer. 93–129.

Walkerdine, V. (1984). Developmental Psychology and the Child-centred Pedagogy. In J. Henriques, W. Holloway, C. Unwin, C. Venn and V. Walderdine (eds), *Changing the Subject: Psychology, Social Regulation and Subjectivity*. London: Methuen.

Warnock, H. (1978). *The Warnock Report (1978) Special Educational Needs Report of the Committee of Enquiry into the Education of Handicapped Children and Young People*. London: Stationery Office.

Wedell, K. (2008). Inclusion: Confusion About Inclusion: Patching Up or System Change? *British Journal of Special Education*. 35 (3). 127–35.

Part IV

Education and society

Chapter 10

Embracing diversity in the classroom

A cross-cultural perspective

Lynn Ang and Rosie Flewitt

Chapter summary

This chapter offers a critical discussion of diversity and children's role as active participants and co-constructors in their own learning across home and educational settings in two distinct cultures. We argue that addressing issues of diversity and child agency requires an understanding of the broader context of children's learning within and beyond the early years setting – such as the family, home and community as key sites of socialisation which inform children's development. The discussion begins by considering different conceptual frameworks of development and learning, including neo-Confucian philosophy on the importance of human and social relationships in child development. We also look at western theorisations of learning as discursive and social (Vygotsky, 1978) and at the concepts of habitus, field, social and symbolic capital as a theoretical framework (Bourdieu, 1977) to explore and understand the ways in which children around the globe draw upon their social and cultural networks to negotiate their identity and position as learners. Finally, we discuss the implications of these conceptual frameworks for early years and primary practitioners in terms of evaluating their own pedagogical practice when engaging with children from diverse backgrounds and in diverse cultures.

During a recent interview with a nursery teacher in an inner-city primary school in England, the experienced teacher briefly described the diverse group of young children who, year after year, begin their formal education in her class:

> TEACHER: It's very much representative of our area, a very multicultural class with a high number of children with English as a second language and children coming in at a lower level than the national average.
>
> RESEARCHER: In what way?
>
> TEACHER: Speaking, listening, emotionally ... personal health and social ... and their imaginative play, in most areas, probably their worldly experiences are quite limited and we have quite a large number of special needs. (Interview conducted by Cremin *et al.*, 2013)

The nursery teacher, Jean,[1] went on to describe how she uses playful pedagogy to encourage all children to be active participants in their own learning in the belief that play underpins understanding. Yet she had found creating the conditions to promote playful learning very challenging, partly due to the difficulties of enabling play among such a diverse group of young learners, but also due to the early education climate of account-ability in England, where teachers, in Jean's view, 'have all these pressures from the curriculum, from many parents, from the Head' to produce hard evidence of young children's learning. Faced with these daunting challenges, how can early years and pri-mary practitioners help children by enriching their personal and social resources through opportunities to play?

We address this fundamental question by placing the notion of educational equality at the heart of this chapter. We foreground the importance of thinking creatively about building inclusive learning communities that embrace diversity for our youngest mem-bers of society, whatever their background. All children live in diversity along intersec-tions of gender, race, culture, class, ability and other differences, which contribute to their holistic experiences and emerging identities as effective and competent learners. Children's experience of diversity and difference constantly evolves and equips them with varying degrees of cultural and social capital from which they are able to negotiate their understanding of the world. Through illustrative examples of practice in England and Singapore, we emphasise the importance of providing opportunities for children from diverse backgrounds to contribute and engage in the learning process, by creating pedagogical spaces from which practitioners are able to innovate and challenge normative approaches to practice, especially when working within the structure of a mandated curriculum. We begin by reflecting on neo-Confucian and Vygotskian conceptualisations of learning as community-based, discursive and social, then we move on to Bourdieuian concepts of habitus, field and social and symbolic capital.

Children negotiating their position as learners

Within the field of early years and early primary education in the western and non-western world,[2] there has been widespread recognition of the important role children play in negotiating their position as active learners in their everyday environments (for example, Anning *et al.*, 2009; Clark and Moss, 2001; Prout and James, 1997; Li *et al.*, 2012). In sociological research, children have come to be viewed as co-constructors of their own lives and cultures, through observing and participating actively in the community and society in which they live (Rogoff and Wertsch, 1984; Rogoff, 2003; Mayall, 2002; Corsaro, 2005; Tobin *et al.*, 1991; Tobin, 2007).

Research has shown that cultural traditions and differences are vital in shaping the norms of teaching and learning across educational settings (Rogoff and Wertsch, 1984; Rogoff, 2003; Tobin, 2007; Li *et al.*, 2012; Wong, 2008), and that distinct, localised philosophical and theoretical frameworks influence the way that children and their learning are constructed. In a non-western context, the childhood historian Dardess (1991) traces the history of childhood in pre-modern China and highlights the central role of Confucianism in shaping pedagogy and children's learning in Chinese societies. He contends that Confucian teachings are aimed at fostering in children at an early age a distinctive social and cultural identity as defined by primordial ties within ethnic, kin-ship and familial groups. The notions of 'childhood' and 'a Confucian child' are first and foremost intertwined with the child's identity as part of the Chinese culture and community as a lived reality, rather than as an independent identity or sense of self. More recent literature also highlights the influence of Confucianism and its modernised form of neo-Confucianism on educational practice, as commonly observed in contemporary early years settings and primary classrooms in many Chinese societies (Li *et al.*, 2012; Tang and Maxwell, 2007).

As the cornerstone of Chinese tradition, Confucianism continues to have a pervasive influence on Chinese educational thought and practice. The overriding philosophy is that children's learning takes place in social and communal contexts, and that the traditions and norms of the society and community make a critical difference to the way children learn or feel. The findings of an ethnographic study of two Chinese kindergartens, for example, reveal that children are encouraged to become active learners in a communal learning environment, with a pedagogical emphasis on group learning and a collective teaching approach rather than focusing on independent learning and the individual child (Tang and Maxwell, 2007). From the teachers' perspectives, the study showed that such an approach was particularly effective for both pedagogical and practical reasons, given the large group of learners. Research also shows that the influence of neo-Confucianism as a philosophy and theory of education has been instrumental in promoting the cultivation of children's sense of cooperation and collaboration in the classroom. While recognising the inherent hybridities and variations within cultures, researchers have foregrounded that these principles of collectivity and collegiality are highly valued in Chinese societies, based on the belief that children learn best from each other as active and social learners, and that cultural values and social beliefs play a key role in shaping children's learning strategies and educators' teaching practices (Wong, 2008; Li *et al.*, 2012).

In a western context, much of the work on children's role as active learners builds on the ground-breaking socio-cultural theory of cultural psychologist Vygotsky (1978) whose works highlight the participatory nature of learning, where children appropriate the conceptual resources of the cultural world they are born into. From this socio-cultural perspective, development is viewed as a process of gradual internalisation proceeding from the social (*interpersonal*, i.e. between people) to the individual (*intrapersonal*, i.e. within the mind of an individual). For learning to occur, both interpersonal and intrapersonal processes must be experienced: at the interpersonal level, the learner's understanding is hazy, whereas at the intrapersonal level the learner tries to make sense of new knowledge and connect it to what he or she already knows (Vygotsky, 1978, p. 57). Vygotsky argues the learner is often reliant on the support of either an adult or more knowledgeable peer to guide and share problem-solving, in situations where the child can take the initiative but is supported when necessary. Gradually, the child can begin to take control and the adult or peer can step back and act as a less involved yet sympathetic supporter. In this way, the child becomes more familiar with new concepts and, over the course of time, these concepts become incorporated into the child's repertoire of understandings. Of course, children can learn on their own, but Vygotsky argues that there is always a 'zone of proximal development' (ZPD), i.e. an area of learning between what a child can do independently and what the same child can do when supported by a more knowledgeable other (Vygotsky, 1978).

Applying Vygotsky's socio-cultural perspective of learning to their observations of mother/child dyadic interaction, Wood *et al.* (1976) developed the concept of *scaffolding* to describe how mothers offer contingent, graduated assistance to help their children achieve complicated tasks which they would not be able to complete on their own. The concept of scaffolding subsequently led to changes in how the role of the teacher was perceived in classroom contexts: teachers were encouraged to scaffold learning by constructing external knowledge in classroom discourse, so that knowledge could be internalised by children and this process would gradually contribute to their own understanding (see Edwards and Mercer, 1987; Edwards and Knight, 1994). However, the principles of scaffolding are based on mothers guiding individual children through one-to-one interaction within relationships that are characterised by high levels of trust and intersubjectivity. These favourable conditions for learning only rarely occur in classroom situations, where one or two teachers may be responsible for up to 30 children (or more in some cultures) and this makes it difficult for teachers to offer contingent support for each child. There may also be a lack of shared language and certainly an imbalance of power and knowledge between the teacher and child.

Furthermore, activities in the classroom are usually initiated by the teacher rather than the child, so a child might not feel motivated to engage in a particular classroom-based learning activity. Research into scaffolding in the primary classroom suggests that if classroom learning is pre-planned and teacher-led, then it risks becoming ritualistic rather than principled, with children going through the motions of completing the tasks they are set, but with no final handover of knowledge (Edwards and Mercer, 1987). To resolve this problem, Mercer (1994) proposes that scaffolding in a group situation can work if teachers adopt a democratic teaching style and allow the synergy of a learning group to develop, where children are able to see the reasons for learning and are free to experiment with and talk about tasks. Bruner (1996) adds that it is incumbent on the teacher to understand what individual children already know, to ensure they are familiar and comfortable with the language and format of activities, and to maintain collaboration and negotiation.

However, a pedagogic model of scaffolding largely assumes that knowledge can be 'handed over', and does not fully allow for the idiosyncratic world views held by different teachers and different learners. In this chapter, we argue that Bourdieu's (1977) theorisation of *field, habitus* and *social* and *symbolic capital* offers a complementary and nuanced understanding of classroom practice which takes account of the diversity and idiosyncrasies of how individuals' personal, social and cultural knowledge and experience shape their active participation in learning.

In Bourdieu's theory of practice (Bourdieu, 1977) human action is viewed as being constituted through a dialectical relationship[3] between the individual's thought/activity (the habitus) and the objective world (the field). Bourdieu conceives of social and cultural spaces as 'fields' in which individuals learn certain ways of being, doing and interacting. For example, the field of education is characterised by its own aims, objectives and principles, yet these change as learners move through different phases (such as the sub-fields of early years, primary, secondary and tertiary education) and are mostly implied tacitly rather than made explicit.[4] As individuals move from one field to another, such as from home to nursery or from nursery to primary school, their interactions in the new setting become dependent upon the affinity and/or disaffinity between the more familiar field (home/nursery) and the new field or sub-field (nursery/primary school).

Habitus describes how, through ongoing social interaction in different fields, each individual subconsciously observes and assimilates the principles of practical action in each new field and in so doing acquires a system of generative schemes and dispositions in each field. By existing in social spaces, individuals encounter familiar and unfamiliar fields, but they always carry with them their previous experiences and the generating structures that characterise their habitus. In a familiar field, there is a high degree of congruence between the habitus and the field, but in an unfamiliar field, such as experienced by young children during the early days, weeks and months of nursery education, there may be a low degree of congruence. The congruence will inevitably vary from child to child: if there is a high degree of congruence between the social, cultural and linguistic backgrounds of the learner, the teacher and the modus operandi of a phase of education, then educational 'success' is more likely. If there is a low degree of congruence, then 'success' is less likely. But these are not fixed states of being. Rather, there is a dialectical negotiation between the individual's habitus and the field, with the potential for the field to become embodied in the habitus and for the habitus to constitute the field as a meaningful world endowed with sense and value. Through ongoing social interaction in new fields, each individual *subconsciously* acquires and adjusts to the systems, the kinds of language, generative schemes and dispositions they encounter in those fields, and, in so doing, equips themselves with what Bourdieu (1977) terms *social, cultural* and *linguistic capital*. If a child feels they belong to a new field, then the values and modus operandi of the new field gradually become a part of the individual's habitus.

Bourdieu's theory is, therefore, highly compatible with Vygotsky's: the habitus is formed in response to external social structures and can be viewed as the internalisation of those relations. But the process of internalisation is not assured – it is dialectical and any knowledge exchange is always contingent on the degree of fit between the field, an individual's habitus and how successful they are at adapting to the social, cultural and linguistic capital that characterise the new field. As a young boy and native speaker of Gascon (a now dead language of the French Atlantic Pyrenees), Bourdieu himself felt out of place when he first started boarding school, and came to realise:

> Rather than providing equal opportunities and a meritocracy, schools were a kind of cultural filter through which children passed. Those with the necessary cultural dispositions gained from their family backgrounds found themselves to be as if a 'fish in water', swimming with the current; those without such prerequisites had the opposite experience and were themselves continuously ill-at-ease in the academic environment.
>
> (Grenfell, 2009, p. 440)

Bourdieuian theory has made a significant contribution to our thinking about childhood – children are no longer viewed as passive and vulnerable beings whose development and learning are determined by a physiological and biological process. Rather, they are competent individuals whose realities and experiences are socially and culturally constructed, and mediated by a complex web of values and beliefs. We adopt this approach to describe how young children participate actively in the social world of nursery education, and how teachers can include familiar frames of reference and resources to enable young children to build social networks and to appropriate cultural knowledge. We suggest that this sociological framework allows for children to be viewed as able and active agents who have the competence and capacity in their own right to understand and make meaning of the world, and recognises children's competence in strategically negotiating their roles and agency as expert individuals and learners.

Key questions for reflection

What problems do teachers face if they try to employ the theoretical concept of scaffolding to support learning in the classroom?

In what ways can the work of Bourdieu help us to understand how school systems can serve to reproduce social and cultural inequalities and to create more equitable educational environments?

Early years and primary education as pedagogical spaces for embracing diversity

Given the well-established links between children and their socio-cultural context, the role of early years and primary educators in creating a pedagogical space for children to be valued as participants and co-constructors of their own learning is crucial. Ang (2010) argues that, as cultural and educational institutions, early education settings are microcosms of the wider society. They reflect the inherent complexities of a world that is typified by diversity and plurality, offering children opportunities to understand and learn about the complexity of the world around them. Issues of diversity and child agency therefore remain at the heart of education practice as those who work with children on a daily basis share a commitment to providing high-quality educational experience where all children feel valued as active co-constructors of their learning.

However, mandatory national curricula tend to reflect, explicitly and implicitly, the values of dominant social and cultural forces and, in the case of the revised *Early Years Foundation Stage (EYFS)* (DfE, 2012) and *National Curriculum* (DfE, 2014) in England, to base normative models of development on linguistically, socially and culturally specific criteria. These normative expectations can act to compound wider issues of inequality and social justice which in turn remain problematic in practice.

Key questions for reflection

In what ways can early years educators be responsible for the delivery of statutory curricula facilitate, recognise and responsive to the diverse realities of children in their setting?

How can children be supported and empowered to respond positively to diversity?

Example 1

In this first example of creating pedagogical spaces that embrace diversity and promote child agency, we focus on data from a study of young children in an inner-city nursery and primary school in England, in the classroom of the nursery teacher, Jean, who was introduced at the beginning of this chapter. In this study, we were asked to evaluate a particular teacher training programme for storytelling and story-acting, called the Helicopter Technique (Cremin *et al.*, 2013), and we observed how the programme was delivered in three nursery and three reception classrooms (three- to five-year-old children). These settings were all operating within the revised *EYFS* (DfE, 2012) which places a strong emphasis on normative models of linguistic and cognitive development. The teachers were keen to counter some of these rigours by creating learning spaces where all the children in their classrooms would engage actively in their own learning. The Helicopter Technique is based on the storytelling and story-acting curriculum developed by Vivian Gussin Paley in the 1980s, which is used fairly widely in the USA, but remains comparatively unknown in other countries (see Paley, 1990, 1992, 2004).

In essence, this story-based pedagogy involves the teacher listening to short stories told by individual children during the course of a school day (around four or five stories in total each day) and transcribing the stories verbatim, usually in a dedicated 'Story Book'. There are a few fixed rules: the child's story can be about any topic of the child's choosing, but only as long as one page in the Story Book, and the teacher must not suggest any corrections or changes to what the child says. Later the same day, the story is acted out by the whole class on an improvised stage, which is made quite simply by creating a large rectangle with masking tape around which the children and teacher(s) sit. The storytellers can choose which character they would like to be in their own story, and subsequent roles are assigned to each child in turn around the stage. Paley argues that these rules have proven to be the most democratic way to ensure each child is offered an equal opportunity both to tell and to act out a story (Paley, 1992). At no point are children coerced into taking part in story-acting or storytelling if they prefer not to. Over time, we observed in each class how all children opted to take part in the storytelling and story-acting after just a few weeks. From a Bourdieuian perspective, we can argue that, among the complexity of activity the children experienced in the *field* of the nursery classroom, the predictability of the Helicopter Technique, with its clear parameters and set format, offered an increasingly familiar territory where the children felt valued, safe and motivated to become active participants in an enjoyable and shared activity.

Initially, the teachers enrolled in this training programme had many concerns: that 'doing anything with this class as a whole class is quite challenging'; that the technique would be too intimidating for 'shy' children or for those with low 'resilience'; that the story-acting session might fail as 'just keeping them focused is quite hard work'. Teachers were particularly concerned about the value of the technique for young children in the early stages of learning English, and that by telling their stories children would expose the 'differences in the way that they're using language'.

However, as the teachers' confidence grew, and as more and more children opted to become actively involved in this new activity, the teachers' fears were assuaged. As Jean commented towards the end of the training programme, she found the technique was 'fantastic for their development and for their understanding of the diversity in the classroom'. So why was it so successful? Here, we present two short examples which illustrate the potential of the Helicopter Technique as an inclusive activity where children in classroom communities that are characterised by diversity are all included as active and valued participants.

Jean described one English-speaking four-year-old boy, Adair, as 'very, very shy'; although he seemed to enjoy role play, he was reluctant to speak in class: 'Normally, when you ask him to come and do something with you, you just get one or two words.' However, during an interview conducted during the sixth week of the training programme, Jean described how Adair soon took to the Helicopter Technique, and began to participate actively after watching other children tell and act out their stories in class: 'in that situation he's really confident, and he must have realised that I was totally relaxed. I was writing down what everybody was saying, and not sort of expecting something from him.'

Jean explained that Adair tended to choose characters 'from stories that we've done in school, and presumably stories he has at home'. For example, during the second week of the programme, he told a story which drew on the traditional tale of Little Red Riding Hood:

> The big bad wolf skipped to the Grandma's house. And gobbled the Grandma up. Red Riding Hood came to Grandma's house. And she can't stop him. And he started to gobble up Little Red Riding Hood.

The underlined words were roles Jean identified for children to act out later: to promote the inclusion of multiple child actors for each story, roles were assigned to both animate and inanimate story components. Here, roles were assigned to the wolf, Grandma's house, Grandma and Red Riding Hood. By week 7, Adair continued to build his narratives around traditional tales, and to add in characters from popular culture:

> The buffalo and three cows and Donald Duck came and Mickey Mouse came. And the duck was in the pond crying because the water went. And the little duck ate breadcrumbs. The little bear came and had a sleep. And then Goldilocks came. Goldilocks took her clothes off and had a sleep. And then it was raining and they all had their umbrellas.

Jean commented how the technique allowed quiet children in her class, like Adair, to 'shine' and gave them 'a voice and an arena that they wouldn't have otherwise'. The storytelling started to build bridges between the field of the school environment and the individual children's 'habitus', allowing teachers to gain insights into children's personal interests, concerns and home reading practices which they quietly and confidently shared through their stories.

Similarly for bilingual and multilingual children, the technique offered a collaborative environment for self-expression. Four-year-old Elana, of North European and Nigerian parentage, was learning English as her third language when she joined the nursery classroom, and Jean commented how much she had learned about Elana through her stories, which had 'the same theme all the time ... it's always something to do with home and coming to school'. Some were very short, as the following example illustrates:

> My mum drive me to school. And we take off school bag now. We play with (girl's name) and (girl's name) too.

By sharing her stories in class, Elana was able to bring herself and her home world into the classroom. This in turn enabled the teacher and support workers to understand her interests and concerns, and to incorporate these in their support for her learning. Normally quiet and withdrawn, Elana began to enjoy acting out roles, and Jean particularly valued the opportunities the acting provided for children to engage with the meanings of words by attempting to represent their materiality through embodied action:

> Elana did a very good house and I was quite impressed with that and she's EAL as well so I think it's working quite well with our EAL children because all the courses I've been with to do with EAL and language it's about them knowing the objects to be able to know the words, and for her to know the word and to then act out that word that's quite impressive.

To summarise, the Helicopter Technique offered opportunities for children to exercise their agency, self-determination and decision-making as young literacy learners in the classroom. Overall, we observed approximately 130 children taking part in the programme, and focused on eighteen case study children from diverse backgrounds. We found strong evidence that the technique contributed positively to children's self-expression and confidence in the classroom; also teachers commented how it enhanced individual children's 'profile within the class', and how they 'are able to show themselves in a different light to the other children because they might be very good at making up stories or acting out stories which other children will enjoy'. Through their ongoing participation in the technique, individual children appeared subconsciously to acquire the kinds of language and participatory dispositions expected in the storytelling and story-acting, and, in so doing, equipped themselves with a small but significant quota of social and linguistic capital.

Example 2

A short narrative observation from an ethnographic study of preschools in Singapore offers a second interesting example of practice which illustrates the importance of children's role as active participants not only in their own development but also as co-constructors of skills and values that afford them social and cultural capital. The nursery, Dixie Kids Childcare Centre, is a preschool in Singapore which offers full and partial day care for preschool children aged eighteen months to six years.

The term 'preschool' in Singapore generally refers to two main types of provision: childcare centres and kindergartens, which differ mainly in their function and hours of provision. Kindergartens cater for three- to six-year-old children and offer daily sessional educational programmes, ranging from two to four hours per session, while childcare centres generally provide full day care, with many settings also offering infant care for children aged two to eighteen months. In addition to these main providers, there are also private for-profit settings, religious-based kindergartens and semi-government-funded and voluntary not-for-profit settings. Primary schooling in Singapore refers to compulsory education which lasts six years for children aged seven to twelve years. While compulsory education and the primary school curriculum are regulated and maintained by the Singapore Ministry of Education, preschools are relatively more autonomous, having the independence to determine the curriculum and stipulate their own goals and approaches (Retas and Kwan, 2000). As with many predominately Chinese societies in the Southeast Asia region, where Chinese make up the majority ethnic group, Singapore's education landscape is influenced by traditional Asian, neo-Confucian values rather than the more individualistic values of western societies, with a strong emphasis on the values of social cohesion and community-building to create a learning culture in educational settings, and ultimately in the wider society (Mortimore *et al.*, 2000).

Like most childcare centres in Singapore, Dixie Kids is open six days a week, 7am to 7pm during week days and 7am to 1pm on Saturdays. Over 90 per cent of the 64 children enrolled attend full time. The children and families are diverse, reflecting the plurality of the population and multicultural community living in the surrounding local neighbourhood. The setting was part of an ethnographic study which explored the nature and diversity of preschool provisions in Singapore. Sustained observations undertaken of the setting over two years for three to six weeks at a time showed a distinctive feature of the centre was its emphasis on group learning and socialisation, particularly mixed-aged interactions where the children are often encouraged to play and interact across the age groups. The routine at Dixie Kids allowed a large proportion of time and ample opportunities in the curriculum for extended mixed-age and group socialisation from the toddlers to the older five- to six-year-olds. When asked if there was one aspect of the setting's practice that she thought was particularly important for the children's learning, Rena, the setting's principal, responded: 'learning to be part of a group, mixing with different children, all children in the centre from the groups and classes, learning to get along with one another'.

The setting was organised according to age-related criteria: a playgroup for children eighteen months to two years, a nursery class 1 (N1) for two- to three-year-olds, N2 class for three- to four-year-olds, kindergarten 1 (K1) for four- to five-year-olds, and kindergarten 2 (K2) for five- to six-year-olds. However, during the observations it became clear that while these categorisations were necessary for administrative purposes of documentation and registration, the divisions between them were not always sustained in practice. The physical environment of the setting, with its open plan layout and low-level shelves used as improvised partitions, led to children across the ages constantly streaming in and out of the 'classes' throughout the day, interacting and stopping to chat with each other or just pausing to observe what the other children were doing. When, as often happens, a child gets distracted and wanders off to another group, the practitioner or children from the other group incorporates them into their activity. Communal spaces were also included in the design of the centre, and these further encourage the children to play together. Older children frequently interact with the younger ones as they go about their daily activities, helping them with everyday tasks such as putting their shoes on, getting their water bottles, resolving peer conflicts or simply walking the younger children to the toilet. The children spontaneously move around the open space of the centre and interact with each other throughout the day across the different groups.

In many ways, the children's free movement is facilitated by the setting's layout, reflecting the pedagogical emphasis on group work and collaboration, with the more confident ones helping the less confident. The daily curriculum was structured around mixed-aged activities, where all the children (from two- to six-year-olds) would come together to engage in communal activities such as during meal times, morning assemblies, play and nap time, early evening get-togethers before leaving for home, or playing outdoors in the neighbourhood playground with other local children. The children are taught to learn together and learn from each other, rather than explore their learning individually. This pedagogical practice may seem markedly distinct from many early years settings such as those in the UK, where the organisation of children by age groups remains the norm. Dixie Kids' practice encourages us to rethink the age-based determinations which govern the way early years provision is delivered in many settings, and instead offers a view of early years education which prioritises peer learning and children's active engagement in their social contexts. In their study of *Preschool in Three Cultures*, Tobin et al. (1991) contend that preschools are essentially cultural institutions that both reflect and support the cultures of which they are a part. It could be argued that the pedagogical practice in Dixie Kids is culturally imbued and influenced by the neo-Confucian philosophy of the importance of human relationships and social relations rather than a more individualistic approach to development and learning. There is a harmony in the way the design and pedagogy in this centre steer children towards group participation, and provide them with opportunities to experience being members of a community where they can learn from each other and, in the process, acquire social and cultural capital by becoming imbued with the skills and values that are most highly prized in their community and beyond. When considering the children's experiences in Dixie Kids, there is, therefore, a need to acknowledge that the broader discourse of culture, community practices and socialisation are significant for the way children negotiate their own learning and identities. These experiences afford the children in the centre what Bourdieu (1991) refers to as *habitus*, acquired social dispositions and frames of reference, where they can develop different ways of thinking about and acting upon their social interactions in their cultural worlds. These frames of reference serve to equip the children in Dixie Kids with the symbolic capital that they need to engage with others in their everyday lives within and outside the setting (Bourdieu, 1991).

New visions

In describing how children and their learning are conceptualised in various parts of the world, we are faced with different cultural descriptions of children's role as learners within a broader, richer perspective of how children develop and learn. The examples above remind us that early years and other educational settings are essentially key sites of socialisation which inform and are informed by children's experiences as active learners, albeit in contrasting cultural and geographical contexts. From a cross-cultural perspective, both communities in which the above two examples are placed generate their own meanings of children's experiences and ways of learning. The purpose of the examples is not to be representative of particular cross-cultural assumptions as no comparison can be accurate or straightforward; what they do show, however, is that, with given variations, the children in both contexts show the situated nature of learning as a form of social practice and negotiation that is richly embedded in cultural values. Both vignettes illustrate how children learn and develop in myriad ways that are more often than not centred around their spontaneous 'everyday' socialisation and informal activities that are not 'designed' or created artificially through the enactment of a formal prescribed curriculum. It is also clear from the examples of practice that there exist varying degrees of cultural and social capital which children are able to draw on from both within and outside the early years setting to negotiate their classroom-based socialisation and co-construct a shared learning space. We suggest that Bourdieu's concepts of habitus, field, social and symbolic capital offer valuable insights that can deepen understandings of young children's active meaning-making. As early years practitioners know all too well, a child's knowledge is only made evident when it is exercised, but there can be many mechanisms at play in an early years environment that mitigate against young children exercising their agency and displaying their competency. In this regard, the concept of *habitus* is particularly well suited to the study of interaction in diverse social environments and offers a useful tool for understanding the impact of context on young children's meaning-making.

Yet, it is ironic that even as research shows a key feature of young children's learning is its contextual and contingent nature, situated in localised social and cultural practices, practitioners are increasingly expected to work within the confines of a mandated national curriculum which assumes a standardised context and universal, normative measures of children's development and achievement. The danger is that the role of early education under such conditions is relegated to preparatory support for formal schooling, tasked with the prime goal of meeting national and international educational performance targets, rather than as a key site for personal, localised socialisation and agency. As Dahlberg and Moss (2005) suggest, 'preschools are increasingly bounded by other normalising frameworks either required by government or offered by experts: standards, curricula, accreditation, guidelines on best practice, inspections, audits, the list rolls on'.

The move towards a 'school readiness' agenda in a climate of educational accountability and assessment, as brought about by changes to the early years curriculum in England in recent years, has fuelled deep concerns that the increased emphasis on educational targets, learning goals and professional accountability has become a major characteristic of early years practice (Ball, 2003; Pugh, 2010; Moss, 2006).

Key questions for reflection

How appropriate is it to implant a standardised educational framework onto children whose learning and backgrounds are so diverse and still very much evolving?

How can early years settings offer an empowering pedagogical space for children to learn and develop within a domain of their own design at their own pace?

The potential for children's individual and collective agency is immense. In this chapter we have drawn on the work of Bourdieu (1977, 1998) to understand how school systems can serve to reproduce social and cultural inequalities and to discuss how teachers can create ways in which children are proactively engaged not only in the shaping of their own learning and social environment but also shaping and supporting the learning of other children. We argue for the importance of thinking creatively about building inclusive learning communities for our youngest, for the need to offer opportunities that involve children in empowering ways which recognise children's competences, interests and experiences. Children's meaning-making is inextricably interwoven within the contexts of their socio-cultural environment as they build their knowledge and experiences with others around them. Drawing on the discourse of the sociology of childhood and socio-cultural theory, it is, therefore, important to understand how children's agency shapes, and at the same time is influenced by, their experiences in the family, early years setting and wider community life. The challenge for practitioners and all those who work in the early years is to take seriously the agency and rights of children in their own learning and development, especially in the midst of increasing surveillance and accountability in a highly politicised and evolving sector.

Notes

1 All participant names and locations are pseudonyms.
2 The authors recognise the complexities in the use of language, especially in polarised constructs such as 'western' and 'non-western', 'East' and 'West'. While acknowledging the need to problematise these concepts, the phrase 'western and non-western world' is used here in the broadest sense to refer to the largely contrasting geopolitical borders between Euro-America, Africa and Asia, and the varying differences in histories, traditions and cultures within and across the regions.

3 The term 'dialectic' implies the presence of disagreement, and it is not synonymous with *debate* or *discourse*. In the latter, there can be discussion without fundamental disagreement, whereas in dialectics there is always a tension to be resolved (or not). Here, the tension is between an individual's habitus and the particular field encountered by that individual.

4 For more detailed discussion, see Grenfell and James, 1998.

Further reading

Young, M. (2013). Overcoming the Crisis in Curriculum Theory: A Knowledge-based Approach. *Journal of Curriculum Studies*. 45 (2). 101–18.

This journal article discusses the term 'curriculum' and offers different theoretical perspectives of how the term can be conceptualised. It is useful in problematising our understanding of the nature of curriculum (what it is for and for whom) and the implications for pedagogy and teaching practice.

Ball, S. (2003). The Teacher's Soul and the Terrors of Performativity. *Journal of Education Policy*. 18 (2). 215–28.

This academic paper discusses the origins, processes and effects of performativity on education. It argues that performativity is a new mode of state regulation which makes it possible to govern in an 'advanced liberal' way, but which requires individual practitioners to respond to targets, indicators and evaluations and to set aside their personal beliefs and commitments.

Bourdieu, P. (1998). *Practical Reason: On the Theory of Action*. Cambridge: Polity Press.

In this book Pierre Bourdieu clarifies his theoretical approach and his 'philosophy of action', which is condensed in the key concepts of habitus, field and capital. He emphasises the two-way relationship between the objective structures of social fields and the incorporated structures of the habitus. This is not an easy read, but provides an accessible route into Bourdieu's theories.

Paley, V. G. (1990). *The Boy Who Would be a Helicopter: The Uses of Storytelling in the Classroom*. Cambridge: Harvard University Press.

In this book, Paley describes her pioneering work on storytelling, focusing on the challenge posed by the isolated child to teachers and classmates in the classroom community. It tells the story of Jason, described as 'a loner and an outsider' and how, through his storytelling, he ultimately became included in the social world of his classmates. As Paley recounts Jason's struggle, she presents a vision of the classroom as a crucible where the young discover themselves and learn to confront new problems in their daily experience.

References

Ang, L. (2010). Critical Perspectives on Cultural Diversity in Early Childhood: Building an Inclusive Curriculum and Provision. *Early Years*. 30 (1). March. 41–52.

Anning, A., Cullen, J. and Fleer, M. (2009). *Early Childhood Education: Society and Culture*. 2nd edn. London: Sage.

Ball, S. (2003). The Teacher's Soul and the Terrors of Performativity. *Journal of Education Policy*. 18 (2). 215–28.

Bourdieu, P. (1977). *Outline of a Theory of Practice*. Trans. R. Nice. Cambridge: Cambridge University Press.

Bourdieu, P. (1991). *Language and Symbolic Power*. Trans. G. Raymond and M. Adamson. Cambridge: Polity Press.

Bourdieu, P. (1998). *Practical Reason: On the Theory of Action*. Cambridge: Polity Press.

Bruner, J. (1996). *The Culture of Education*. Cambridge, MA: Harvard University Press.

Clark, A. and Moss, P. (2001). *Listening to Young Children: The Mosaic Approach*. London: National Children's Bureau and Joseph Rowntree Foundation.

Corsaro, W. A. (2005). *The Sociology of Childhood*. 2nd edn. Thousand Oaks, CA: Pine Forge Press.

Cremin, T., Swann, J., Flewitt, R., Faulkner, D. and Kucirkova, N. (2013). *Evaluation Report: Executive Summary of MakeBelieve Arts Helicopter Technique of Storytelling and Story Acting*. Faculty of Education and Language Studies: Open University. Available at: http://static.squarespace.com/static/53ad7934e4b0a25fee7c47b2/t/53baaba4e4b0afc035d38a2d/1404742564651/Executive+summary.pdf

Dahlberg, G. and Moss, P. (2005). *Ethics and Politics in Early Childhood Education*. Oxfordshire: RoutledgeFalmer.

Dardess, J. (1991). Childhood in Premodern China. In M. Hawes and R. Hiner (eds), *Children in Historical and Comparative Perspective*. Westport, CT: Greenwood Press.

Department for Education (DfE) (2012). *Early Years Foundation Stage*. Available at: https://www.education.gov.uk/schools/teachingandlearning/assessment/eyfs. Accessed 27 April 2014.

Department for Education (DfE) (2014). *National Curriculum for England*. Available at: https://www.gov.uk/government/collections/national-curriculum. Accessed 27 April 2014.

Edwards, A. and Knight, P. (1994). *Effective Early Years Education*. Milton Keynes: Open University Press.

Edwards, D. and Mercer, N. (1987). *Common Knowledge*. London: Methuen.

Grenfell, M. (2009). Bourdieu, Language, and Literacy. *Reading Research Quarterly*. 44. (4). 438–48.

Grenfell, M. and James, D. (1998). *Acts of Practical Theory: Bourdieu and Education*. London: Falmer Press.

Li, H., Rao, N. and Tse, S. K. T. (2012). Adapting Western Pedagogies for Chinese Literacy Instruction: Case Studies of Hong Kong, Shenzhen, and Singapore Preschools. *Early Education and Development*. 23. 603–21.

Mayall, B. (2002). *Towards a Sociology for Childhood*. Buckingham: Open University Press.

Mercer, N. (1994). 'Neo-Vygotskian Theory and Classroom Education'. In B. Stierer and J. Maybin (eds), *Language, Literacy and Learning in Educational Practice*. Buckingham: Open University Press.

Mortimore, P., Gopinathan, S., Leo, E., Myers, K., Stoll, L. and Mortimore, J. (2000). *The Culture of Change: Case Studies of Improving Schools in Singapore and London*. London: Institute of Education, Bedford Way Press.

Moss, P. (2006). Possibilities for Re-envisioning the Early Childhood Worker. *Contemporary Issues in Early Childhood*. 7 (1). 30–41.

Paley, V. G. (1990). *The Boy Who Would be a Helicopter: The Uses of Storytelling in the Classroom*. Cambridge: Harvard University Press.

Paley, V. G. (1992). *You Can't Say You Can't Play*. Cambridge, MA: Harvard University Press.

Paley, V. G. (2004). *Child's Play: The Importance of Fantasy Play*. Chicago: Chicago University Press.

Prout, A. and James, A. (1997). A New Paradigm for the Sociology of Childhood? In A. James and A. Prout (eds), *Constructing and Reconstructing Childhood: Contemporary Issues in the Sociological Study of Childhood*. 2nd edn. London: Falmer Press.

Pugh, G. (2010). Improving Outcomes for Young Children: Can We Narrow the Gap? *Early Years*. 30 (1). 5–14.

Retas, S. and Kwan, C. (2000). Preschool Quality and Staff Characteristics in Singapore. In C. Tan-Niam and M. L. Quah (eds), *Investing in Our Future: The Early Years*. Singapore: McGraw-Hill. 53–65.

Rogoff, B. (2003). *The Cultural Nature of Human Development*. New York: Oxford University Press.

Rogoff, B. and Wertsch, J. (eds) (1984). *Children's Learning in the 'Zone of Proximal Development'*. San Franciso: Jossey-Bass.

Tang, F. and Maxwell, S. (2007). Being Taught to Learn Together: An Ethnographic Study of the Curriculum in Two Chinese Kindergartens. *Early Years*. 27 (2). 145–57.

Tobin, J. (2007). An Ethnographic Perspective on Quality in Early Childhood Education. In J. X. Zhu (ed.), *Global Perspectives on Early Childhood Education*. Shanghai: East China Normal University Press.

Tobin, J., Wu, D. Y. H. and Davidson, D. H. (1991). *Preschool in Three Cultures: Japan, China and the United States*. New Haven and London: Yale University Press.

Vygotsky, L. (1978). *Mind in Society: The Development of Higher Psychological Processes.* Cambridge, MA: Harvard University Press.

Wong, M. N. C. (2008). How Preschool Children Learn in Hong Kong and Canada: A Cross-cultural Study. *Early Years.* 28 (2). 115–33.

Wood, D., Bruner, J. S. and Ross, G. (1976). The Role of Tutoring in Problem Solving. *Journal of Child Psychology and Psychiatry.* 17 (2). 89–100.

Chapter 11

Families, society and school choice

Georgina Merchant

Chapter summary

The main concern for teachers is the learning and development of children in their class. Teachers also understand that the communities that children live in are an important element of education. Schools' contact with families begins with the process of parents choosing a school, the topic which is central to this chapter. The chapter begins with a short history of school choice as a means to better understand current developments. Other sections in the chapter address the ways that parents may negotiate school choices, and some of the consequences of England's current system of allocation of school places. The chapter concludes with some recommendations for policy and for the ways in which society should support those most in need.

As the nail in the 'for sale' sign was given a final hammer into place, a tinge of sadness was felt by Jill. Her house had been a happy place to live, and she had thought it might be that 'forever home' that many hanker after, with its generous garden, bright living room and the homely kitchen that had been the focus of much DIY. Jill's son Alex was clinging round her leg, while at the same time enjoying his banana, something that reminded Jill of the reason that they were to move to a small flat 'with potential', as the estate agent had put it. A move of house was her only hope of getting Alex into Hilltop School, with its 'outstanding' Ofsted rating and its pupil test scores that were well above the national average. This would also hopefully mean avoiding the Lowland School down the road that was still deemed to be 'requiring improvement'.

Jill reflected on the contrasting situations of her two sisters and their children. Alison's rural location meant her only realistic choice was the local village school which had been a 'good' school for many years. Her other sister Frances, on the other hand, preferred her children to go to a private school, which her husband's salary as a lawyer enabled them to afford.

The choices that Jill was presented with in the fictional example above raise many issues, some of which are addressed in this chapter. One of these issues is something that has become more common in wealthy nations, the option for some parents to move house in order to be in the catchment area of a desired school. This option is only open to parents who have the resources, and social capital, that enables them to move house. One feature of such a scenario is that, in spite of attempts by governments and local authorities to ensure that entry to schooling is based on fair and reasonable criteria, parents with greater social capital are able to subvert systems to ensure advantage for their children. Another key issue is the way that national educational monitoring systems, such as inspectorates and national testing, result in a further distortion of the distribution of pupils to schools perceived as good or otherwise by parents and their children.

An important starting point for choosing a school is knowing what kinds of schools are available. In England the main types of schools are as follows:

- Community school – state schools (formerly county schools). Admissions mainly based on proximity of family home to the schools and on whether siblings have been or are at the school.
- Foundation school – mainly former grant-maintained schools. A governing body owns the land, employs staff and is the admission authority in consultation with the local education authority (LEA). There is LEA representation on the school's governing body.
- Voluntary aided school – these are owned by a voluntary body, usually religious, who appoint most of the governors. LEA funded except building and repair costs, which are shared between governing body, LEA and government. Governing body is the admissions authority, in consultation with the LEA. Voluntary aided schools are allowed to include the religious denomination of families as part of their admissions criteria.
- Voluntary controlled school – similar to voluntary aided, but with mainly LEA-appointed governors. The LEA is the admissions authority.
- Community special school and foundation special school – these are for pupils with significant special educational needs.
- Academy schools and free schools – schools in England which are directly funded by central government (specifically, the Department for Education) but are independent of direct control by local authority.

Most children in England attend one of the kinds of schools in the list above. A relatively small proportion of parents can afford to send their children to private schools for which the cost is more than £10,000 per child per school year. A minority of parents opt to educate their children at home. Although there don't appear to be government statistics on this, some people estimate 'that there are around 60,000 (approximately 0.6%) UK children of compulsory educational age who are currently (2012) being home educated' (http://www.home-education.org.uk).

In any local authority the various types of school are able to establish their own admissions criteria within certain guidelines. For example, voluntary aided schools (some of which can be called 'faith schools') may require affiliation with particular religions. Other criteria include straight-line distance between home and schools as part of the concept of 'catchment area'. Another criteria may be the priority that a parent has indicated about the school in a numbered list. This could mean that if a parent has ranked a school number one in the list the school would be more likely to accept their child.

Anecdotally, we know that parents of early years and primary children have conversations with their children to see what kind of schools they would like to attend, if there is a choice of school, which at primary level is less common. However research evidence in relation to young children's school preferences is scarce, beyond studies of the kinds of preferences children have for teaching and learning more generally. Even very young children can be asked their views about educational settings that they might attend, or are attending. Older primary pupils have been shown to raise very important issues when asked about schools choice, although research studies in relation to this age of child are rare. One study examined the impact of school choice policy on the decisions made by black and minority ethnic (BME) parents. Although the study was focused on selection of secondary schools it did include data from primary-age pupils. For example, the primary pupils commented on issues such as the ethnic mix and ethnic groups in schools:

> CJ: [In Eastown Boys'/Girls'] it's not mixed and it's just like full of Asians.
> RISHA: Look at yourself in the mirror.
> CJ: I like to be mixed. It's boring just Asians. It's nearly [an] Asian school.
> RISHA: No, my sister has lots of friends and none of them are Asian.
> CJ: It's just boring. If you're mixed it's like quite fun and stuff. If you just stay like Asians that's just boring.
> RISHA: But you can make friends with other people too. After school. Eastlea Primary, Year 6 children (Weekes-Bernard, 2007, p. 49)

Rather worryingly the primary pupils suggested stereotyping on the part of teachers as part of their reflections about friendships:

> MICHAELA: If we are all the same, some of us get into trouble. We have a group of friends and we're all like the same kind of and we always get told by the teachers [that] we're black clouds and we need to split up. They call us black clouds and we need to split up even though we do talk to other people.
> RUBUS: They don't call you that because of your skin colour.
> DALE/MICHAELA: You lot never get told off – it's only our colour [who do].
> MASTEESHA: It's a bit like you're not allowed to hang out with your own friends. If you make friends with somebody who's the same colour, it doesn't matter.
> DALE: Some people like Rubus' colour, if they see [him] playing with any colour they [older children] try and kill you. If you mix with other people at Northfields High or Northtown Secondary.
> MICHAELA: You have to hang around with your own colour or they beat you up.
> JANE: I've got a friend and she's Sikh and if that were to happen then I wouldn't be able to play with her and she's my best friend.
> DALE: Why should we stop because some people are racist?
> MICHAELA: But when this lot make groups and everything it's just not a problem because that teacher doesn't go up to them and say oh you're on the white side. We've asked him [the teacher] what do you mean and he says 'You're all black people hanging around together,' so it's not about how our personalities are, it's because of how we look and I made sure I asked before I jumped to conclusions.
> MASTEESHA: The teacher that we're talking about [who's] always shouting at us for being in certain colour groups, he's also a bit of a hypocrite because he's …
> MICHAELA: … the same colour as us. (Year 6 pupils, Northgrove Primary)

For state-funded schools, councils provide booklets about schools' criteria and how to apply. Admission criteria are different for each school. For example, schools may give priority to children:

- who have a brother or sister at the school already
- who live close to the school
- from a particular religion (for faith schools)
- who do well in an entrance exam (for selective schools, e.g. grammar schools)
- who went to a particular primary school (a 'feeder school' to a secondary school)
- who are in local authority care (all schools must have this as a top priority).

Parents complete a form which is sent to the local authority who then assigns pupils to schools based on the application, on the individual admissions criteria and on the availability of school places.

The concept of school choice in this chapter is contextualised as the parental right to express a preference for the school that they would most like their child to attend. The chapter focuses on the issues that parents and children face as part of choosing a school, and the issues that competition for places in schools raises. It begins with an exploration of the history of school choice in England. In particular, this section focuses on the ways in which the ideology of free market economics influenced educational policy, leading to greater competition between schools as they sought to be chosen by parents seeking places at the best schools for their children. Research on the issues considered by parents and children when choosing schools, and the impact on different groups in society, is the main focus of the next section of the chapter. The consequences of the particular system of choice that exists are explored, and some possible ways forward are recommended at the end of the chapter.

Key questions for reflection

How did your parents choose your school?
Was it their first choice for you?
    Look online at your local authority website to see what the process for admissions is in your local area.

A short history of school choice in England

The idea of making a link between the economics of schooling and parental choices has a long history. Johnson (1990) notes the work of philosophers Adam Smith in England, and Tom Paine in the USA, who, in the eighteenth century, argued for funding for schools to be given to parents who would be obliged to use it in educating their children. Smith viewed this as being a means by which a more effective education would be provided through market forces. The 1944 education acts in England saw the seeds of 'choice' being sown for parents and their children. In addition to the responsibility given to local education authorities to provide access to suitable schools, there was also reference to wishes of parents.

> The Minister and local authorities shall have regard to the general principles that, so far as is compatible with the provision of efficient instruction and training and the avoidance of unreasonable public expenditure, pupils are to be educated in accordance with the wishes of their parents.
>
> (Education Act 1944, section 75)

However, the intention was not to provide parents with choices between similar schools but rather to align denominational schools with the state system while maintaining faith school provision (Adler et al., 1989).

In the years that followed the Education Act 1944 some parents began to challenge local authorities and submit appeals in relation to the school their children were allocated to. Subsequently, clarification was offered by the Ministry of Education in *Circular 83: Choice of Schools* (Ministry of Education, 1946), and procedures for appeal were laid down for local education authorities. Circular 83 primarily addressed selection criteria; however, it also made it clear that parents still did not have complete freedom of choice and, generally, were expected to select according to the age of their children in relation to the school's provision, and proximity of the school to their home. A subsequent manual of guidance suggested that parents could cite factors such as costs they might incur, and/or overcrowding as reasons for preferences. Hence the concept of a balance of needs between the local education authority and parents was established.

A key moment in the modern history of educational policy was the Conservative Party Manifesto of 1974, where the balance of power for choice was tipped in parents' favour by propositions framed in 'A Parents Charter of Rights' whereby state and local authorities would have an obligation to consider the wishes of parents. This proposal included the establishment of a new system of appeals for parents. However, although parliamentary proposals for this Charter were presented in parliament twice, it did not become law (Adler et al., 1989).

Proposals for parental choice in the 1979 Education Bill included some compromise around the issue of appeals, specifically to what degree the appeals process would be independent from local education authorities, who feared that complete autonomy of appeals panels would strip them of power. Ultimately, it was agreed that appeal committees would have both independent and LEA members.

The key in the subsequent Education Act 1980 was politicians' belief that parents were demanding more choice; an increasing need to manage numbers of schools' places in the face of falling school roles; and the problems ensuing from an increase in the number of appeals (Stillman and Maychell, 1986). The 1980 Act required all LEAs to permit parents to express their preferences and these were to be upheld unless this would:

- prejudice the provision of efficient use of resources;
- clash with the principles of voluntary aided or special agreement school; or
- clash with selective principles. (Stillman, 1994, p. 29)

In 1987, Kenneth Baker, who was Secretary of State for Education, looked back to the Education Act 1944 Act to underpin his Education Bill of 1987:

> If we are to implement the principle of the 1944 Education Act 'that children should be educated in accordance with the wishes of their parents', then we must give

consumers of education a central part in decision making … it means encouraging the consumer to expect and demand that all educational bodies do the best job possible. In a word, it means choice … For the first time they [local education authorities] will face competition in the provision of free education, so standards will rise in all schools as we introduce a competitive spirit into the provision of education – and at no extra cost to the consumer.

(Hansard, cited in Hughes *et al.*, 1994, p. 10)

This was the first time that parents had been cast into the roles of consumers so explicitly and was reflective of wider political views of the period. Thus funding for a particular school was dependent upon the number of pupils that it could attract and consequently a raising of competition among schools based upon an endeavour to exhibit higher academic standards was envisaged.

A subsequent twelve acts over the next thirteen years of Conservative government introduced a number of additional factors pertinent to the issue of choice: an increase in school governor responsibility for providing information to parents; the highly significant Education Act 1988 that included the introduction of the National Curriculum, grant-maintained schools, technical colleges and 'open' enrolment. In 1992 this was followed by requirement for annual reporting to parents; league tables of school statutory test scores; and the inspection system the Office for Standards in Education (Ofsted). Grant-maintained schools became seen as an 'escape route from local government control rather than a means of becoming something different' (Hirsch, 1994, p. 63). Some saw grant-maintained schools as a political means of releasing schools from Labour Party-dominated local authority control. Additionally, rules were introduced preventing roles from falling below a nominated capacity.

The very recent addition of free schools and academies has added to the mix of 'choice' for parents, and the potential for more diversity as these schools are funded by the state yet free from local authority control and implementation of England's National Curriculum of 2014. The Academies Act (2010) authorised the creation of free schools and allows all existing state schools to become academies. Academies are self-governing and all are constituted as not-for-profit trusts. They may receive additional support from personal or corporate sponsors, either financially or in kind. They must meet the requirements for a broad and balanced curriculum in common with other state schools, and they are also subject to inspection by Ofsted. Free schools were introduced by the Conservative–Liberal Democrat coalition following the 2010 general election, making it possible for parents, teachers, charities and businesses to set up their own schools. Free schools were an extension of the existing 'academies programme' that began under the New Labour government (1997 to 2010).

The origins of these particular links between economics, competition and choice can be traced back to the influence on the development of the 1988 Education Reform Act of an influential group of right-wing educationalists during the late 1970s and 1980s (Hughes *et al.*, 1994). Donald Hirsch, writing for the OECD (1994), suggested a number of reasons that choice became prominent. He identified it as partly stemming from a 'neo-liberal' approach prevalent in a number of different countries that had a dependence upon free markets to drive the management of public finance. In school choice terms, this puts the parent and child into the role of consumers, and makes schools reliant upon attracting those consumers and their associated funding. The concept of education as being a marketable commodity theoretically positions parents and their children as consumers with spending power in terms of funding that is attached to their enrolment at a particular school. At its heart it was envisaged that, like other consumer-driven aspects of society, schools would have to cater to the new powers of parents. Parents could 'vote with their feet' by taking their children to a school of their choice, not necessarily the one closest to their home, hence competing schools would have to raise standards in order to win children.

Key question for reflection

What sources of information do you think parents should consult in order to evaluate the relative merits of schools? Once you have listed some sources, arrange the list in order of preference in terms of what you think is their importance in relation to a child's progress in school.

Parents negotiating school choices

Schools that are in demand in a particular area cannot expand the number of places for children endlessly, so, despite the ideological commitment to choice, this cannot be guaranteed. As a result, parents find ways to negotiate the admissions procedure to try to gain a preferred place for their child. Much media attention focuses on the academic standards of schools as measured by national testing and exams, yet research internationally suggests that the picture is more complex than suggested in the media. Parents are mainly interested in three factors when thinking about school choice: academic attainment, proximity of the home to the school and socio-economic context of the school (Burgess *et al.*, 2009). But the reasons for school preferences as stated by parents have been shown to differ to some degree from those that they finally make. Research by Burgess *et al.* (2009) shows that, despite better test results being indicated to be a greater factor in choice for more educated parents, proximity to the school is strong driver for all. They also found that higher socio-economic status (SES) parents were likely to opt for those schools with lower free school meal roles within the choice of schools available to them. Similarly, a study in America (Hastings *et al.*, 2005) found that proximity was important to parents and that higher SES and greater levels of education were attributes of those parents that opted for schools that demonstrated better test scores.

The negative aspects of choice leading to stratification of children within schools are evidenced by studies such as that of Buckley *et al.* (2006) in Chile. Although parents of all backgrounds cited that they rated academic performance, the study found parents did not consistently choose those schools with highest performance but rather those with similar pupil demographics. In Michigan, Buckley *et al.* (2006) found that parents claimed to make choices base upon teacher quality and academic excellence but the tracking of online search behaviours indicated a prevalence for looking at the pupil demographic as a key source of information under consideration. This finding is reinforced by other studies such as that of Tedin and Weiher (2004), carried out in Texas. They found that race is a strong predictor of parental preference.

More recent research has suggested the concept of the 'feasible choice set' that is also influenced by social class. Burgess *et al.* (2009) found that parents of lower SES, and those who had no educational or vocational qualifications, had more common access to schools with greater number of pupils with the following characteristics: entitlement to free school meals (used in England as an indicator of deprivation); for whom English was an additional language; identified as having special educational needs, than did their higher SES counterparts and those who had, as a minimum, a degree. Burgess *et al.* (2009) demonstrate that a 'favourite' school will not necessarily be the first choice on parents' application forms as a result of the differing demands of admissions procedures. They also found that parents with higher SES were more likely to make the choice of a higher-performing school and one with lower levels of pupils eligible for free school meals. Parents with lower SES were found to be less likely to apply to these schools because these schools were not seen as part of their feasible choice set. Further evidence of the restrictions on choice that the feasible choice set shows may be figures such as those in England in 2014 indicating a national figure of around 90 per cent of parents getting their first choice of school with variations across regions. For example,

- Cornwall: 94 per cent first preference (93.1 per cent in 2013)
- Durham: 92 per cent first preference (94 per cent in 2013); 5,153 applications in total (5,072 in 2013)
- Leeds: 85 per cent first preference (unchanged from 2013); 9,774 applications (9,355 in 2013)
- Liverpool: 89 per cent first preference (90 per cent in 2013); 4,894 applications (4,664 in 2013). (Adams *et al.*, 2014)

This data should be viewed in the context of my previous arguments regarding the degree to which this is indicative of the *actual* preferences of parents.

Ball and Gewirtz (1996) categorised three groups of 'choosers': 1. privileged and/or skilled choosers who are almost exclusively middle class; 2. semi-skilled choosers who are from a variety of class backgrounds; and 3. the 'disconnected' who were almost all 'working class'. This study of parents choosing secondary schools concluded that the matching of children to particular types of schools was not as prevalent among those categorised as disconnected choosers. One important factor was the view of parents that their child's abilities and attainment was 'fixed' and not likely to be altered by the context of the school environment. The working-class parents in the study were less likely to view themselves as 'consumers', and sometimes in preference to determining school choice on the basis of test outcomes these parents sought schools that might offer better support for children who had lower attainment, and where they perceived fairness and friendliness of teachers.

Parental preferences are subject to the systems at national and local levels that determine how school places are allocated. Parents, if they have the capacity, have to develop strategies in order to 'play the system'. For example, if parents know that a school is over-subscribed they may prioritise another good school that they feel their child is more likely to be offered a place at, rather than risk not getting either school, if the system takes into account whether a school has been nominated by a parent, and the rank order of those nominations.

The impact of the choice of other people, such as friends and family, has been found to be an influential and valued source of knowledge about schools and how to access them. Ball and Vincent (1998) considered this in terms of the possible impact of the 'grapevine', defined as the informal knowledge afforded to one through social net-works, which they found to be very significant in influencing choice. The advent of the internet has meant that the nature of social networks has been added to dramatically. One currently prominent example is Mumsnet. Mumsnet is an online forum for information and 'chat' which was founded in 1999 by mother of twins Justine Roberts, who is a former financial analyst in the city of London and, subsequently, a journalist. In 2014 Mumsnet was influential, indicated by its £3m turnover, with more than a million unique users every month and 25,000 daily posts on discussion boards. The site includes guidance on school choice, with the recognition that this is far from a straight-forward process:

> How to choose a school: the theory. Armed with Ofsted reports and league tables, the discerning parent visits all the schools in the local area and makes a decision as to where their child will best thrive. Parent applies and child is offered a place.
>   How to choose a school: the practice. Having made the key decision, the parent finds out that in order to get into the appropriate school they will need to move to within a metre of the school gates, convert to Catholicism and come up with an elder sibling already at the school.
>
> (Mumsnet, 2014)

The Mumsnet site recommends that parents should do the following: access their local authority booklet on the applications process; check the league tables of academic results; read Ofsted reports; and visit the school. There are notes of caution when taking account of academic results and inspection reports with the recognition that they represent 'a snapshot' so things can change quickly – for example, with the arrival or departure of key teaching staff, especially in primary education.

Although the Mumsnet guidance above is logical, as I have shown so far in this chapter the issues are rather more complex. For example, research indicates that the 'impact of racial and ethnic disadvantage makes the issue of knowledge and choice particularly problematic, both because of the lack of requisite social expertise and knowledge of the system within particular communities and because of the structural constraints on the choices available to parents in economically deprived areas' (Weekes-Bernard, 2007, p. 1). The School Choice and Ethnic Segregation project (Weekes-Bernard, 2007) explored the experiences of parents and children. It makes a clear connection between the 'choice' agenda and inequality in education:

> Perhaps most importantly, the report states that for the majority of Black and Minority Ethnic (BME) parents, school choice remains an illusion rather than a reality – that for BME families there is often no choice and that this has serious knock-on effects for processes of ethnic, racial, religious and classed segregation, community cohesion and individual achievement.
>
> (Weekes-Bernard, 2007, p. 2)

In general this research, and other studies cited in the chapter, leads me to question the likelihood of improved education being a result of competition between schools. The more likely outcome appears to be greater social stratification.

Key questions for reflection

Discuss your initial reaction to the following news headlines:

'More children miss out as baby boom puts squeeze on places' (Woolcock and Bassett, 2014)

'Revealed: the legal loophole letting pushy parents "rent" the best state school places' (Herrmann, 2013)

'Children are battling for best primary school places from age of TWO as record numbers of youngsters are denied chosen school' (Clark, 2014)

Select one of the articles (or other more recent relevant article) to read and think about.

Some consequences of education as a 'commodity'

The concept of schools as a marketable commodity theoretically positions parents and their children as consumers, who have spending power in terms of funding that is attached to each pupil's enrolment at a particular school. There are a number of social effects created by this idea of marketable commodities. One particularly worrying effect is the additional stratification of schools, and greater segregation between pupils at different schools as a result of homogeneity within schools. This wider societal issue is one of social justice. Parents may make choices that are not concurrent with the needs of society as a whole. For example, choices may lead to racial or religious segregation. One could well imagine a scenario whereby the choices agenda might also result in schools conforming to the wants and needs of the articulate middle classes, resulting in those pupils with more 'expensive' needs being forced to attend less popular schools meaning increased pressure on those schools' resources. Critics of these kinds of market-driven school choice policies assert that middle-class parents are more motivated and informed regarding availability of educational options. As early as 1994, Hirsch saw the result of the advantages taken by middle-class parents as being increasing polarisation of schools, with some becoming viewed as being 'middle class' or working class' and social cohesion being threatened.

Paradoxically, although the free market ideology of education is built on the idea of maximum choice it has also been accompanied by policies and practices that reduce choice. For example, the idea of a national curriculum that must be followed by all schools in order to assure educational quality denies an element of choice, that of choice over different kinds of curricula. As Hughes *et al.* (1994) pointed out in relation to England's first national curriculum from 1988 onwards, the resultant tension was clear:

> Parents are to be free to choose a school for their children but not free to choose what is taught there, which is the exclusive territory of the Secretary of State ... freedom of choice over curriculum matters is to be curtailed for schools, teachers, parents and pupils. The proffered freedom of choice is illusory: parents are free to choose which institution will slavishly teach the Secretary of State's curriculum to their children.
>
> (Bash and Coulby, p. b114, as cited in Hughes *et al.*, 1994).

However, in 2014 the context in relation to choice and the curriculum took another dramatic turn (see Chapter 4 for more on the curriculum). Schools that become academies or free schools do not have to follow the national curriculum. Hence the financial incentives that initially come with Academy status to adopt an ideological policy that puts schools in direct control of the Secretary of State for Education rather than, for example, local authorities, are matched with the incentive of greater freedom over the curriculum – something, that should be open to all schools, teachers and their pupils.

The final consequence addressed in this chapter appears to be a recent phenomenon in England, but one that perhaps could have been predicted to follow the establishment of the ideology of free market competition. The price rises of houses that are within desired target schools' catchment areas. This in turn means that certain schools become only accessible to those with the financial and social capital to negotiate places at these schools. This has led to further narrowing of the diversity of children able to access such schools. With the stakes for particular places in particular schools rising so highly, a consequence for children who do not get their first choice could be dissatisfaction and a lack of engagement. The impact is not just on the child and their family, but also on the ethos of the school.

New visions

There does not appear to be any robust evidence that the ideology of schools operating in a free market, supported by the use of high-stakes national assessments and league tables, has resulted in higher standards of teaching and learning. The evidence suggests that the issue of school choice weighs heavily upon the parents of all children in England, and the constraints and possibilities that it may offer are challenging to negotiate. A particular concern for society is the disadvantages for families from lower SES and the greater stratification of schools, with consequent narrowing of diversity of school populations. The emphasis of policy should be excellent neighbourhood schools for all, with the expectation that the proximity of the home to the school would be the main criterion for admission.

Primary schools in England have been slower than secondary schools to take up academy status, although the financial incentives for the first five years of new academies has been so lucrative that the numbers of primary schools has been increasing steadily. The freedoms offered to academies – for example, over the curriculum – are potentially interesting. However, these freedoms should not come at the expense of the requirement to loosen ties with local authorities and come under the direct control of the Department for Education. All schools should have the power to innovate supported by strong local authorities, whose role should be to encourage evidence-based innovation and practice. Local authorities are also in an ideal position to encourage fairness and equity in school choice for all.

At the time this book was written the general election of 2015 was imminent so it was, of course, difficult to predict how different configurations of government would change educational policy. In view of the fact that New Labour established the ideal of academy schools, and that this was continued by a Conservative–Liberal Democrat government, it seems unlikely that a large-scale return to local authority control of schools will happen. Nor does it seem likely that the emphasis on national testing and competition will change. In this context, it is essential that the disadvantages likely to be faced by the poorest families in society are addressed. For example, a lottery for places at popular schools is possible, as is access to free transport to pupils that fall outside a particular catchment area. At a more basic level, it is also important to ensure that parents and children most in need of support are helped to access key information regarding the possibilities for school choice.

A serious problem for a significant proportion of children in England's schools is the impact of not securing a school place that is most appropriate for their needs and development. Most political parties have a commitment to helping children most in need of education, although their means for achieving this differs. It seems contradictory to have a strong emphasis on high standards of learning for all, and particularly those children at greatest risk, but at the same time supporting a school choice system that seems too often to disadvantage those very children. Most parents know instinctively that good schools and good teaching are a vital component of their children's learning. Therefore, access to the best schools and the best teachers is essential for those most disadvantaged families. Indeed, if this access was improved there could be a major positive effect on standards of learning, negating the need for other expensive ways to drive up standards.

Further reading

Ball, S. J. (2003) *Class Strategies and the Education Market: The Middle Classes and Social Advantage.* London: RoutledgeFalmer.
Using evidence from parent and child interviews, this book examines the strategies and considerations drawn upon by the 'middle classes' at key moments of decision-making regarding education for their children.

Hansen, K. and Vignoles, A. (2010) Parental Choice of Primary School. *Millennium Cohort Study Briefing 5.* London: Centre for Longitudinal Studies, Institute of Education.
This briefing draws upon data from the Millennium Cohort Study tracking children from birth and covers a wide-ranging topic base. It examines information that reveals the extent to which parents actually choose primary schools rather than simply opting for schools in their locality. In addition, it considers the reasons driving choice.

Cowan, N. (2008). *Swedish Lessons.* London: Civitas.
This book considers the Swedish model of choice in schools and the ways that these may influence views upon what policies in England should be.

Weekes-Bernard, D. (2007). *School Choice and Ethnic Segregation.* London: Runnymead Trust.
Research study that found the complex factors, such as risk avoidance related to race and religion, facing BME parents when making school choices with their children.

References

Adams, R., Ratcliffe, R. and Elvin, E. (2014) Primary School Places: Fewer Parents get First Place. *Guardian.* Available at: http://www.theguardian.com/education/2014/apr/16/primary-school-places-parents-first-choice
Adler, M., Petch, A. and Tweedie, J. (1989) *Parental Choice and Educational Policy,* Edinburgh: Edinburgh University Press.
Adnett, N. and Davies, P. (2002). Education as a Positional Good: Implications for Market-Based Reforms of State Schooling. *British Journal of Education Studies.* 50 (2). 189–205.
Ball, S. J. and Gewirtz, S. (1996). Education Markets, School Competition and Parental Choice in the UK: A Report of Research Findings. *International Journal of Educational Reform.* (5) 2. 152–8.
Ball, S. and Vincent, C. (1998). I Heard It On the Grapevine: 'Hot' Knowledge and School Choice. *British Journal of Sociology of Education.* 19 (3). 377–400.

Buckley, J. and Schneider, M. (2002). What Do Parents Want from Schools? Evidence from the Internet. *Educational Evaluation and Policy Analysis*. 24 (2). 133–44.

Buckley, J., Elacqua, G. and Schneider, M. (2006) School Choice in Chile: Is it Class or In the Classroom? *Journal of Policy Analysis and Management*. 25 (3). 577–601.

Burgess, S., Greaves, E. and Vignoles, A. (2009) *Parental Choice of Primary School in England: What 'Type' of School do Parents Choose?* Bristol: CMPO.

Clark, L. (2014). Children are Battling for Best Primary School Places from Age of TWO as Record Numbers of Youngsters are Denied Chosen School. *Daily Mail*. Available at: http://www.dailymail.co.uk/news/article-2605668/Children-battling-best-primary-school-places-age-TWO-record-numbers-youngsters-face-denied-chosen-schools.html

Department of Education (2013). The National Curriculum 2014. Available at: https://www.gov.uk/government/collections/national-curriculum

Hastings, J., Kane, T. and Staiger, O. (2005). *Parental Preferences and School Competition: Evidence from a Public School Choice Program*. Cambridge, MA: NBER.

Herrmann, J. (2013). The Legal Loophole Letting Pushy Parents 'Rent' the Best School Places. *London Evening Standard*. Available at: http://www.standard.co.uk/lifestyle/london-life/revealed-the-legal-loophole-letting-pushy-parents-rent-the-best-state-school-places-8878941.html

Hirsch, D. (1994). *School: A Matter of Choice*. Paris: Centre for Educational Research and Innovation, OECD.

Home Education UK. Available at: http://www.home-education.org.uk/

Hughes, M., Wikeley, F. and Nash, T. (1994). *Parents and their Children's Schools*. Cambridge: Blackwell.

Johnson, D. (1990). *Parental Choice in Education*. London: Unwin Hyman.

Mumsnet (2014) *Choosing a Primary School*. Available at: http://www.mumsnet.com/

Ministry of Education (1946). *Circular 83: Choice of Schools*. London: Ministry of Education.

Stillman, A. (1994). Half a Century of Parental Choice in Britain? In J. M. Halstead (ed.), *Parental Choice in Education*. London: Kogan Page.

Stillman, A. and Maychell, K. (1986). *Choosing Schools: Parents, LEAS and the 1980 Education Act*. London: Routledge.

Tedin, K. L. and Weiher, G. R. (2004). Racial/Ethnic Diversity and Academic Quality as Components of School Choice. *The Journal of Politics*. 66 (4). 1109–33.

Weekes-Bernard, D. (2007). *School Choice and Ethnic Segregation*. London: Runnymead Trust.

Woolcock, N. and Bassett, H. (2014). More Children Miss Out as Baby Boom Puts Squeeze on Places. *The Times*. Available at: http://www.thetimes.co.uk/tto/education/article4061640.ece

Chapter 12

Politics, policy and teacher agency

Susan Taylor, Sue Bodman and Helen Morris

Chapter summary

This chapter looks at a case of teacher decision-making and how it is influenced by politics and policy. The case is embedded in early literacy teaching and contrasts policy approaches that empower the teacher to make strong links between theory and practice, and those which disempower the teacher, creating a less coherent approach to teaching negatively influenced by prevailing policy decisions. This chapter argues for teacher autonomy in raising standards of attainment. It suggests that professional autonomy is underpinned by both effective initial teacher preparation and continuing professional learning that include explicit discussion of interactions between student,[1] syllabus, curriculum and policy.

Ben had been in school for one year and enjoyed listening to high-quality children's stories read aloud by his teacher. He shared books at home and knew how to hold a book and turn pages. Ben enjoyed reading simple caption books and understood that the few changes on every page were highly supported by the illustrations. Sometimes he enjoyed making up parts of the story when reading books that were, as yet, too hard for him. Ben had learned to recognise many letters and relate them to the sounds he heard. He sometimes used these letters to help him read. He considered himself a reader.

Ben's previous class teacher had passed on assessment records which indicated knowledge of some letters and sounds. However, it was clear to his new teacher that Ben was not making the same progress during the first few weeks in his new class as the other five- and six-year-olds. Ben's new class teacher observed him during the daily phonics sessions. Ben joined in and was able to orally separate words into their constituent sounds – '/c/a/t/ – cat'. He tried to use his knowledge of letters and sounds to read books but became frustrated when sounding out didn't help him access the stories he loved so much. Ben was now struggling to read the words in the simple books he was being presented with during reading lessons and his previous enjoyment of books was being negatively affected. He tried to use the strategy of 'calling sounds' modelled by his teacher when reading but could not make sense of what he was saying, so stopped. She did not consider him a reader.

Approaches available for a teacher to help Ben and investigate his poor progress differ across educational contexts internationally (Tan, 2012). In some policy contexts (Schleicher, 2012), a teacher is enabled to engage in a comprehensive assessment process to identify a student's strengths and weaknesses. How governments view teachers and teaching shapes policy, directly affecting the education students receive and the ways that teachers are able to teach. Policy determines how much leeway the teacher has for decision-making. In some policy contexts, teachers are enabled to engage in a comprehensive assessment process to identify a child's strengths and weaknesses. They are supported by policy that demonstrates trust in professional decision-making (Schleicher, 2012). Curricula descriptions provide evidence that those governments understand that learning and teaching are complex, and that teachers need to continue to receive professional learning opportunities throughout their professional lives. In some contexts, professional learning prepares teachers to respond to students' slow progress and consider their needs, drawing on robust and meaningful evidence to design suitable learning programmes. In other contexts, teachers are told how to respond through professional learning about how to enact highly prescribed curricula. In such contexts, policy prescribes teaching content, style of teaching and teaching sequence. Teachers are instructed to ignore the context of learning, what is already known, what has been taught before and how the student learns effectively. There is little room for autonomous professional decision-making based on expertise, professional knowledge and assessment of the individual. The teacher is reduced to delivering content rather than developing effective pedagogies to respond to individual students' needs. The nature of policy, we suggest, communicates to the teacher how much she is trusted to respond appropriately and how government and society in general understands teaching and learning.

So what happened next for Ben? How did the current prescriptive policy of teaching reading through a strict sequence of phonics support the teacher and provide guidance? Current policy prescribes that the first steps of teaching should focus solely on learning letter–sound correspondences and applying this phonic knowledge to the reading process. Therefore, Ben's teacher consulted his records of phonic knowledge and reassessed him. He appeared to have learned just, and only, what had been taught. Ben's teacher was at a loss as to what to do next; she had followed the step-by-step policy of phonics teaching but Ben was not learning at the same rate or in the same way as most of the other students. Ben's teacher was not able to provide instruction that developed the book-handling and language skills that he had in place. She had to focus on the aspects that he found most difficult before using interesting stories and information books written in language structures that Ben was familiar with. Despite continued letter–sound instruction in class and extra catch-up sessions on phonics with the teaching assistant, Ben fell further behind his peers. He became confused, resentful of teacher attention and put a lot of energy into avoiding reading and writing activities. These and similar experiences led Ben's teacher to believe that attainment in reading is solely about success in phonics instruction and that those students not able to learn in this way are somehow lacking or 'slower' than others.

Unfortunately, this situation is not unique. Ben's teacher did not want him to fail. She wanted to help unravel his confusions and avoid the ensuing negativity. She had faithfully followed the national and school policy on phonics instruction and it had worked for the majority of students. She wondered about adopting an approach centred on Ben's knowledge and understanding but was concerned how such an approach would 'fit' within the prescriptive current government policy. Her adherence to national policy was carefully monitored by middle and senior management at the school. She was aware that, during school inspections, there would be scrutiny of her teaching in relation to national policy and that student data would be used as a way of monitoring her teaching of reading. She was not enabled to take a fresh approach and her understanding of her role did not support her conviction that as the teacher she had the power, or agency, to act as she felt suited the needs of the student. She recognised that the teaching indicated by policy was not helping empower a young reader, but she felt powerless to search for alternative responses. She was unsure of the level of autonomy allowed in making changes to pedagogy within the particular education policy context. Her teacher's pay was linked to her performance management targets, which focused partially on the attainment of the students in her class. Attainment in this age group of students was measured primarily by phonic knowledge. The school's policy followed the national curriculum on the primacy of phonics teaching but Ben's learning needs presented a challenge to the prevailing pedagogy determined by policy, so it was considered he had less of a capacity to learn effectively than his peers.

The example that started this chapter, and the analysis of teacher response, indicate clear tensions between what the teacher felt was needed to support literacy learning and a government policy on literacy instruction. In the remainder of this chapter we explore ways of theorising and understanding these tensions and suggest ways that professional learning can help overcome feelings of helplessness and re-engage teachers with decision-making founded on knowledge, skills and assessment evidence.

Key questions for reflection

In what ways is policy supportive of individual students' literacy learning?
    In what ways could teachers fulfil policy requirements yet still control pedagogy to meet the needs of individual students in their class?

The international drive for standards

The challenges faced by Ben and his teacher will be recognisable by teachers in many contexts. Educational policy internationally appears to be becoming more specific and prescriptive (Schleicher, 2012). Do those prescriptions represent positive moves forward for the teaching profession? Do they support teachers to develop a view of themselves as autonomous decision-makers? The move to prescriptions about curricula and pedagogy was an international response to improving standards and removing the stress of teacher decision-making through the creation of universal curricula (Schleicher, 2012). But have such policies back-fired? We explore shifts in policy throughout the latter part of the twentieth century into the twenty-first century that have influenced teacher professional learning and autonomy.

The latter part of the twentieth century saw political interest in education focus particularly on the achievement of universal literacy and numeracy (Fullan *et al.*, 2001; OECD, 2010). Technology began to be used to generate large amounts of student data and paved the way for assessment of narrow aspects of curricula. These large data sets led to the development of international league tables against which individual nations could be compared. In turn, there was a heightened interest in the kinds of curricula and the methods of teaching that might lead to improvements in the international rankings of particular countries in the Programme for International Student Assessment (PISA) (OECD, 2010).

In relation to literacy skills, this interest focused on the methods used in learning to read, reported in the Progress in International Reading Literacy Study (PIRLS) (Twist *et al.*, 2012). The focus of both of these studies is evaluation and measurement, looking at test scores, rather than how students learn, to make comparisons between attainment within and across education systems.

With the advent of international league tables in addition to national results, governments endeavour to create policies that aspire to achieve high outcomes for all students. This and similar foci on systemic strategies that enhance students' learning is both a moral and societal goal. However, not all systematic strategies will work in the same way; some weaken professional autonomy. For instance, Ben's teacher rigorously followed the advice of English policy about the teaching of reading and seemed to have neither the professional knowledge nor the opportunity to consider more appropriate ways to approach Ben's learning difficulties. The effect of lack of professional autonomy can be identified in policies that aim to improve educational standards through control: telling teachers what to teach, when to teach it, and how to teach it. Policies which try to ensure quality through control turns teachers from 'autonomous professionals into ... technicians' (Gray, 2006, p. 30). Ben's teacher is a product of such an approach; she has been offered one methodology and when it fails she has no other way of understanding and responding to Ben's difficulty. She can only repeat the same teaching approach, either at a slower pace or reducing the numbers in a teaching group led by a teaching assistant, or both.

When understandings of what teaching entails are reduced to lists of standards and checklists that can be easily identified, monitored and measured, the subtlety and nuance that teaching requires can be devalued and neglected (Tan, 2012). A top-down approach to monitoring teacher standards is now common in many nations. It has been interpreted as having more to do with control and conformity than raising the quality of teaching and learning (Evans, 2011). The way teachers teach, their view of themselves as teachers and their expectations of students are the result of the ways that policy represents their professional skills, the content and curricula and the way in which learning for teachers is valued.

The use of top-down control and increased surveillance in performance and accountability are evident in the standards for teachers in England. Other factors contribute to feelings of professional insecurity and lack of value. There is competition for their role from a growing workforce of teaching assistants and other para-professionals. This is accompanied by increased marketization, with a commercial approach to education concurrent with reductions in funding. A failing respect or recognition for the professional knowledge of teachers is also reflected in the media, which often perpetuates the government view that teachers are solely and directly responsible for standards. This, in combination with the other policy features above, undermines teachers' perceived and actual autonomy even further.

We do not wish to suggest that policy designed to raise standards is in essence a bad thing. System improvement and consequent improvement in student outcomes is an admirable goal which we do not dispute. However, we will argue that achieving positive outcomes is driven by developments in pedagogy not through accountability measures. In analysing the approaches typically chosen by leaders in countries such as Australia and the USA, Fullan (2011) considers policy features that do and do not support 'the moral imperative of raising the bar (for all students) and closing the gap (for lower performing groups) relative to higher order skills and competencies required to be successful world citizens' (2011, p. 3). He concludes that the key to successful reform is to capture the energy of educators and students as the driving force. He suggests that the energy comes from 'doing something well that is important to you' and 'makes a contribution to others as well as society as a whole' (Fullan, 2011, p. 3). We interpret this conclusion as an indication that successful reform requires teachers to understand the interactive relationship between their practice in the classroom, the theories surrounding those practices and the moral purpose of the need to ensure student progress, as they reflect on their practice. This understanding is called praxis (Kemmis and Smith, 2008). One way to ensure that teachers develop a praxis stance is to make it a key focus of professional learning: the collection of activities, training and critical reflection that teachers do, to make sure that they are always working for improved student outcomes.

Professional learning opportunities focusing on praxis, may involve:

- teachers working collaboratively on problem-solving activities to find solutions and discover causal connections between their instruction and student outcomes (Gallimore et al., 2009);
- opportunities to share goals for particular student groups and plan collaboratively with colleagues;
- observing colleagues teaching with a focus on specific students or learning goals such as lesson study;
- training on particular approaches;
- professional development focused on student improvement and built on theory and evidence.

It provides many opportunities for teachers to talk about why we do what we do; define what must be done to achieve our purposes and goals; creates clearly understood ways and practices of 'being a teacher'; and identifies goals for that practice. This concept of professional learning is in sharp contrast to the top-down approaches focused on teacher control discussed earlier in the chapter. It is effective because it builds competence, capacity, culture, expectation and action in combination.

Capacity building, collaboration, pedagogy and coherence of all aspects of the 'system' are effective in improving attainment 'because they work directly on changing the culture of schools systems' (Fullan, 2011, p. 5). In Fullan's view, accountability on the basis of test results is less effective, relying on individual teacher quality rather than collaboration, expecting technology alone to raise standards and using fragmented rather than systemic approaches. Such 'drivers' should not be used to lead change since they merely change structures and procedures of the system, 'and that is why they fail' (Fullan, 2011, p. 5). However, they are attractive to governments since they may bring about short-term, observable shifts which indicate that policy is being enacted by teachers. This may serve to protect the reputations of ministers 'by having new programmes to announce which can demonstrate that they are driving forward the process of reform' (Moss, 2009, p. 166). National testing of students and measurement of teacher quality are by-products of government attempts to establish the success of their policies and seek 'evidence' that their policy is succeeding or that further change is needed. When policy contexts seem to invest less in teacher decision-making, and privilege accountability, there is a consequent risk not only to professionalism, but also to student outcomes.

The ways of working that Fullan describes as effective for improvement imply the need for particular kinds of professional learning. A focus on the 'wrong drivers' can lead to the adoption of linear approaches to professional learning, and to prescribed curricula, as experienced by Ben's teacher. She was powerless to think for herself and act accordingly – she was denied the right to develop 'agency'. Reforms adopting a linear approach of spreading and demanding particular teaching approaches can give rise to a limited capacity for teacher agency where a teacher's role is to faithfully replicate a chosen approach (Coburn and Stein, 2010). On the one hand, there is programme and policy, based on what is seen to work for most students and, on the other hand, the teacher is confronted by the evidence of observation of how the approach plays out in the classroom with individual students. Returning to the example of Ben and his teacher, we can see a clear dissonance between policy assumptions of 'what works' and the reality of what works for individuals. The focus on one method of interpreting and responding to a student's needs caused a negative impact on the range of skills Ben's teacher was able to use to help him. This is a clear example of how teachers have been prepared professionally to follow a narrow and prescribed curriculum but have had only limited preparation for, and even less perceived choice about, alternative pedagogies and practices and how to adapt them to meet the needs of all students. Next, we consider the particular case of English education reform.

The case of educational reform in England

Curriculum development and teacher professional development in England focuses on aspects of learning that can be easily measured. For example, in 1993, as part of a national curriculum, the national literacy and numeracy strategies were developed. The strategies were based on large-scale cascade models of professional development and learning, linked to teaching practices with the goal of raising attainment in literacy and numeracy. Nationally provided opportunities for professional development became inextricably linked to what could be measured through student outcomes and increased teacher accountability. It also became linked to school inspection processes and an expanded inspection system was introduced, heightening the role of accountability using both student outcomes and teacher performance to evaluate and compare schools through league tables and linking teachers' pay to student performance.

Over time, education in England moved from a service ethic to a performance ethic (Barnett, 2008). A drive to shape teacher agency through government reform has led to a 'demanded' professionalism, focusing predominantly on teachers' behaviours rather than their dispositions or how they think about pedagogy (Evans, 2011). A statutory system of 'performance management' was introduced in 2007, along with published 'professional standards' (Training and Development Agency, 2007). The updated standards (Department for Education, 2012a) are a simplified version with a single set of standards which applies to all teachers. These standards conceptualise teachers' pedagogy as relating to subject or curriculum knowledge (Department for Education, 2012a). The White Paper, *The Importance of Teaching* (Department for Education, 2010), indicated the Conservative–Liberal Democrat government's intentions for teacher professionalism with a narrowing of the standards, leaving a remaining structure and a goal of using these to identify and deal with unsatisfactory performance. The thrust of the proposals in the White Paper represents a particular philosophy which implies control of the teacher, rather than facilitating teachers' decision-making (Evans, 2011). Further politicisation of teacher training is evident in the suggestion from government that the standards will not be mandatory for any schools which choose to move to academy[2] status. This has potential to further weaken the collective professional status of teachers and reduce the agency they have to be decision-makers.

Teacher agency

Teacher agency is shaped by the interaction between teachers' own learning and experience with the wider context of policy and accountability. Teachers' learning includes their own experiences as students; their initial and continuing professional learning as teachers; their knowledge and understanding of the classroom contexts; and their observation of the needs and responses of students, which builds up a case knowledge over time. Factors relating to the wider context include government policies on teaching and learning and on teacher education; accountability processes such as testing and inspection; national and local priorities frequently changing and not always being congruent with the learning trajectories of teachers.

How a teacher thinks about their own professional learning and knowledge is an important aspect of their professional agency (Opfer *et al.*, 2011). The teacher we aspire to be has an impact on the development of our own and others' perceptions of us as a teacher (Day *et al.*, 2006). The ways in which teacher agency is understood and experienced may impact on our decision-making processes (Beijaard *et al.*, 2004). Informed professional autonomy such as this is the backdrop of this chapter. In our example, Ben's teacher lacked professional agency and, therefore, the ability and autonomy to make decisions about Ben's next steps and support him to become a reader. Her perception of herself as a teacher reflects this inability to make pedagogic decisions in the classroom that differ from current policy and is consequently a threat to her agency.

Teacher agency can be self-initiated or demanded by others, be planned or incidental, be in an individual or social context. The ways in which teacher learning is developed may result in an increase or decrease in teacher agency and therefore in decision-making. The extent to which teacher learning develops and maintains agency, depends on a range of factors. Teachers learn to interpret and reflect on what occurs in student learning from a standpoint of continuous development of professional knowledge, 'having high standards and (a) strong drive to learn … and to be responsive to students' needs' (Tan, 2012, p. 7). How and what teachers learn from their own experience of practice and from observing the practice of others can be underestimated (Gallimore *et al.*, 2009).

Professional knowledge

According to Eraut (1994), knowledge can be categorised into four main kinds: replicative, applicative, associative and interpretive. Table 12.1 outlines these four categories with an illustrative example of Ben and his teacher.

Replicative and applicative knowledge are the most prevalent forms of knowledge construction teachers experience in professional learning programmes within policy-driven curicula. Teachers are conceived as 'corporate agents, grasping and executing the organisation's mission' (Newman and Clarke, 2009, p. 82) rather than agentic decision-making

Table 12.1 Categories of knowledge

Category	Features	Application	Implications for Ben and his teacher
Replicative	Positions teacher as scholar with more knowledge than student	Imparted didactically. Used in similar contexts/ conditions. Relates to specific knowledge of topic. Taught to particular age phase. No reflection	Ben's teacher followed prescriptive guidance from policy-makers
Applicative	Application of knowledge to new contexts	Some adaptation and differentiation for age phases or ability groups	Ben's teacher knew the phases in phonic instruction, had assessed Ben and identified which phase he was working within. She knew which sounds Ben had learned and applied this knowledge to her instruction for him
Interpretive	Implies knowledge generated at the point of practice	Allows for teacher agency. Links with Schön's (1991) reflection-in-action leading to decisions about possible next learning steps for the student	Ben's teacher needed an explanation for why he was not learning how to read despite his his letter–sound knowledge. She was beginning to reflect on her practice and on Ben's learning
Associative	Draws not only on knowledge of pedagogy and subject, but also intuitive elements of reflection	Role of reflection prior to, during and after practice. It is knowledge *in* action, knowledge *on* action and knowledge *for* action that leads to professional agency	Ben's teacher had not yet taken the next step in turning that reflection into action and did not feel she had the agency for rethinking a pedagogy that would support Ben's learning to read

professionals (Billett, 2008). Any sense of agency under such circumstances seems to be conceptualised as externally awarded to teachers and limited to the level of choice about programmes and materials rather than methods.

Currently, there is world-wide interest in the Finnish education system as both politicians and educators look for successful models (Niemi, 2012). Despite contextual differences, what should not be ignored is the investment in teacher development in Finland: teachers have a seven-year course of study, having to attain a Master's degree to be accredited, and are respected decision-makers with autonomy to adapt a loose national curriculum to suit the local needs of their students (Niemi, 2012). They have time and dedicated spaces in the school environment to collaborate with colleagues and also have access to continuing professional learning classes throughout their careers. This style and concept of teacher learning appears to align more with the professional learning associated with a professional agency that is fundamental to the success of students like Ben. It resonates with Fullan's description of the 'right drivers' for educational improvement – working directly on changing values, norms, skill, practices and relationships (Fullan, 2011, p. 5). This professional agency arises through particular types of teacher learning. In the next section we consider two types: linear and conceptual.

Key questions for reflection

How does the drive for standards – for instance, through national testing and inspection – affect how you develop pedagogy in your classroom?
What opportunities do you feel you have for autonomy?
How does your view and application of knowledge fit with Eraut's categories?

Models of professional learning

Earlier in the chapter we introduced the notion of a linear approach to professional learning (Coburn and Stein, 2010). Linear approaches to teacher learning may or may not be informed by research and frequently go through a development stage before being rolled out to a wider context. The goal of linear approaches is to rapidly change teachers' behaviours to align them with current policy – practical tools such as schemes of work and lesson plans are sometimes foregrounded to rapidly alter classroom practice as a means of shifting teachers' thinking (Coburn and Stein, 2010).

In England, the policy at the time of writing on the teaching of early reading represents a linear approach to teacher professional learning. By privileging one component skill – synthetic phonics, taught systematically (SSP[3]) – materials for teachers, from a range of commercial providers, have been confined to sequences of described and prescribed content. All providers of phonics phase teaching materials, nevertheless, have to be in alignment with government policy and need to ensure that the teaching sequence and phases conform. As the prescribed teaching materials merely give a sequence and a practice to be followed, the underlying theories and research on teaching reading are not accessible for teachers to draw into their pedagogical decision-making. Therefore, the complexity of reading theory is largely hidden from teachers. The linear professional learning in SSP has emphasised replicative and applicative types of knowledge described above and is closer to a 'training' model, with outcome measures based on the number of teachers adopting the approach (Coburn and Stein, 2010). The adoption of SSP has been evaluated by monitoring the numbers of schools which have responded to an offer of matched funding to purchase government-approved phonics resources (Department for Education, 2012b). This approach demonstrates an assumption that materials can change practice and that the teacher's role is to replicate and apply knowledge. Replicative and applicative types of knowledge which teachers can learn in linear professional learning approaches are not sufficient to equip them for decision-making as described in the example of Ben's teacher above. Opfer *et al.* (2011) found that supporting teacher agency through professional learning opportunities was not a sequential process and that 'assuming that belief change leads to practice change or that practice change leads to belief change may not be helpful in understanding the complex processes at work' (2011, p. 143). Teacher learning was found to be a complex interaction between changes in belief, changes in practice and changes in students, which depended significantly on teachers' orientation to learning. Developing interpretive and associative knowledge (Eraut, 1994) is critical to achieving the goal of developing generative learning processes (Taylor and Bodman, 2012) which extend beyond the time-frame of professional learning sessions.

Failure to improve student outcomes in linear models is often attributed to a lack of correct application of the programme mandated by policy (Coburn and Stein, 2010).

Student outcomes are an accountability tool in the SSP policy and so we can perhaps understand the dilemma of Ben's teacher. She is accountable for the progress of all the students in her class, yet, despite following this linear approach and the government policy on SSP teaching, Ben was not meeting expected outcomes. Standard assessment tasks in reading for seven-year-old students in England offer one measure demonstrating no improvement of student outcomes indicating falling standards which in turn can trigger inspection as discussed above.

Through examples of policy in England we have demonstrated how a linear model of professional learning casts teachers as conduits for policy decisions rather than developing their professional agency and allowing them to act as professionals in the fullest sense. The flexibility with which teachers are able to interpret curriculum is diminished by narrowing the scope of teacher professional learning programmes and linking them to accountability measures (Richards, 2012). This can result in an imbalance since the policy, which by its nature is a general one, is not intended to be reinterpreted at the level of the classroom. Policy which demands a particular approach to teaching reading focuses on behavioural aspects of the role: what teachers will do and be seen to be doing when monitored. It fails to take into account two other key aspects: first, teachers' orientations (for example, beliefs, perceptions, views held, self-perception, values, motivation, job satisfaction and morale) and, second, the intellectual component of professionalism (knowledge bases, the amount and degree of reasoning applied to practice, analytic skills and what they understand) (Evans, 2011).

There is an alternative to a top-down linear approach to reform: conceptual approaches to teacher professional learning can offer greater potential in developing teacher agency.

New visions

Effective contexts for conceptual approaches to teacher professional learning create interactive spaces where teachers can collaboratively draw on theory and practice and develop reflective dispositions driven by observation of their students. This interaction takes into account the learning that practitioners do as they enact practices and is focused on shifting teachers' cognitions and increasing their knowledge, enabling them to make responsive, practical decisions day-by-day (Coburn and Stein, 2010). This kind of professional learning may have enabled Ben's teacher to make moment-by-moment decisions based on her knowledge of his progress. A conceptual approach foregrounds the professional capacity of teachers and promotes a positive professional self-perception as a teacher as well as teacher agency.

Taylor and Bodman (2012) observed the positive impact on student learning that occurs when teachers become self-teaching learners through extended periods of related professional learning opportunities. Hattie (2009) also indicated efficacy of professional learning models which occurred over an extended period of time but which were led by external experts rather than by in-school initiatives and aimed to deepen teacher knowledge and extend skills, thereby positively impacting student outcomes. Importantly, professional learning programmes needed to challenge teachers' prevailing discourse and conceptions through dialogue with colleagues grounded in student learning (Hattie, 2009).

An example of professional learning that follows a conceptual approach is the initial and ongoing professional learning opportunites built into the literacy intervention, Reading Recovery. Students who have made little or no progress in reading and writing catch up with their peers (Burroughs-Lange and Ince, 2013; Department for Education, 2011;

Douëtil, 2011). Teachers, through extended professional learning opprotunities, are empowered to draw on moment-by-moment observations of the learning interactions with students. Opportunities to discuss and critically reflect upon personal and observed practice, linking theory and practice in continual cycles, are built into all instances of professional learning. Learning opportunities are ongoing over extended periods of time and facilitated by 'experts' (Taylor *et al.*, 2013). From these observations of pupils, teachers construct hypotheses about the pupil's learning, using assessment knowledge together with newly learned theories of literacy learning to determine the next steps for that particular student. Teachers learn to critically reflect and to act on their reflections to make informed decisions thereby increasing teacher autonomy. This is a clear example of a professional learning design which develops and maintains agency as one of its core purposes.

A key factor in the success of Reading Recovery pupil outcomes is its approach to professional learning for teachers (Department for Education, 2011). It represents an investment in the planned development and maintenance of teacher agency by recognising that high-quality decision-making is dependent on teachers' knowledge and their ability to critically reflect on the application of that knowledge. This tenet links to the previously discussed applicative and associative areas of professional knowledge. A key practical feature is the use of a one-way screen behind which a member of the teacher learning group teaches a student. Together the group describes, theorises and then critically reflects in real-time dialogue to provide supportive and constructive feedback for their colleague and to draw out new insights for the group that will help their decision-making processes with struggling literacy learners. The leader of the learning coaches the group to become 'more flexible and tentative, to observe constantly and alter their assumptions in line with what they record as children work. They need to challenge their own thinking continually' (Clay, 2009, p. 237). One-to-one coaching also takes place in each teacher's own school context. In this example, professional learning has several design elements that seem to work together to promote professional agency: building and applying theory based on practice and close observation of that practice; discussion grounded in teachers' work with learners; and sustained and ongoing learning.

A distinctive feature of professional learning in Reading Recovery is that theoretical understandings are considered core to pedagogical decision-making underpinning the intervention practices. This theoretical base is articulated for teachers in a series of core texts. These are not handbooks or schemes of work, but are used as a reflective tool during professional learning sessions and as reflection on teaching in teachers' own contexts. This is unusual among guidance and publications for professional learning activity, particularly for the teaching of literacy skills among low-attaining groups. Such materials are often confined to sequences of described and prescribed content (Wasik and Slavin, 1993). This building and applying theory is fundamental to a sense of professional agency being forged by such professional learning practices.

Ben might benefit from literacy instruction with a teacher who can reflect on observations not only of his progress of phonic knowledge, but also on his other reading behaviours. Ben's teacher would praise what he does correctly and model how to apply that knowledge or partial knowledge to problem-solving ways of reading new words to make sense of the 'story'. She would observe and reflect on how Ben approaches his reading with his newly acquired reading strategies and would support him making his own decisions and problem-solving. She would be able to incorporate national policy with informed teaching decisions based on what she knows of Ben and his needs.

Teachers working in Reading Recovery are asked to reflect on the ways that working with individual students has taught them something about learning more generally. They are referring to the opportunities for critical reflection on practice. Their daily teaching of students provides opportunities for newly acquired theories of teaching and learning to be tested and reformulated (Pinnell, 1997), thereby allowing teachers the opportunity for an agentic role. So Ben's teacher would learn not only how to support him, but also, more generally, how to support other learners, and be empowered to make decisions about all her students' learning. The model of professional learning espoused above has been described as 'enquiry-based', with teaching and learning interwoven through a 'reflective/ analytic experience' (Pinnell, 1997, p. 9). Teachers bring their experiences of working with students to professional learning sessions and engage in collaborative dialogue about challenges they have encountered in their teaching. Each teacher sees the situation through a different lens, triggering a reflective loop 'around theory, practice and observation, with critical reflection operating at its hub' (Taylor *et al.*, 2013, p. 98). It is important to note here that Reading Recovery operates internationally and works successfully in all policy contexts, including those such as England, where the curriculum is prescribed.

Teacher professional learning is never seen to be complete in an enquiry-based professional development context. Knowledge generated at the intersection between technical procedures and the point of practice provides a demonstration of praxis during which teachers adapt and restructure learning opportunities in ways that might best meet the needs of the students. Within this process, existing professional knowledge is used to develop both reformulated knowledge and new practice as it is occurring. Therefore, it would seem to involve reflection-in-action (Schön, 1991). Designing professional learning opportunities such as these described here draws on not only knowledge of pedagogy and subject, but also intuitive elements of reflection. This view of professional knowledge suggests a dynamism, incorporating replicative and applicative knowledge and prior experience as well as the seminal role of critical reflection as fundamental to the development of professional knowledge: reflection prior to, during and after practice (Schön, 1991).

The model of professional learning we use and advocate represents the transformation of learning opportunities from passive receipt of policy information to one of repeated and upward spiralling of information to support and 'power' the learning process (Carless, 2007). Additionally, the model confronts the importance of attitudinal change, vital to developing and maintaining a professional identity of teacher as powerful decision-maker: knowing not only how to act, but also why, able to rationalise and evidence their decision-making using a theoretical framework for action. To neglect the full extent of what is needed for change is to risk widespread misunderstanding of failure of any given top-down policy (Fullan *et al.*, 2001).

Conclusions

Teacher professional agency and decision-making is in conflict in many international settings such as Korea, Poland and Slovenia (OECD, 2009), caught between a linear model of professional learning with growing accountability and a lack of agency to affect how political policy reforms are played out at the point of learning. Competition rather than collaboration creates a negative climate, with unrealistic claims that all teachers should be outstanding, and the public perception of teachers' competency developed through the media creates a further lever for teacher competency to be used as a political tool. If decision-making lies at the policy level rather than the classroom level, teachers may feel less, not more, responsible for outcomes. They have neither autonomy nor responsibility. Teachers should 'conceive of themselves as "agents of change", rather than "victims of change"' (Whitty, 2008, p. 45). Teachers need to be able to develop as 'imaginative professional(s)' who can make 'creative and articulate responses rather than respond with feelings of hopelessness' (Power, 2008, p. 157).

We argue that the pathway to teachers reclaiming trust and respect and a capacity for developing and using professional knowledge is possible through coherent approaches to continuing professional learning. Longer-term and conceptual models of professional learning which aim to build teachers' interpretive and associative knowledge and privilege a conceptual rather than a linear approach can equip teachers with a well-informed praxis. This in turn enables greater agency and creativity on the part of the teacher and more effective learning outcomes for all students. Rather than acting as a performative robot, enacting policy, the teacher becomes an 'alchemist', planning and leading learning experiences creatively, flexibly and responsibly and able to do so through informed autonomy. If Ben's teacher and others like her felt this level of autonomy and teacher agency, then maybe Ben would become a successful reader as his teacher felt empowered to make decisions based on her observations of Ben's reading behaviours.

Notes

1 In this chapter, we use the term 'student' to mean: child, children, student or pupil and young learners, to make the chapter accessible to all contexts.
2 Academies are publicly funded independent schools where the governing body has greater autonomy.
3 Synthetic phonics teaches the phonemes (sounds) associated with the graphemes (letters). The sounds are taught in isolation then blended together (i.e. synthesised), throughout the word.

Further reading

Burroughs-Lange, S. G. and Ince, A. (eds) (2013). *Every Child a Reader: History, Politics and Practice*. London: Institute of Education.
By providing a comprehensive description and critique of how Every Child a Reader was operationalised in England, this book provides a recent case context of autonomy and decision-making agency within a prescriptive policy system.

Lyons, C. A. and Pinnell, G. S. (2001). *Systems for Change in Literacy Education: A Guide to Professional Development*. Portsmouth, NH: Heinemann.
This book offers theories, designs, guidelines, examples and materials needed to bring about school-wide, long-lasting change.

Opfer, D. V., Pedder, D. G. and Lavicza, Z. (2011). The Role of Teachers' Orientation to Learning in Professional Development and Change: A National Study of Teachers in England. *Teaching and Teacher Education*. 27. 443–53.
This article proposes a model of teachers' orientation to professional learning consisting of beliefs, practice and experience and how these impact change in practice.

Tan, O.-S. (2012). *Teacher Education Frontiers: International Perspectives on Policy and Practice for Building New Teacher Competencies*. Singapore: Cengage Learning Asia.
This edited book looks at international perspectives on teacher education and professional learning.

References

Barnett, R. (2008). Critical Professionalism in an Age of Supercomplexity. In B. Cunningham (ed.), *Exploring Professionalism*. London: Institute of Education, Bedford Way Papers. 190–207.

Beijaard, D., Meijer, P. C. and Verloop, N. (2004). Reconsidering Research on Teachers' Professional Identity. *Teaching and Teacher Education*. 20. 107–28.

Billett, S. (2008). Emerging Perspectives on Workplace Learning. In S. Billet, C. Harteis and A. Etelapelto (eds), *Emerging Perspectives of Workplace Learning*. Rotterdam: Sense. 2–15.

Burroughs-Lange, S. G. and Ince, A. (eds) (2013). *Every Child a Reader: History, Politics and Practice*. London: Institute of Education.

Carless, D. R. (2007). Learning-oriented Assessment: Conceptual Bases and Practical Implications. *Innovations in Education and Teaching International*. 44 (1). 57–66.

Clay, M. M. (2009). Implementing Reading Recovery Internationally. In B. Watson and B. Askew (eds), *Boundless Horizons: Marie Clay's Search for the Possible in Children's Literacy*. Rosedale, North Shore, NZ: Pearson Education. 221–49.

Coburn, C. E. and Stein, M. K. (2010). Key Lessons About the Relationship Between Research and Practice. In C. E. Coburn and M. K. Stein (eds), *Research and Practice in Education: Building Alliances, Bridging the Divide*. Lanham, MD: Rowman & Littlefield. 201–26.

Day, C., Kington, A., Stobart, G. and Sammons, P. (2006). The Personal and Professional Selves of Teachers: Stable and Unstable Identities. *British Educational Research Journal*. 32 (4). 601–16.

Department for Education (DFE) (2010). *The Importance of Teaching: The Schools White Paper*. London: Stationery Office.

Department for Education (2011). *Evaluation of Every Child a Reader (ECaR)* London: DfE.

Department for Education (2012a). The Teachers' Standards. Available at: https://www.gov.uk/government/publications/teachers-standards. Last accessed 12 October 2012.

Department for Education (2012b). Match Funding for Systematic, Synthetic Phonics Products and Training. Available at: http://www.education.gov.uk/schools/teachingandlearning/pedagogy/phonics/a00191791/match-funding-for-systematic-synthetic-phonics-products-and-training. Last accessed 12 October 2012.

Department for Education (2012c). Phonics Screening Check Materials. Available at: http://www.education.gov.uk/schools/teachingandlearning/assessment/keystage1/a00200415/phonics-screening-check-materials. Last accessed 10 October 2012.

Douëtil, J. (2011). *Reading Recovery™ annual report for UK and Ireland 2010–11*. London: European Centre for Reading Recovery. Available at: http://readingrecovery.ioe.ac.uk/reports/. Last accessed 13 January 2012.

Eraut, M. (1994). *Developing Professional Knowledge and Competence*. London: Falmer Press.

Evans, L. (2011). The Shape of Teacher Professionalism in England: Professional Standards, Performance Management, Professional Development and the Changes Proposed in the 2010 White Paper. *British Education Research Journal*. 37 (5). 851–70.

Fullan, M. (2011). *Choosing the Wrong Drivers for Whole School System Reform*. Centre for Strategic Education. Seminar Series Paper No. 204. April.

Fullan, M., Rolheiser, C., Mascall, B. and Edge, K. (2001). Accomplishing Large Scale Reform: A Tri-Level Proposition. Prepared for *Journal of Educational Change*, November.

Gallimore, R., Ermeling, B. A., Saunders, W. M. and Goldenberg, C. (2009). Moving the Teaching of Learning Closer to Practice: Teacher Education, Implications of School Based Enquiry Teams. *The Elementary School Journal*. 109 (5). 537–53.

Gray, S. L. (2006). What Does it Mean to Be a Teacher? Three Tensions within Contemporary Teacher Professionalism Examined in Terms of Government Policy and the Knowledge Economy. *FORUM*. 48 (3). 305–16.

Hattie, J. (2009). *Visible Learning: A Synthesis of Over 800 Meta-analyses Relating to Achievement*. London: Routledge.

Kemmis, S. and Smith, T. J. (eds) (2008). *Enabling Praxis: Challenges for Education*. Rotterdam: Sense.

Lyons, C. A. and Pinnell, G. S. (2001). *Systems for Change in Literacy Education: A Guide to Professional Development*. Portsmouth, NH: Heinemann.

Moss, G. (2009). The Politics of Literacy in the Context of Large-scale Education Reform. *Research Papers in Education*. 24 (2). 155–74.

Newman, J. and Clarke, J. (2009). *Publics, Politics and Power, Remaking the Public in Public Services*. London: Sage.

Niemi, H. (2012). Teacher Education for High Quality Professionals: An Analysis from the Finnish Perspective. In O.-S. Tan, *Teacher Education Frontiers: International Perspectives on Policy and Practice for Building New Teacher Competencies*. Singapore: Cengage Learning Asia. 43–69.

OECD (2009). *Creating Effective Teaching and Learning Environments: First Results from TALIS*. Executive Summary. OECD. Available at: www.oecd.org/publishing. Last accessed 29 April 2014.

OECD (2010). *Programme for International Student Assessment 2009 Rankings*. Paris: OECD.

Opfer, D. V., Pedder, D. G. and Lavicza, Z. (2011). The Role of Teachers' Orientation to Learning in Professional Development and Change: A National Study of Teachers in England. *Teaching and Teacher Education*. 27. 443–53.

Pinnell, G. S. (1997). An Inquiry-based Model for Educating Teachers of Literacy. In S. L. Swartz and A. F. Klein (eds), *Research in Reading Recovery*. Portsmouth, NH: Heinemann. 6–17.

Power, S. (2008). The Imaginative Professional. In B. Cunningham (ed.), *Exploring Professionalism*. London: Institute of Education, Bedford Way Papers. 144–60.

Richards, C. (2012). Where to Begin. *Education*. 470. 5–6.

Sachs, J. (2001). Teacher Professional Identity: Competing Discourses, Competing Outcomes. *Journal of Educational Policy*. 16 (2). 149–61.

Schleicher, A. (2012). The Case for 21st Century Teacher Policies. In O.-S. Tan, *Teacher Education Frontiers: International Perspectives on Policy and Practice for Building New Teacher Competencies*. Singapore: Cengage Learning Asia. 21–41.

Schön, D. A. (1991). *The Reflective Practitioner: How Professionals Think In Action*. Aldershot: Ashgate.

Tan, O.-S. (2012). Teacher Education Frontiers: 21st Century Challenges in Teacher Education and Overview. In O.-S. Tan, *Teacher Education Frontiers: International Perspectives on Policy and Practice for Building New Teacher Competencies*. Singapore: Cengage Learning Asia. 1–19.

Taylor, S. and Bodman, S. (2012). 'I've Never Been Asked That Before!' Preparing Teachers for Any Eventuality? In O.-S. Tan, *Teacher Education Frontiers: International Perspectives on Policy and Practice for Building New Teacher Competencies*. Singapore: Cengage Learning Asia. 233–56.

Taylor, S., Ferris, J. and Franklin, G. (2013). Experts Gaining Expertise. In S. G. Burroughs-Lange and A. Ince (eds), *Every Child a Reader: History, Politics and Practice*. London: Institute of Education. 82–108.

Training and Development Agency (2007). *Professional Standards for Teachers*. London: TDA.

Twist, L., Sizmur, J., Bartlett, S. and Lynn, L. (2012). *PIRLS 2011: Reading Achievemnet in England*. Slough: NFER.

Wasik, B. A. and Slavin, R. E. (1993). Preventing Early Reading Failure with One-to-one Tutoring: A Review of Five Programs, *Reading Research Quarterly*. 28 (2). 179–200.

Whitty, G. (2008). Changing Modes of Teacher Professionalism: Traditional, Managerial, Collaborative and Democratic. In B. Cunningham (ed.), *Exploring Professionalism*. London: Institute of Education, Bedford Way Papers. 28–49.

Conclusion

Early childhood and primary education: new visions and a manifesto for change

Dominic Wyse, Rosemary Davis,
Phil Jones and Sue Rogers

Throughout this book we have identified new visions for primary education. The text has explored conceptual 'dialogues' between the study of childhood and the study of education. We have attempted to reunite the phases of education known respectively as early years and primary education through a developmental perspective. Parochialism, ethnocentrism and misplaced nostalgia based on personal reminiscence have been challenged through deployment of theory, evidence and a sense of educational history. We have appraised the effects of globalisation and marketisation and, in so doing, have scrutinised national/international policy control in relation to local agency.

The authors have critiqued a range of current certainties in early years and primary education, and proposed new visions. For this final chapter of the book we crystallise the key ideas from these new visions as a *manifesto for change*.

Surveillance and performativity

The surveillance derived from league tables of pupil attainment (focusing almost exclusively on language/English, maths and science), and the performativity effects that result from this, are based on narrow measures in relation to the overall needs for children's learning. In settings where there is an overemphasis on narrowly defined targets and traditional school subjects the consequences for children may be serious, to the extent that they miss out on other more creative and child-led activity. As Roberts-Holmes (Chapter 5) suggests in the context of England, such approaches need to be challenged. Surveillance and performativity can lead to anxiety, and even fear, for some people, including for parents in the choice of schools, as Merchant (Chapter 11) points out.

Superficially, the choice of educational institutions in England is wide, with state schools, free schools and academies available, in theory, to cater for all preferences. A particular government conception of 'standards' in early years settings and schools is used to heavily monitor and control through statutory testing and assessment, the results of which are publically communicated. Yet true choice to ensure high-quality education is illusory for many parents, and their children. *De facto* intimidation of professionals, children and parents through excessive accountability measures is unacceptable in a modern democracy.

Identity and agency

The agency of teachers and children should be central to future policy and practice, as Eaude (Chapter 7) and several other authors argue. Changes are needed to a system that prioritises monitoring over teacher professionalism: the emphasis should be reversed to prioritise professionalism over monitoring. Rogers and Wyse (Chapter 4) address these concerns, advocating a balance between statutory curriculum content and teacher-determined content. For many of the book's authors, teacher and child agency are connected. They emphasise that nurturing children's sense of agency requires teachers who are supported by training and policies that empower them as professionals rather than treat them as technicians. Roberts-Holmes (Chapter 5) argues that if early years children are to develop positive life-long learning dispositions then government should pay much greater attention to, and trust, early years teachers' professional judgements and considerable knowledge.

The enactment of agency requires space for reflection on complex issues in the classroom. Mintz (Chapter 9) demonstrates an aspect of the complexities in his reflective stance on interventions to support a boy with dyspraxia. Similarly, Ambrossi (Chapter 8) in her discussion of strategies for teaching a foreign language at Key Stage 2 (age seven to eleven) sets out alternatives for knowledge about languages, and the cultural context for languages. Ambrossi's advocacy for team-teaching reminds us that appropriate levels of professional autonomy do not exclude collaboration. Taylor, Bodman and Morris' (Chapter 12) case for teacher autonomy emphasises teacher preparation and development and, in particular, the need for educators to have space and opportunities to develop as reflective practitioners. The necessary reflectivity involves training and support for individuals to make critical decisions on their work, based upon a developing knowledge and understanding of the dynamics between research and practice.

Rhetoric vs reality

With each new government comes the rhetoric of newly identified but familiar problems, then the offer of 'new solutions' that fail to account for the history of educational policy. Too often solutions seem to be driven by a combination of ideology and personal nostalgia rather than rigorous understanding of educational history and research. The rhetoric of 'new dawns' based on technology are legion: the latest iterations are critically evaluated, and more realistic potentials indicated, by Roberts (Chapter 6).

The problem of rhetoric vs reality is most clearly seen in the contrasts between political statements (however well intentioned) and policies, versus the evidence of practice in classrooms and schools. The most serious examples are the longstanding difficulties with protecting children from abuse as Davis (Chapter 2) explains. Children's rights more generally is a particularly extreme example of rhetoric, where globally and nationally children's rights have strong legal backing yet in the education system, particularly, their voices are rarely heard. A more appropriate match between the rights children are due and the lived realities of school life is needed.

Although societal consensus exists over a number of issues – for example, the need for high standards of teaching and learning – the reality of the 'standards' agenda has been seen to be rhetorical, as the reality of negative outcomes of high-stakes assessment reveal (e.g. Roberts-Holmes, Chapter 5). Rogers and Wyse (Chapter 4) uncover the rhetoric of teacher empowerment in a system where curriculum and pedagogic autonomy are reserved for academies, free schools and private schools. The rhetoric of public 'consultation' is also laid bare. Public consultations need to become a genuine democratic vehicle for ground-up change, and their findings and methods subject to independent analysis.

Even the idea of early years and primary teaching as a profession, ideally with Master's-level qualifications developed in university education departments in partnership with schools, is threatened. Eaude (Chapter 7) has perceptive observations about the work and education of primary teachers in relation to teacher education and development, expertise and knowledge.

Development

Consideration of child development requires understanding of the range of needs, interests and contexts that affect children. Ang and Flewitt (Chapter 10) illustrate diversity using a cross-cultural perspective, particularly relevant in the UK's multicultural population. In recognition of a more globalised world, they stress the importance of teachers evaluating their own pedagogical practice. Mintz' (Chapter 9) reflections on his own practice, in the light of the child Dougie's behaviour, are indicative of the depth of reflection on child development and learning that is necessary. For teachers, reflectivity means being supported to understand development, and to exercise autonomy to support children. For children, their development can also be supported by attention to their voice, the main concern for Davis (Chapter 2), and illustrated by Jones (Chapter 1) in his research into primary school children's perceptions of their development and their transition into secondary school. In Jones' chapter the children's voices were made 'audible' through building up images of children's hopes and fears for the new world of school that awaited them. Robertson's (Chapter 3) enquiry into children's metacognition recognised the importance of children being encouraged to reflect on their own learning in support of their development.

Alternatives

All the new visions proposed in this chapter, and throughout the book, are alternatives and/or significant changes to current educational systems. But the need for politicians and policy-makers to have recommendations, in accessible forms, from rigorous theory and research, rooted in the reality of children's and teachers' lives lead us to conclude the book with a series of three essential points per chapter that we think should be enacted for children and their education in the twenty-first century (see Table C.1).

The most important theme of our book is that children's agency and teachers' agency should be central to early years and primary education. One key aspect of agency, and other desirable features of education, is 'voice'. The starting point for the book was the voices of the authors (themselves steeped in the practice *and* research of education). The voices of the authors are evident in their rallying call for the empowerment of children, their teachers and teacher educators; key people in the educative process. The necessary fulfilment of children's rights, needs, wishes and passions can only become reality in education through recognition and sensitivity to what children say (or do not say) and communicate through their actions. Teaching and learning enacted through research-informed pedagogy, in an education system which hears and responds to voice, will empower children in the co-construction of knowledge, and is a fundamental element in the vision of this book. We hope you will respond to our manifesto for change.

Table C.1 Essential points for action

Themes of the book	New visions	Chapter number	Chapter title
Surveillance and performativity	All people involved in education should champion children's rights worldwide as reflected in the United Nations Convention on the Rights of the Child	2	The Child's Voice – Rosemary Davis
Surveillance and performativity	Change the emphasis on high-stakes national testing and target-setting to an emphasis on child-centred formative teacher assessment	5	High Stakes Assessment, Teachers and Children – Guy Roberts-Holmes
Surveillance and performativity	Emphasise collaboration using new technology more than excessive individualisation as part of teaching and learning	6	Technology and Education – Lynn Roberts
Surveillance and performativity	Replace the punitive emphasis of national education systems by much greater emphasis on trust in teachers and children	7	Expertise, Knowledge and Pedagogy – Tony Eaude
Surveillance and performativity	Ensure less emphasis on statutory testing and other performativity mechanisms, and more emphasis on teacher autonomy	7	Expertise, Knowledge and Pedagogy – Tony Eaude
Surveillance and performativity	Give all schools the power to innovate, e.g. over the curriculum, working closely with local authorities rather than controlled by the Department for Education	11	Families, Society and School Choice – Georgina Merchant
Rhetoric vs reality	Increase emphasis on evidence, rather than ideology, in the education system	1	Childhoods and Contemporary Practices – Phil Jones
Rhetoric vs reality	Ensure more rigorous attention to evidence, not ideology, as part of public consultations	4	Agency, Pedagogy and the Curriculum – Sue Rogers and Dominic Wyse
Identity and agency	Conceptions of childhood should reflect a sophisticated understanding located between romanticised views of all children as fully capable vs deficit views of children as all completely incapable	1	Childhoods and Contemporary Practices – Phil Jones
Identity and agency	Children's voices should be repeatedly and actively listened to and constructively acted upon	2	The Child's Voice – Rosemary Davis
Identity and agency	Children should be consulted on all matters that affect them	2	The Child's Voice – Rosemary Davis
Identity and agency	Give all teachers, irrespective of the kind of school they work in, the power to create their curriculum and to 'own' the pedagogy to implement their curriculum	4	Agency, Pedagogy and the Curriculum – Sue Rogers and Dominic Wyse
Identity and agency	Place more emphasis on teachers' professional judgements	5	High Stakes Assessment, Teachers and Children – Guy Roberts-Holmes

(Continued)

Table C.1 Essential points for action (Continued)

Themes of the book	New visions	Chapter number	Chapter title
Identity and agency	Motivate teachers' personal interests in human triumphs, defeats and inventiveness, including the study of empire and conflict	8	Language and Culture in Foreign Language Teaching – Paula Ambrossi
Identity and agency	Empower teachers to select and use specialist knowledge to construct appropriate pedagogy for all children, including those with SEN	9	Inclusion or Special Educational Needs? Uncertainty in the Twenty-first Century – Joseph Mintz
Identity and agency	Take seriously the agency of children as part of providing for their educational needs	10	Embracing Diversity in the Classroom: A Cross-cultural Perspective – Lynn Ang and Rosie Flewitt
Development	Put more emphasis on children thinking about their thinking and their learning, not simply being consumers of education	3	Children's Thinking – Anne Robertson
Development	Liberate children from the insularity of an undue focus on the grammar of language alone	8	Language and Culture in Foreign Language Teaching – Paula Ambrossi
Development	Help children shape their own learning and resist reproduction of social inequality though greater understanding of human capital	10	Embracing Diversity in the Classroom: A Cross-cultural Perspective – Lynn Ang and Rosie Flewitt
Alternatives	Early years and primary education should reflect a matrix of dialogues between child, professional and social and cultural contexts	1	Childhoods and Contemporary Practices – Phil Jones
Alternatives	Professional development opportunities for teachers should be provided to support their understanding of dialogic teaching for metacognition	3	Children's Thinking – Anne Robertson
Alternatives	Children and teachers alike need space and time to reflect	3	Children's Thinking – Anne Robertson
Alternatives	Achieve an equal balance between more general national educational curriculum aims and teacher-determined and child-determined curricula	4	Agency, Pedagogy and the Curriculum – Sue Rogers and Dominic Wyse
Alternatives	Replace the dominance of the 'school readiness' approach with an approach that emphasises development as part of a through curriculum	5	High Stakes Assessment, Teachers and Children – Guy Roberts-Holmes
Alternatives	Emphasise the role of computer programming as a language to express and explore powerful ideas	6	Technology and Education – Lynn Roberts
Alternatives	Focus on the pedagogy when using new technology, not just the technology	6	Technology and Education – Lynn Roberts
Alternatives	Place more emphasis on pedagogical knowledge than subject knowledge	7	Expertise, Knowledge and Pedagogy – Tony Eaude

Alternatives	Include cultural understanding as an aid to understanding foreign language learning	8	Language and Culture in Foreign Language Teaching – Paula Ambrossi
Alternatives	Support teachers to use theoretical diagnostic information about special needs sensitively alongside their professional knowledge of the children they teach	9	Inclusion or Special Educational Needs? Uncertainty in the Twenty-first Century – Joseph Mintz
Alternatives	Ensure greater emphasis on Special Educational Needs in teacher training and development	9	Inclusion or Special Educational Needs? Uncertainty in the Twenty-first Century – Joseph Mintz
Alternatives	Ensure greater emphasis on inclusive learning	10	Embracing Diversity in the Classroom: A Cross-cultural Perspective – Lynn Ang and Rosie Flewitt
Alternatives	Change policy to emphasise excellent neighbourhood schools for all with proximity as main criteria for selection	11	Families, Society and School Choice – Georgina Merchant
Alternatives	Give priority to the most disadvantaged families to access the best schools and the best teachers	11	Families, Society and School Choice – Georgina Merchant
Alternatives	As part of professional development for teachers emphasise conceptual approaches that create interactive spaces for reflection on theory, research and classroom practice	12	Politics, Policy and Teacher Agency – Sue Bodman, Susan Taylor and Helen Morris
Alternatives	Refocus the goals of professional development to create teachers who have ownership of their own learning and needs	12	Politics, Policy and Teacher Agency – Sue Bodman, Susan Taylor and Helen Morris
Alternatives	Encourage critical reflection throughout the education system, not least because it is vital to the development of professional knowledge	12	Politics, Policy and Teacher Agency – Sue Bodman, Susan Taylor and Helen Morris

Index

Page numbers in italic denote tables and figures.